NEW EDITION

first certificate

Gold

coursebook

Richard Acklam

with Sally Burgess

Longman

Contents

Reading	Listening	Speaking	Writing
Why do we risk it? (matching pictures to paragraphs)	*Disaster at sea* (note taking, True/False)	Comparing and contrasting photographs	An informal letter and checking accuracy
Would you set yourself on fire for £75 a day? (gapped text)	*Unpopular jobs* (multiple matching) Song: *9 to 5* (Dolly Parton)	Discussing: 1) value of different jobs 2) qualities/abilities different jobs require Explaining how to play a sport	A transactional letter (1) Using sequencers
Twins (True/False) *Open house* (multiple matching)	*Man's best friend* (ordering pictures) (Yes/No questions)	Discussing 1) being an only child, a twin 2) care of pets	Drafting and redrafting (article)
The real Mona Lisa? (multiple matching) *War of the Worlds?* (gapped text)	*Lies* (multiple matching) *Extracts* (multiple choice)	Discussing: 1) fakes and forgeries 2) presenting a case 3) lies 4) UFOs	A short story
Extract from *Wuthering Heights* (reading between the lines)	Song: *Your song* (Elton John) *Do you take this man?* (multiple matching)	Discussing: 1) music 2) good books 3) marriage customs	Background reading texts
The mind machine? (multiple matching)	*Exam fever* (note taking)	Discussing: 1) purpose of schools and the qualities of good students/teachers 2) exams	An article and punctuation
Eight years old and worth his weight in gold (gapped text: paragraphs)	*The psychology of fame* (True/false) *Stagefright* (multiple matching)	Roleplay: giving advice Roleplay: landlord/unhappy tenant Discussing fears	A report (1)
Supermodel sensation (jigsaw reading) *Why laughter is the best medicine* (gapped text)	Song: *Blue suede shoes* (Elvis Presley) *Designer row!* (comprehension questions)	Discussing fashion Describing an accident, an illness, etc. Roleplay: parent and son/daughter discuss party rules	A descriptive composition (person)
Irish Stew (multiple choice) *Are you hooked?* (multiple matching)	*An addict's story* (True/False) *Shop complaint* (ordering pictures)	Discussing eating and cooking Explaining how to cook something Discussing shopping Roleplay: making a complaint	A formal letter (complaint)
Leaders of the Pak (gapped text: sentences)	*Inventors* (note taking)	Discussing money Problem solving: 1) awarding a scholarship 2) ranking inventions	An application
Weird weather facts (question formation)	*Biosphere 2* (significance of key words)	Discussing environmental issues Problem solving: selecting personal items	A transactional letter (2) and informal/formal style
The Eiffel Tower conman (gapped text: sentences) *TV ration box* (question formation)	*Radio advertisements* (assessing effectiveness)	Roleplay: product presentation Creating a new TV channel	A discursive composition (1) and linkers
Mad as a hatter or geniuses at work? (multiple matching)	*Vampire woman* (comprehension questions)	Discussing eccentricity Describing animals Discussing different types of accommodation	A descriptive composition (place)
Batman (comprehension questions)	*Guardian Angels* (True/False)	Roleplay: deciding what to do with a young criminal Ordering a picture story Discussing the role of vigilantes	Making your writing more interesting
Chatting with chimps (selecting correct sentences) *Graffiti* (multiple choice)	Song: *I wish it would rain down* Extracts (multiple choice) *Handwriting* (True/False)	Discussing: 1) differences between people and animals 2) graffiti	A report (2) A discursive composition (2)

Communication activities p.199   Language index p.207

Exam information

Overview

The Cambridge First Certificate Examination in English consists of five papers. Each paper tests a different area of your ability in English and is worth twenty per cent of your total result. After you take the exam you will receive a grade: A, B and C are pass grades; D and E are fail grades.

Paper 1 Reading

This paper contains four parts. Each part has at least one text with a task. There is a total of 35 questions. A variety of types of texts may be used, including letters, advertisements, extracts from works of fiction, newspaper articles and information from brochures. You will have 1 hour and 15 minutes to answer all the questions.

Part 1: Multiple matching

You match headings or summary sentences to each paragraph of a text. There are 6/7 questions and an example (0) at the beginning. (See similar tasks on pp. 36–37; pp. 58–59; pp. 130–131.)

Part 2: Multiple choice

You choose between four alternatives to answer questions or complete statements about a text. There are 7/8 questions. (See Exam Focus pp. 64–65 and similar tasks on p. 89 and p. 157.)

Part 3: Gapped text

Sentences or paragraphs have been removed from a text. You decide where in the text these sentences or paragraphs should be placed. There are 6/7 gaps in the text but 7/8 sentences or paragraphs. The first gap is an example (0). (See similar tasks on pp. 22–23, pp. 68–69, p. 85, pp. 98–99 and pp. 120–121 and Exam Focus on pp. 114–115.)

Part 4: Multiple matching

You read a text divided into sections and then answer specific questions about each section. There are 13–15 questions and an example (0) at the beginning. (See Exam Focus on pp. 10–11 and a similar task on p. 92.)

Paper 2 Writing

In this paper you have two tasks. You will have 1 hour and 30 minutes to complete the two tasks and you will be required to write between 120 and 180 words for each task.

Part 1 is compulsory and requires you to write a 'transactional' letter based on information and prompts. (See example on p.20 Exam focus, and model text with notes in Writing Reference p.179.)

In **Part 2** you have a choice from four tasks. These will be a selection of the following:

- a letter, which could include a 'letter of application' (See example on p.12 Writing, and model texts with notes p.181 and p.184.)
- an article (See example on p.126 Exam focus, and model text with notes p.183.)
- a report (See example on p.73 Exam focus, and model text with notes p.182.)
- a discursive composition (See example on p.158 Writing, and model text with notes p.185.)
- a descriptive composition (See example on p.81 Writing, and model text with notes p.186.)
- a short story (See example on p.44 Writing, and model text with notes p.180.)
- a composition, article, report or letter on one of the background reading texts (See example on p.51 Writing, and model text with notes p.186.)

Paper 3 Use of English

This paper contains five parts with a total of 65 questions. You will have 1 hour and 15 minutes to answer all the questions. The five different parts are as follows:

Part 1: this consists of a multiple choice cloze text. This is a text with 15 gaps, followed by 15 four-option multiple choice questions. The focus is on vocabulary. (See example on p.143 Use of English and p. 106 Exam Focus.)

Part 2: this consists of an open cloze text. This is a text with 15 gaps which you must fill with an appropriate word. The focus is on grammar and vocabulary. (See example on p.135 Exam focus.)

Part 3: this consists of 10 'key' word transformations. You are required to complete a sentence using a given word, so that it means the same as a previous sentence. The focus is on grammar and vocabulary. *(See example on p.83 Exam focus.)*

Part 4: this consists of an error correction text. This is a text where some lines are correct and some contain an extra and unnecessary word which must be identified. The focus is on grammar. *(See example on p.28 Exam focus.)*

Part 5: this consists of a word formation exercise. You will read a text in which there are 10 gaps. You are given the stem of the word which you must use to complete each gap. The focus is on vocabulary. *(See example on p.19 Exam focus.)*

Paper 4 Listening

This paper contains four parts with a total of 30 questions. In each part you will hear the text(s) twice. The texts will be a variety of types, possibly including phone messages, lectures, news, stories, interviews, advertisements, conversations, quizzes and extracts from plays. There will be a mixture of native and non-native speaker accents. This paper will last approximately 40 minutes.

Part 1: you will hear 8 short, unrelated extracts and have to answer a multiple choice question about each one. You may be asked to decide on, for example, the general subject of the text, the relationship of the speakers or the purpose of the conversation. *(See example on p.146 Exam focus.)*

Part 2: you will hear a monologue or conversation lasting about 3 minutes. You will have to take notes or fill in blanks to complete missing information. *(See example on p.91 Exam focus.)*

Part 3: you will hear a series of short, related extracts of about 30 seconds from monologues or conversations. While you listen you complete a multiple matching task in which you match the speakers to given prompts. *(See example on p.17 Listening.)*

Part 4: you will hear a monologue or conversation lasting about 3 minutes. You will have to answer questions which involve selecting between 2 or 3 possible answers, for example True/False, Yes/No, which speaker said what, multiple choice, etc. *(See example on p.148 Listening.)*

Paper 5 Speaking

This paper contains four parts. The standard format involves an interview between two candidates and two examiners. One of the examiners is an interlocutor who speaks to the candidates; the other examiner only assesses the candidates and does not speak. In Parts 1 and 2 of this paper candidates speak mainly to the interlocutor. In Parts 3 and 4 the candidates speak mainly to each other. The different parts are as follows:

Part 1: the interlocutor asks each candidate to say a little about themselves, for example where they come from, what they like doing in their free time, etc. This will last approximately 3 minutes.

Part 2: candidates compare and contrast two photographs they are given by the interlocutor and talk about them in relation to themselves and their own experience. This will last approximately 4 minutes. *(See a similar task on p.13 and an example on p.53 Exam focus.)*

Part 3: candidates are given visual prompts (e.g. photographs, line drawings, diagrams, maps) and are asked to carry out a task together which may involve planning, problem solving, decision making, prioritising or speculating. This will last approximately 3 minutes. *(See a similar task on p.102 and an example on p.104 Exam focus.)*

Part 4: the interlocutor develops the topic covered in Part 3 and asks the candidates to discuss and give opinions on more general questions related to the same theme. This will last approximately 4 minutes.

In total this paper will last approximately 14 minutes. *(For an example of a complete Paper 5 interview see pp.124–125 Exam focus. There are practice test materials for Paper 5 on pp.187–195.)*

1 A sense of adventure

Speaking

1 Look at the picture below and discuss the following questions.

1 Why do you think the man is doing this?
2 Would you be prepared to try this? Why?/Why not?
3 What type of character would you need to have to do this?

2 Complete the questionnaire opposite. Then compare your answers with other students in the class and find someone whose answers are similar to your own.

Are you a THRILL-SEEKER?

Choose the alternative that best describes your likes or dislikes, or the way you feel.

1a) I sometimes like to do things that are a little frightening. ....X..
 b) Sensible people avoid dangerous activities. ......
 c) I love being terrified! ......

2a) I enter cold water gradually, giving myself time to get used to it. ......
 b) It's fun to dive or jump right into the ocean or a cold pool. ......
 c) I won't go in the water unless it's very warm. ...X..

3a) When I go on holiday, I want a decent room and a bed at least. ......
 b) I like going camping and doing without the conveniences of everyday life. ......
 c) I expect a bit of luxury on holiday. ...X..

4a) My friends are pretty crazy. ......
 b) I prefer calm, conventional people. ..X..
 c) I like having a mix of friends of all different types. ......

5a) I think it would be really exciting to do a parachute jump. ......
 b) Jumping out of a plane, with or without a parachute, is crazy. ......
 c) I'd consider doing a parachute jump if I had proper training. .X....

6a) I think it would be fun to be hypnotised. ......
 b) I wouldn't mind being hypnotised by a professional. ......
 c) I would hate to be in the power of a hypnotist. ......

7a) People who ride motorbikes must have some kind of unconscious desire to hurt themselves. ..X..
 b) Riding a motorbike at high speed is one of the most exciting things you can do. ......
 c) Motorbikes are just another means of transport. ......

To see how you did on the test, turn to page 199.

Vocabulary: feelings

1   Look at the groups of words below and answer the following questions. Use your dictionary where necessary.

1   Which word is the odd one out in each group? Why?
2   On which syllable does the main stress fall in each word?

EXAMPLE: *ex 'cited – second syllable stress*

a) frightened excited terrified scared
b) happy lucky thrilled glad
c) depressed miserable sad confused
d) astonished upset amazed surprised
e) angry cross furious nervous

Watch Out! *nervous*

1   Please stop whistling. It's making me *nervous./It's very irritating*.
2   I get very *nervous/irritated* just before an exam.

Which is the most likely alternative in each sentence?

---

2   Decide which is the correct form of the adjective in each of the following sentences.

1   I had never done a parachute jump before. It was very *frightening/frightened*.
2   I had never done a parachute jump before. I was very *frightening/frightened*.

Which of the other adjectives in Exercise 1 have an *-ed* form and an *-ing* form?
Grammar reference p.162 (1.1/1.2)

3   Complete the following sentences with a suitable adjective from Exercise 1 in the correct form.

1   That film was very frightening all the main characters died!
2   I was scared to hear that he had passed his exams because he never seemed to do any work. It's so annoying!
3   It makes me so nervous when people drop litter in the street!
4   Mike was glad when they asked him to be godfather of their first child. Nothing could have made him happier!
5   It was a very exciting match. The score was 2–2 until just before the end.

4   Tell a partner how you would feel in the following situations and what you would do next.

1   You hear you have passed all your exams.
2   You are in a lift which suddenly stops and won't move.
3   Your brother/sister/flatmate has borrowed some of your clothes without asking permission.
4   You are walking home late at night and you think someone is following you.

5   Choose three more adjectives from Exercise 1. Tell your partner the last time you felt like that.

6   How are you going to record new vocabulary?

1   Are you going to have a special vocabulary notebook? If so, are you going to organise it:

- by day (like a diary)?

  EXAMPLE:

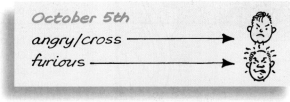

- by topic area?

  EXAMPLE:

- alphabetically (like a dictionary)?

  EXAMPLE:

  A

  amazed /ə'meɪzd/ adj.: to feel very surprised
  e.g. They were all amazed by her new hairstyle.

2   What information are you going to put in your vocabulary notebook? It is a good idea to include the following things:

- the part of speech e.g. noun, verb, adjective, etc.
- a definition
- an example sentence
- the translation
- the phonemics and word stress

Reading

1 Look at the pictures below and describe what you can see happening in each one.

2 Now read the text opposite and decide which paragraph each picture belongs to. Then tell a partner how each picture relates to the text.

3 In most texts you read there will be some words that you do not understand. It is important that you are able to make sensible guesses as to what these words might mean from the surrounding context.

1 The words opposite come from the text. Look at each word in context and choose the correct meaning a) or b).

Why do we risk it?

Ordinary people all over the world are willing to risk their lives for the ultimate experience – an 'adrenaline buzz'. What basic human need is driving them to do it?

RISK SPORTS are one of the fastest-growing leisure activities. Daredevils try anything from organised bungee jumps to illegally jumping off buildings. These people never feel so alive as when they are risking their lives. In their <u>quest</u> for the ultimate sensation, thrill-seekers are thinking up more and more elaborate sports. 'Zip wiring', for example, involves sliding down a rope from the top of a cliff suspended by a pulley attached to your ankle.

So why do some people's lives seem to be dominated by the 'thrill factor', while others are perfectly happy to sit at home by the fire? Some say that people who do risk sports are reacting against a society which they feel has become dull and constricting. David Lewis, a psychologist, believes that people today <u>crave</u> adventure. In an attempt to guarantee safety, our culture has eliminated risk. 'The world has become a <u>bland</u> and safe place,' says Lewis. 'People used to be able to seek adventure by hunting wild animals, or taking part in expeditions. Now they turn to risk sports as an escape.'

Risk sports have a positive side as well. They help people to overcome fears that affect them in their real lives. This makes risk sports particularly valuable for executives in office jobs who need to stay <u>alert</u> so that they can cope when things go wrong. They learn that being frightened doesn't mean they can't be in control.

Of all the risk or adrenaline sports, bungee jumping is proving the most popular. Worldwide, one-and-a-half million people have tried it. You <u>hurtle</u> towards the ground from 200 metres up and, at the last moment, when you are about to hit the water or land and death seems certain, a rubber band <u>yanks</u> you back to life. You can decide whether to jump from a crane, a bridge or a balloon. Attached to a length of elastic rope, jumpers experience a free fall of nearly 100 mph, before they're slowed by a quickly increasing pull on their ankles.

After five or six bounces jumpers are lowered on to a mattress and set free. Almost <u>inarticulate</u>, they walk around with idiotic grins on their faces. Their hands can't stop shaking, they can only use superlatives and say repeatedly how amazing it was. 'As you're falling, all you see are things flying around as you turn,' says one breathless bungee jumper. 'You don't think you're ever going to stop and when you rebound, it's like weightlessness. You feel as if you're floating on air. My legs are like jelly, but I feel so alive!'

from *Focus* magazine

1 quest *(noun)*	a) search	b) fear
2 crave *(verb)*	a) want very much	b) dislike strongly
3 bland *(adjective)*	a) frightening	b) without excitement
4 alert *(adjective)*	a) full of anxiety	b) quick to notice what is happening
5 hurtle *(verb)*	a) move very fast	b) be sick
6 yank *(verb)*	a) hit violently	b) pull suddenly
7 inarticulate *(adjective)*	a) unable to speak clearly	b) unable to move

2 Now choose two other words that you don't know in the text and try to work out their meaning from the context.

Grammar: questions

1 Here are some incorrectly formed questions. Try to correct them. Then read the information about QUESTIONS opposite and check your ideas.

1 Why people take such dangerous risks?
2 Can you tell me how did you feel afterwards?
3 Did he was waiting for you to jump?
4 Let's go home, do we?
5 When you went bungee-jumping?
6 Are you agree?
7 How many time have you been doing this sport?
8 Of what are you afraid?
9 Who did asked the instructor?
10 Do you know if is he coming?
11 He used to hate motorbikes, wasn't he?

2

1 Question tags are used to check information.

EXAMPLE: *You've got two brothers,* **haven't you?**

- If you are fairly sure that your information is correct, your voice should <u>fall</u> on the question tag.
- If you are not very sure whether your information is correct or not, your voice should <u>rise</u> on the question tag.

Listen and decide if the person saying the above sentence is fairly sure or not very sure that their information is correct.

QUESTIONS

a) Questions are often formed in this way:

Question word(s) +	**auxiliary verb** +	**subject** +	**main verb**
How much	*does*	*this bag*	*cost?*
When	*did*	*he*	*go?*
What	*have*	*they*	*done?*

b) *Be, can* and *have (got)* just change the order of the subject and auxiliary verb.
e.g. *He is watching TV.* > **Is he watching** *TV? They can swim.* > **Can they** *swim? You have got time.* > **Have you got** *time?*

c) If *who/which/what* is the **subject** of the sentence, do not use *do/does/did*.
e.g. **Who invented** *the telephone?* (**not** ~~Who did invent the telephone?~~) **What happened** *to Mike last night?* (**not** ~~What did happen to Mike last night?~~)

d) With 'indirect' questions the word order of the subject (and auxiliary) and main verb is the same order as in statements.
e.g. *Do you think* **he is doing** *his homework? Are you going to ask me what* **I bought?**

e) Question tags are generally formed with the auxiliary of the verb in the first part of the sentence. Positive statements generally have negative question tags, negative statements generally have positive question tags.
e.g. *You don't like him,* **do you?** *They haven't taken it,* **have they?**

shall we is the question tag used after *Let's*
e.g. *Let's watch TV,* **shall we?**

did/didn't is used in the question tag after *used to*
e.g. *You used to like swimming,* **didn't you?**

f) Prepositions generally come at the end of questions (except in very formal situations).
e.g. *Who did you go to the cinema* **with?** (**not** ~~With whom did you go to the cinema?~~) *What were you talking* **about?** (**not** ~~About what were you talking?~~).

g) To ask about a period of time we can use *How long ... ?*
e.g. **How long** *have you known him?* **How long** *are they staying?*

Grammar reference p.171 (13)

---

2 Listen to five other people using question tags. Are they fairly sure or not very sure that their information is correct?

3 Work with other students and check what you know about them using question tags and the appropriate intonation.

EXAMPLE: *You're eighteen,* **aren't you?**

3 In small groups consider the following two problems. Try to solve the problems by asking your teacher questions which she/he can answer 'Yes' or 'No' to. Your teacher will not answer your questions unless they are grammatically correct.

Cindy and Sebastian are lying dead on the floor. They are surrounded by broken glass and water. The window to the room is open and the curtains are flapping in the breeze.

Who are they? How did they die and why?

EXAMPLE: *Were they murdered?*

A man is lying dead on the floor. Next to him is a piece of wood, some sawdust and a gun. Another man comes to the door, opens it, looks in, sees the dead man and smiles. He walks away extremely happy.

How did the man die? Why is the second man so happy?

EXAMPLE: *Did the second man kill the first man?*

4

1 A young Australian actress was recently interviewed for a popular magazine. These were the answers she gave. Work with a partner and try to imagine the kinds of questions she might have been asked. See how many different questions your class can think of for each answer.

   a) About two years now.
   b) Chocolate cake with fresh cream.
   c) Heights.
   d) Madonna, I suppose.
   e) Biting my nails.
   f) Getting up before 8.00 in the morning.
   g) About once every five years.
   h) No, actually, I'm twenty.
   i) Yes, but I gave up a few months ago.
   j) He's a good friend. Nothing more.
   k) My hair. I wish it was blonde.
   l) The fact that I am very loyal.
   m) My mother. I tell her everything … nearly.

2 Now choose some of your questions and interview a partner.

5

1 Work with a partner. Together, choose two famous people that you are both interested in. Write at least six questions that you would like to ask them.

2 Now take it in turns to be a journalist and the famous person. One of you should ask the questions, the other should answer as if you were that famous person. Be as imaginative as you can in your answers.

Exam focus

Paper 1 Reading: Part 4 (multiple matching)

About the exam: In Paper 1, Part 4 you read a text divided into sections and then answer between thirteen and fifteen questions. In this part of Paper 1 you need to find specific information in the text.

Procedure

1 Make sure you look at the title and /or the subheading or introduction of the text before you start reading. This should give you a good idea of what to expect. (Do this for all parts of Paper 1.)
2 Read the text through quickly to get a general idea.
3 Look at the first question carefully. Scan each section to find the relevant information. Watch out! Sometimes information in more than one section will relate to a specific question. Make sure you choose the information that matches the question exactly.
4 Work through all the questions in this way. Leave any you can't do and come back to them at the end.

You are going to read a magazine article about the publisher of some famous travel guides and the information they receive from travellers. For questions **1–15**, choose from the travellers **(A–D)**. There is an example at the beginning **(0)**. In the actual exam you would mark your answers on a separate answer sheet.

Which of the travellers A–D:

> **A Sarah Ellison**
> **B Scott Williamson**
> **C Donna Cotter**
> **D John Nevison**

had some rather frightening experiences?	**0** C
warns other travellers about something?	**1**
was travelling with someone else?	**2**
tells other travellers what to take with them?	**3**
recommends a particular season?	**4**

mentions three good things about public transport?	**5**
does not mention public transport?	**6**
talks about a place that not many people know?	**7**
describes the natural beauty of the place?	**8** **9**
visited a place where it is often wet?	**10**
met some local people?	**11**
says you can prepare for other trips here?	**12**
says what kind of luggage they were carrying?	**13**
mentions accommodation?	**14**
wants to repeat the experience?	**15**

The Lonely Planet guidebooks have been treasured for years by travellers who are looking for adventure. Today Lonely Planet also has its own website where travellers are invited to send electronic postcards with news and tips for others who might be planning a trip. Here are some examples.

A Tenerife is home to Spain's highest mountain, Teide. Towering at almost 4000 metres, it dominates the island and is snow-capped for most of the year, sometimes as late as May. The one way to get up to the top is to stay at the refuge halfway up overnight. You get up at 3 a.m. to walk to the summit for the sunrise. The mountain lies at the heart of the Teide National Park, Spain's most visited park, and the surrounding scenery is breathtaking. Other 'must dos' include the Masca valley in the west with its picturesque villages and the Anaga peninsular in the north. Transport on Tenerife is cheap. Bright green buses run all over the island, they are regular and run on time.
Sarah Ellison, USA

B Greece is ideally suited to a cycle-touring holiday. The roads are of good quality, with wide shoulders and little traffic. The weather in spring is perfect for cycling, with lots of sunshine, little rain and comfortable temperatures. The scenery in Greece is spectacular, and there is no better way to enjoy it than by bike: golden sandy beaches, rocky headlands and high sea cliffs making up the coastline, olive groves, lush green hillsides and rugged snow-capped mountains in the interior. The colourful wildflowers in spring add to the already impressive landscape. You will come across a lot of hills when travelling in Greece but keep in mind: the higher you go the better the view. Aside from the natural scenery, there are the ancient ruins and picturesque towns that add to the Greek experience. The food is excellent, especially the creamy yoghurt, warm loaves of bread fresh from the oven and delicious desserts. On a more practical note all the larger towns have bike shops where repairs can be made and spare parts bought. Bikes can be easily transported on boats, trains and even buses.
Scott Williamson, New Zealand

C Hitchhiking in Africa is an interesting experience! While hitching through Zambia, me and my six-and-a-half-foot, 20-stone fiancé were picked up by a small truck already carrying no less than nine people and a chicken in the back and four in the front (including a lady with a baby tied around her waist hanging over the edge!). Feeling very tired we climbed aboard with our rucksacks. The truck was soon travelling at speeds of up to 150km per hour and going down some hair-raising hills. This made us a little concerned especially when we saw that one of the wheels was slowly coming off. We finally got them to pull over to inspect it only to find that all the wheels were loose! The owner of course already knew this and was saying 'no worry, no worry'. Somehow we made it to our destination at Lake Kariba only to be woken up in the night by an earthquake! But I would do it all again.
Donna Cotter, Australia

D If you're looking for an escape from the high-tech facades and interiors of Singapore's Orchard Road, you should go to the MacRitchie Reservoir north of the city centre, where a walk or run around the MacRitchie Loop, located in the 2000 hectares of the Central Catchment Nature Reserve, is excellent training for rainforest treks elsewhere in South-East Asia. Surprisingly few people go to the Loop, which is why it remains one of Singapore's best kept secrets. The 11km circuit should not be taken lightly. A reasonable level of physical fitness is required. Carry water, a small umbrella and sun protection. After heavy rains, a near-daily occurrence in Singapore, the trail is muddy and slippery. Storms can leave entire trees uprooted and blocking the paths. When the sun does appear, it burns fiercely. To get there, take the metro (the MRT) to Bishan and then bus 136.
John Nevison, Singapore

from Lonely Planet Website

destination   eKno   on the road   the thorntree   postcards   propaganda   health   the scoop   FAQ   subWWWay

Writing:
informal letters

1   Look at the example of an informal letter opposite written in answer to the following question:

> You have recently got back from a holiday. You decide to write back to an English friend who wrote to you some time ago. Apologise for the delay in replying and tell her/him about your holiday.

Unfortunately, the letter contains a number of spelling, grammar and vocabulary mistakes. Try to find and then correct them. The number of mistakes is indicated at the end of each sentence.

2   Before you practise writing an informal letter, answer the following questions about how you write informal letters in English.

1   Where do you write your address?
2   Do you write the address of the person you are writing to in the letter?
3   Where do you write your name?
4   Where do you write the date?
5   How do you usually begin an informal letter?
6   How can you finish an informal letter?
7   Do you need to write your address in the exam?

Apartado 134,
02640 Almansa,
(Albacete),
Spain
5/8/95

Dear Chris,

Thanks for your last letter. I am really sorry I didn't write back earlier, but I have only just got back from holiday. I went with three friends to a little place called Mojacar which is near of Almeria, but it wasn't exactly that we expected (2)!

We booked some rooms in hotel in the village, but when we arrived to the hotel, we were very disappointing (3). It was very old, rather dirty and we couldn't to see the sea (1). So, we decided change (1).

The next hotel was perfectly (1). It was very clean and it had the bigest swiming pool I ever seen (3). But it was one problem – it was so much expensive (2)! We stay one night, but then there was time to change again (2)!

On the end we found the beautiful apartment with a balcony and it was cheap (2). Unfortunatly, we only had four days of our holiday left (1)!

Anyway, I must go and unpack my suitcase! I will write again soon.

Love,

Natalia.

3   Now write an informal letter in answer to the question in Exercise 1 in 120–180 words. Your letter should follow this order:

- Apologise for not writing sooner and explain why.
- Say where you went on holiday and who with.
- Say why you enjoyed/didn't enjoy your holiday and describe any special things you did.
- Say when you hope to see or contact your friend.

When you have finished, show your work to a partner who should check your grammar and spelling.

4   When your teacher has corrected your letter, make a note of some of your spelling, grammar and vocabulary mistakes.

EXAMPLE:

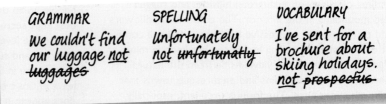

GRAMMAR
We couldn't find our luggage *not* ~~luggages~~

SPELLING
Unfortunately *not* ~~unfortunatly~~

VOCABULARY
I've sent for a brochure about skiing holidays. *not* ~~prospectus~~

- Build up a list of your common mistakes and try to avoid them in your future writing.

Vocabulary: transport

1 How many different ways can you think of to travel by sea, air or land?

EXAMPLE: *by sea > submarine, canoe, motor-boat, etc.*

2 Put the words in the box into categories according to whether they relate to *ships, trains, planes, cars* or *buses*. Which of the words can go in more than one category?

> a dual carriageway   to check in   the fast lane   a guard   Customs
> roadworks   a lifeboat   a lay-by   a platform   a compartment
> a fare   a ticket   a cabin   a seatbelt   a deck   a liner   a cruise
> a passenger   a port   a single   an inspector   a stop   to take off
> a parking meter   a ferry   a departure lounge   a life-belt   a flight
> first-class   a track   a driving test   a steward   a yacht

3 Complete the following table.

	car	bicycle	train	motorbike	plane	bus
get into/ out of	✔	✗				
get on/ off						
drive						
ride						
catch/ miss						

Watch Out! *journey/trip/travel*

1 I've got to go on a business *journey* to Rome next weekend.
2 The *travel* to New York was long and tiring.
3 *Trip* makes you more sensitive to other cultures.

What is the mistake in each of these sentences?

Speaking

Compare and contrast the photographs in each pair by discussing these questions.

1 **Photos 1 and 2**
1 What are the similarities between these ways of travelling?
2 What are the differences?
3 Have you ever travelled by plane or ship? Which do you prefer?

2 **Photos 3 and 4**
1 What are the similarities between these ways of getting to work?
2 What are the differences?
3 Which scene is more common in your country? Which do you think is worse?

Listening: disaster at sea

1 Look at the picture above and discuss the following questions.

1 What can you see happening? What do you know about this ship? Why is it so famous?

2 How do you think these words will be important in the story of this ship?

carefully   control   freeze

| iceberg | look-out | bridge (of a ship) | sink | icy | lifeboat |

2 Listen to the first part of the story and see if your ideas were correct.

3 Listen again and make a note of the significance of these numbers.

a) 2,300 *passengers*   d) 22 knots *speed of Titanic*
b) 11.40 p.m. *time of warning* e) 16 *life boats*
c) 1,513 *life lost*

4 What do you think happened next on board the *Titanic*? Discuss your ideas with a partner and then listen to the second part of the story to see if you were right.

5 Listen to the second part again and decide if the following statements are True or False.

T 1 The passengers of the *Titanic* weren't particularly worried at first.
F 2 Emily Richards had just left the USA.
F 3 She had her two children with her.
T 4 She regrets not being able to save more people.
F 5 The ship was completely under the water at 2.20 a.m.
T 6 Music was heard as the ship went under the water.
F 7 Megan Roberts wrote a novel based on the story of the *Titanic*.

6 Discuss the following questions.

1 Who do you think was responsible for the sinking of the *Titanic*?
2 Have you seen the film *Titanic*? Is it a love story or a disaster movie?

Vocabulary: word formation

● *And so began two hours and forty minutes of **dis**belief ...*

1 What do the following prefixes in **bold** mean?

EXAMPLE: *re-* means 'again'.

1 **re**play/**re**do
2 **dis**belief/**im**polite/**il**logical/**un**usual/**ir**responsible/**in**visible
3 **over**crowded/**over**charge *too much*
4 **under**estimate/**under**weight *too little*
5 **post**graduate/**post**mortem *after death*
6 **ex**-husband/**ex**-President *previous*
7 **sub**marine/**sub**way *under*

2 What parts of speech (nouns, adjectives, or adverbs) do the suffixes in **bold** indicate?

1 quick**ly**/back**wards**
2 employ**ment**/happi**ness**/infl**ation**/social**ism**
3 employ**ee**/teach**er**/conduct**or**
4 fam**ous**/sunn**y**/hope**ful**/brown**ish**/use**less**

3 Make as many words as you can by combining different parts of the box.

dis	excite	ful	ment
un	appoint	less	ness
im	honest	able	ion
	patient	ly	
	success	y	
	direct	ship	
	kind		
	profit		
	help		
	friend		
	luck		
	like		

4 Choose six words you formed and write a sentence for each to illustrate the meaning.

1

Match the two halves of the following conversations. Imagine who is speaking and where they might be.

1 A return to Manchester, please.	a) Look, I'm really sorry, but I had it a minute ago. **3**
2 I can't believe it. We've been stuck in this traffic jam for hours!	b) Oh, well … why don't we go and have a look round the Duty Free shop? **4**
3 Tickets, please.	c) And did you ever have dinner with the captain? **5**
4 The 19.30 Los Angeles flight will be delayed by one hour due to poor weather conditions.	d) Will you be coming back today? **1**
5 We generally got up early and went for a walk round the deck before breakfast.	e) Can you wait for a second because I think there's a petrol station just a bit further on? **6**
6 Can you stop at the next lay-by? I think there's something wrong with my seatbelt.	f) There are probably roadworks ahead. **2**

2

Use the word given in capitals at the end of each line to form a word that fits in each space in the same line. There is an example at the beginning (0).

THE DRIVING TEST

I knew I would have to (0) *retake* my driving test as soon as   **TAKE**
I saw the (1)........... . He didn't even say 'hello' and seemed   **EXAMINE**
very (2)............. I was a little bit late I suppose as I had slightly   **FRIEND**
(3)........... how long it would take me to get there. As usual   **ESTIMATE**
in this (4)...........city all the buses were packed and I had had to   **CROWD**
wait more than twenty minutes before a (5)............ would let me   **CONDUCT**
get on a bus. I knew apologising would be (6) .... so I just   **USE**
got in the car. (7) .... I wasn't feeling particularly nervous   **LUCK**
but this horrible man stared at me in (8) .... as I began to   **BELIEF**
drive off. I put the car into gear, but it went (9) .... so fast   **BACK**
I couldn't believe it – straight into a wall. I was so (10) ....   **APPOINT**
when he told me I had failed that I thought I might cry.

3

Look at the pictures and think of a word to describe how the people are feeling. What do you imagine has made them feel this way?

A   B   C   D   E

4

This informal letter contains various mistakes of organisation and punctuation. Rewrite the letter correcting the mistakes.

Chris Parker
19/5/96
181 Dover House Rd.,
Putney,
London SW5 5AE

Dear Natalia,
Thanks very much for your letter, your holiday sounds like it was very interesting! I have been very busy at work recently, but Sam and I are going on holiday to Greece next week for ten days, We are really looking forward to it. I promise I'll send you a postcard! Hope to see you soon, best wishes,
Chris

5

Put the words in these questions in the correct order. Then answer the questions in complete sentences.

1 free do doing like you what time your in ?
2 place the been what most to is ever interesting have you ?
3 holidays best of what you kind like do ?
4 studying for English long been you how have ?
5 English learning thing the you about find do what difficult most?
6 pass exam you you the Certificate do think will First ?

UNIT
2 Work and play

A

B

C

D

E

G

H

F

Speaking

Look at the pictures of people with different jobs and discuss who you think should be paid the most/the least and why.

Vocabulary: jobs

1 Describe what these different people do in their jobs.

EXAMPLE: *A nurse takes care of people who are not well.*

a nurse   a debt collector   an undertaker   a referee   a tax inspector   VAT a bouncer   a plumber   a traffic warden   a conductor   a bookmaker a social worker   a surgeon   a dustman   an artist   a chef   a miner a private investigator   a librarian   a caretaker   a stockbroker an editor   a vet   a wrestler   a lifeguard

2 If you had the necessary skills/qualifications, which of these jobs:

1 might you be interested in? Why?
2 would you definitely not be interested in? Why?

3 Work with a partner.

1 Choose one of the jobs from Exercise 1, but don't tell your partner which one you have chosen.

2 Your partner must ask you questions to find out what the job is.
   EXAMPLE: A: *Do you wear a uniform?* B: *Yes.*

3 You can only answer 'Yes' or 'No' to the questions. When your partner has discovered the job, change over.

4 See who can discover the other person's job in the least number of questions.

Listening: unpopular jobs

a private investigator

1 You are going to hear four people talking about their jobs. Each job appears in the box in Vocabulary Exercise 1. Listen and decide what each person's job is.

2 Now listen again and decide which speaker each of the following sentences applies to. (One of the sentences does not apply to any of them.)

A This person says she/he was physically threatened. *bouncer*
B This person says her/his salary is the most important thing.
C This person has actually cried at work. *tax inspector*
D This person most enjoys the contact with people = *bouncer*
E This person has had an embarrassing experience at work.

a private investigator

3 Look at the phrasal verbs with *on* in the sentences below and decide if the common meaning of them all is:

a) to move
b) to complete
c) to continue
d) to change

hang on

- One individual did say he would break my legs if I *kept on* asking him for money. *continue*
- Let's *hold on* for a little bit longer. I'm sure he will be here soon. *Wait*
- I will *carry on* working here until I can find a better job. *continue*
- The book was so interesting that she wanted to *go on* reading it until she had finished. *continue*

4 Discuss the following questions.

1 Would you be interested in doing any of the four jobs that you have heard about?
2 What qualities/abilities do you need to do each of these jobs well?

Grammar: present tenses

1 Read the following rules for when the Present Continuous is used. Then match one of the sentences below to each rule.

The Present Continuous (or Progressive) is used for:

1 actions happening now or over a period of time around now.
2 changing/developing situations.
3 temporary situations.
4 future arrangements.
5 annoying habits.

a) Why are you always telling me what to do?
b) The level of unemployment is getting worse.
c) I'm sorry, but he is doing his homework right now.
d) We are having dinner with Julie on Friday night.
e) She is staying with friends in York for a few days.

a: 5
b: 2
c: 1
d: 4
e: 3

Grammar reference p.175 (17.2)

2 Now do the following exercises with a partner to practise the Present Continuous.

1 Think of members of your family or close friends and say what you think they are probably doing at the moment.
EXAMPLE: *I think my father **is probably having** a meeting in his office.*

2 Think of the same people again and tell your partner about any annoying habits they may have.
EXAMPLE: *My younger brother **is always leaving** his shoes and socks around the house.*

3 Tell your partner what things you have arranged to do this weekend.
EXAMPLE: ***I'm meeting** Maria on Saturday morning and **we're going** shopping together.*

4 Tell your partner if you think the people you know and the place where you live are changing. Think about things such as: fashion/unemployment/ cost of entertainment/pop music/inflation/ pollution/the weather.
EXAMPLE: *The pollution where I live **is getting worse** all the time!*

train timetable
town

3 Read the following rules for when the Present Simple is used. Then match one of the sentences below to each rule.

The Present Simple is used for:

1 routine or regular, repeated actions.
2 time clauses after *when, as soon as, if, until*, etc.
3 permanent situations.
4 the future as expressed in timetables.
5 scientific or natural laws.
6 with 'state' verbs (which we do not usually use in the continuous form) e.g. *be, believe, feel, hate, hear, know, like, look, love, prefer, realise, remember, see, seem, smell, suppose, taste, want*.

a) Water freezes at 0°C.
b) I work five evenings a week.
c) I'll ask him when I see him.
d) I live in Athens.
e) It's the people I like most about the job.
f) The train arrives in Edinburgh at 5.00 p.m.

Grammar reference p.175 (17.1)

4 Now do the following exercises to practise the Present Simple.

1 Complete the following sentences with the Present Simple or Future Simple (*will*) form of the verbs in brackets.
   a) I ......*will*...... (paint) the kitchen when I ......*have*...... (have) some free time.
   b) We ......*won't*...... (start) the meeting until everybody ......*arrive*...... (arrive).
   c) If she ......*...*...... (find) a better job, I think she ......*will*...... (leave).
   d) They ......*will*...... (move) house as soon as they ......*find*...... (find) a buyer.
   e) When he ......*...*...... (come) back, I ......*will*...... (tell) him what we have decided.

2 Write five sentences about yourself in the Present Simple. Each time you should use one of the words/expressions in the box below.

> quite frequently/about two or three times a year/
> very often/from time to time/hardly ever/
> as often as I can/never/once or twice a week/
> more often than I'd like to

EXAMPLE: **I visit** my grandmother **as often as I can**.

3 Work in a group with two other students. Describe your typical routine at the weekend. Are there any major differences between your routine, and the routines of the other students in your group?

EXAMPLE: *I usually **get up** at about 7.00 a.m. and **have** a shower. Then I ...*

5 Complete the following dialogue with the Present Continuous or Present Simple form of the verbs in brackets.

RUPERT: Hi, Nigel! How are you?
NIGEL: Fine, fine. It's been a long time.
RUPERT: Yes, nearly four years now.
NIGEL: So, tell me about yourself!
RUPERT: Well, I (1) .... (work) in this language school in Cairo.
NIGEL: Oh, really? So what (2) .... (do) here in London?
RUPERT: I (3) .... (have) a holiday.
NIGEL: Oh, I see. And what (4) .... (think) of Cairo?
RUPERT: Oh, I (5) .... (like) it very much. It's a very exciting place.
NIGEL: And what about your job?
RUPERT: Well, I generally (6) .... (get up) about 8.30 and (7) .... (plan) some lessons. Fortunately, with time, it (8) .... (get) easier and easier to plan lessons – in the beginning it took me ages! I usually (9) .... (teach) from 11 a.m. to 1 p.m. and later again from 6.30 to 9.30. We all (10) .... (finish) at 9.30 p.m. and we often (11) .... (go) into town in one big group, to a disco or something.
NIGEL: When (12) .... (go back) to Cairo?
RUPERT: Next week, on Friday. The plane (13) .... (leave) early, about 7.00 a.m.
NIGEL: And how's your brother?
RUPERT: Chris ... oh, he's OK. I (14) .... (see) him as often as I can. He is married with two children and he never (15) .... (stop) telling me that I should get a regular job and settle down! He (16) .... (play) a lot of football at the moment. I (17) .... (think) he (18) .... (try) to get fit!
NIGEL: That's new!
RUPERT: And what about you? What (19) .... (do)?

Vocabulary: employment

1   Read the following questions and check that you understand the meaning of the words in *italics*. Use a dictionary where necessary.

1 What do you think is a good *salary* or *wage* in your country? How much would you like to *earn*?
2 Would you like to work on *commission*? Why/Why not? Do you think people should get paid a *bonus* for especially good work?
3 What different information should you put in a *C.V.*?
4 What should you do to make a good impression at a job *interview*?
5 Think of the job you do at the moment or that you would like to do in the future. What *skills* and/or *qualifications* do you need to do it?
6 How many years' *training* do you need to do before you can become a doctor in your country?
7 Is it common or unusual for *employees* to *go on strike* in your country? Do you have *trade unions*?
8 For what reasons can people be *sacked*? For what reasons can people be *made redundant*? Why do people sometimes *resign* from their jobs?
9 What help do people get from the government if they are *unemployed* in your country?
10 At what age do men and women usually *retire* in your country? Do you think this is early, late or about right? Do they usually get a *pension*?

2   Now discuss the questions in small groups.

Watch Out!   *experience*

1 He did a scientific *experiment/experience* in the laboratory.
2 He has a lot of *experience/experiences* as a salesman.
3 He had some terrible *experience/experiences* while he was travelling in the USA.

Which alternative is correct in each sentence?

Exam focus

Paper 3 Use of English: Part 5 (word formation)

About the exam: In Paper 3, Part 5 you read a text with ten gaps. At the end of each line is a key word. You change the form of the word so that it is the correct part of speech to fill each gap.

Procedure
1 Read the text all the way through.
2 Look at the example **(0)**.
3 Look at each gap. Decide what part of speech is required and whether it needs to be positive or negative.
4 Fill in the gap with a word in the appropriate form.

For questions **1–10**, read the text below. Use the word given in capitals at the end of each line to form a word that fits in the space in the same line. There is an example at the beginning **(0)**. In the actual exam you would mark your answers in a box (like the one below) on a separate answer sheet.

EXAMPLE: | **0** | *laziness* |

FATHER FIRES SON

A businessman sacked his own son because of (0) *laziness*,   **LAZY**
incompetence and (1) .... Stuart Bidwell received   **HONEST**
dozens of letters of (2) .... about his work during   **COMPLAIN**
the ten years he was his father's (3) .... 'He got   **EMPLOY**
(4) .... warnings,' said Stephen Bidwell, Stuart's   **NUMBER**
father, and the (5) .... of the company. 'He was   **MANAGE**
absolutely (6) .... at his job and he didn't   **USE**
even have the right (7) ....' Eventually he was   **QUALIFY**
asked to hand in his (8) .... after being caught making   **RESIGN**
phone calls to a girlfriend in Australia. His (9) ....   **REFUSE**
to resign forced his father to sack him, (10) ....   **FAIR**
according to Stuart, who is now suing his father.

Listening: song

1 What does the expression 'the rat race' mean? Why would some people want to get out of it? What might they do instead?

2 You are going to listen to a song called *9 to 5*. What do you imagine the song will be about? Listen and see if you were right.

3 Here are the words to the song, but in each verse the lines are in the wrong order. Put them in the correct order. Then listen to the song again to check your answers. You have been given the first line of each verse.

And the blood starts pumping
And yawn and stretch
Out on the streets
Tumble out of bed *(1)*
Pour myself a cup of ambition
With folks like me
And try to come to life
Jump in the shower
On the job from 9 to 5
And I stumble to the kitchen
The traffic starts jumping

Chorus
And they never give you credit
What a way to make a living
It's all taking and no giving
It's enough to drive you crazy
Working 9 to 5 *(1)*
Barely getting by
If you let it
They just use your mind

You would think that I
But the boss won't seem to let me
9 to 5 for service and devotion *(1)*
I swear sometimes
Want to move ahead
Would deserve a better promotion
That man is out to get me

Exam focus
Paper 2 Writing: Part 1 (transactional letter)

About the exam: In Part 1 of Paper 2 you must write a letter based on certain information. There is no choice and you must write between 120 and 180 words.

1 Read the following example of a typical task.

> You see the following job advertisement in a local newspaper. You are quite interested but would like some extra information. Read carefully the advertisement and the notes which you have made below. Then write your letter:
>
> a) saying why you think you would be particularly suitable for this job.
>
> b) asking for extra information as suggested by the handwritten notes below.
>
> Write **a letter** of **between 120 and 180** words in an appropriate style. Do not write any addresses.

> ### WORK WITH
> ### ENGLISH-SPEAKING TOURISTS
>
> Have you been looking for a chance to improve your English and earn good money at the same time? Well, this is an ideal opportunity!
>
> Our company specialises in providing package tours for British and American tourists all over the world, and we are looking for local people who are interested in acting as tour guides around major cities and places of national interest. You would also be responsible for looking after the general welfare of your group while they were in your care.
>
> Letters of application should be sent to:
>
> *BritAm Tours,*
> *Empire House,*
> *176 Piccadilly,*
> *London W1 9FQ*
>
> Short-listed applicants will be called for interview locally.

- *when job start?*
- *hours of work + pay?*
- *'be responsible for looking after the general welfare' – what does it mean?*
- *available for interview – evenings only!*

2 Here are two different attempts to answer the question in Exercise 1. Read Letter A and Letter B and then complete the table according to the characteristics which you think each letter has.

	Letter A	Letter B
• answers the question directly and completely	✔	✗
• communicates the message effectively	✓	✓
• begins and ends the letter appropriately = *correctly*	✗	✗
• organises it well with clear paragraphs	✗	✓
• has a good range of grammatical structures and vocabulary	✓	✗
• uses the grammatical structures and vocabulary accurately	✓	✗
• has correct punctuation and spelling	✓	✗
• includes a range of linking expressions e.g. *although, furthermore*	✗	✓
• uses language of an appropriate style	✓	✓

Letter A

Dear Sir/Madam,

I am writing with reference to your advertisment in todays paper concerning possible work with English-speaking tourists. I am very intrested in doing this kind of job and will be available from the begining of next month. I need to know exactly when the job would start, I should say that my level of english is good, I can communication well and fairly fluently. I have spent time on holiday in britain and really enjoy meeting people from other countrys. i have always been interested in the history and cultur of my local area. before I can consider the job I need to know what the hours of work and pay would be. I would like to know more about what 'be responsable for the general welfare of your group' means and what they could inwolve. I am afraid that I will only be available for interview in the evening (due to present work commitements). I look forward to hearing from you in the near future.

Yours faithfuly,

Ingrid Nelson

Letter B

Dear Sir/Madam,

I write about your advertisement in today's newspaper concerning possible work with English-speaking tourists. I am very interested by this job and can be start next month. However, I need knowing when job start.

First of all my English level is quite well. I went to England and very enjoy meeting people from others countries. (Moreover,) I had interested in the all history and culture of my town.

I looking forward hear from you.

Lots of love,

Luis Sanchez

3 Now write your own letter in answer to the question above, trying to incorporate the best features of Letter A and Letter B.

Would *YOU* set yourself on fire for £75 a day?

... OR LAUNCH yourself off the Great Wall of China without a parachute? It's all in a day's work when you're a nerves-of-steel stuntwoman. And as it's a profession where there is very little female participation – there are only sixteen stuntwomen in the whole of Britain – it's a job consideration worth taking seriously. Sue Dando finds out the facts.

Astuntperson is a man or woman who does all the really dangerous bits of acting work in films or on TV. (1 ———) Sarah Franzi, 24, is one of Britain's 16 professional stuntwomen (as against 160 men). Like many of her female colleagues, it was a career she'd never seriously considered. 'From when I was young I'd trained to be a dancer, and for seven years after school I was rarely out of work. A dancer's life is pretty short, though, and it was my father who suggested I should think about doing stunt work after I'd given up dancing. (2 ———) For six months, I worked really hard, every day, all day. I had to learn six different skills – sub-aqua, sky diving, horse riding, stuff like that – to a high standard of training.'

Sarah finished all the requirements in just five months – it can take as long as three years to qualify. Two weeks after Sarah's completed application was accepted by the Stunt Committee, she was launching herself off the Great Wall of China in *Superman IV*. 'I was very lucky to get work so quickly. I had a small part, playing a tourist who fell off the Wall after an earthquake, only to be rescued from death by Superman. In reality, I fell 15 metres onto a pile of cardboard boxes! (3 ———) You just have to suffer the discomfort and fall properly. I was paid £210 a day for it, and because it was considered dangerous, another £200 "adjustment" fee was added for every extra take.' This may sound like a lot but, as Sarah explains, 'The film company is paying for the risk. If I'd broken a bone, that isn't very much money at all when you're out of work for the next few months, and there is a risk involved. Safety procedures are very strict, but it's still a danger. (4 ———).'

As yet, Sarah has received injuries no more severe than bangs and bruises, though she does admit to having been scared on at least one occasion.

'I was set alight for *London's Burning* (a TV programme about the London Fire Brigade). It was a full fire job, which meant that my whole body – I was wearing protective clothing – was set alight. (5 ———) The difficulty with that kind of job is that you're never fully in control of the fire, so it's easier for something to go wrong.

'It's jobs like that which make people think we must be completely mad to do this kind of work.

(6 ———) There are so many safety precautions, with so much mental concentration involved, that what we're really doing is creating an illusion of danger. If people think, "How could you do that? You must be mad!" then we're just doing our jobs properly.'

How to qualify

To be accepted onto the Stunt Register – the official list of qualified stuntpeople, and the only means by which you're able to get work – you have to be between 18 and 30 years old, and a full member of Equity, the actors' union. Once you've got these qualifications, you then have to reach the required standard in at least six of the categories listed below. (7 ———) The groups are:

Group A – Fighting
Fencing
Judo/Aikido/Wrestling
Other martial arts
Boxing

Group B – Falling
Trampolining
Diving
Parachuting

Group C – Riding and driving
Horse riding
Car driving
Motorcycle riding

Group D – Agility and strength
Gymnastics

Group E – Water
Swimming
Sub-aqua

Group F – Miscellaneous
Evidence of a high standard of qualification in a skill not listed e.g. ballet, athletics, dance.

Further help

For more details write to:
Stuntperson Enquiries, Equity, 8 Harley Street, London W1N 2AB.
(Don't forget to enclose a stamped addressed envelope.)

from *Just 17* magazine

Reading

1 Describe to a partner the most dangerous and/or exciting thing you have ever done.

2 Read the text opposite and then answer the following questions. (Certain sentences have been taken out of the text which will be inserted later.)

1 What is Sarah Franzi's job? *stuntperson*
2 What made her decide to do it? *her father*
3 Has she been seriously injured? *just one time*
4 Do you think she is well paid? *No*

3 The sentences below have been removed from the text. Decide which sentence goes in each of the numbered gaps in the text. Here is a **procedure** for doing this type of task:

- Read the text once to make sure that you have a good general idea of what it is about.
- Look at the sentences that have been removed and try to get an idea of the subject of each one.
- Look at each gap in the text in turn, at the sentence before it and the sentence after it. In your mind, try putting in the most likely missing sentences. Look for clues to help you e.g. words like *that*, *it* or *he* which refer to something or someone in the sentence before.
- Decide on one sentence for each gap. If later you want to use a particular sentence again, go back and check where you used it before. There may be a different sentence that would fit in this gap.

A But *that's* not the case at all.
B You can't use anything softer than *that*, like mattresses for instance, because you'd bounce back up into view of the camera.
C I was on fire for 15 seconds and towards the end it was incredibly hot.
D *They* should fall within at least three of the groups, but not more than two categories should fall within any one group.
E *This* can be anything from a relatively simple fall into a swimming pool, to jumping off the top of a skyscraper.
F Fortunately, the risks are one part of the job I really enjoy.
G I did think about *it* for the next two years – then decided to take the plunge and have a real go.

4 Compare your answers with a partner and say what you think the underlined words in Exercise 3 refer to.

EXAMPLE: *In A I think that refers to the idea that stuntpeople must be completely mad.*

5 Discuss the following questions.

1 What would you feel about doing Sarah's job?
2 Have you ever done any of the sports in Groups A–F? Are/Were you good at them? Would you like to do any of them? Why?/Why not?

Vocabulary: sports

1 Match the words in the box to one of the listed sports below. Some of the items go with more than one sport.

a glove   a net   a hole   a set   a ring   a green
a goal   a racket   a round   an umpire   a court
a pitch   a linesman   a club   a referee   to serve

1 tennis *a set*   4 volleyball *a net*
2 golf *hole, green*   5 boxing *a ring*
3 football *a net, green goal*

2 Describe how the following pairs of sports are similar to and different from each other.

1 volleyball/basketball
2 tennis/table-tennis
3 boxing/wrestling
4 football/American football
5 surfing/windsurfing

3 Discuss the following questions.

1 What sport do you enjoy playing most? Are there any other sports that you would like to try?
2 What sport do you enjoy watching most? Do you prefer going to sports events or watching them on TV?

Writing: sequencers

1 Read the text and put the following pictures in the order in which they happen.

Mountain Men

The history of Sumo wrestling goes back over 2000 years. Its origins are connected to the Japanese belief in Shinto, the 'way of the gods', where winning gains favour with the gods. This is why the ritual of a sumo match is taken so seriously.

The clay fighting ring is itself a sacred shrine. On entering it, the enormous wrestler first claps, to attract the gods' attention and indicate his own purity of heart. Having done that, he shakes his apron to drive away evil spirits, and raises his arms to show he carries no weapons. Next comes his most dramatic gesture. With his left hand on his heart and his right arm extended to the east, the huge fighter raises his right leg as high as possible – to send it crashing down with all his force. Then he performs the same earth-shaking stamp with the other leg. After that, he purifies himself and the ring by throwing salt, wiping himself, and rinsing his mouth with water. Finally, the opponents spend three or four minutes trying to intimidate each other with grimaces and threatening postures.

The fight itself is brief and brutal and consists of a thunderous collision that rarely lasts more than ten seconds, which ends when one giant is pushed to the ground or outside the circle.

2

1 What seven different words or grammatical structures can you see in the second paragraph for describing a sequence?
   EXAMPLE: **On** enter**ing** it, the enormous wrestler **first** claps, ...

2 Think about a typical morning in the week. Describe what happens when you wake up. Use some of the 'sequencers' from the text.
   EXAMPLE: *The first thing is that my alarm goes off. Then I get up ...*

3 Work in a group with other students and describe a sport that you know.

- Refer to the following if appropriate:
- where you play
- what you play with
- what you wear
- who you play with
- the object of the game
- the basic rules
- what makes a good player
- Use some of the words and structures from the text to describe sequences.
- If the other students know how to play the sport, they should imagine they don't and make you explain very clearly!

4 Write a short introduction to your particular sport for people who have never played it before. Divide it into paragraphs referring to the different areas listed in Exercise 3 above.

1 Look at the following characteristics and think of two jobs for which each one is necessary. Use different jobs each time.

EXAMPLE: *strength: a wrestler, a bouncer*

1 strength   2 kindness   3 patience
4 reliability   5 creativity   6 attention to detail

2 Explain the difference in meaning between the following pairs of words/phrases.

1 an employer/an employee
2 to win/to earn
3 a salary/a wage
4 unemployed/on a pension
5 to be sacked/to be made redundant
6 a perk/a bonus
7 to retire/to resign

3

1 Write the verb form of the following nouns. Then mark the position of the stress in both forms.

Noun	Verb
qualifi'cation	to 'qualify
resignation	
employment	
advertisement	
application	
replacement	
information	
specialisation	
protection	
concentration	

2 Now write a sentence using either the noun or the verb form of each of the words in the table.

EXAMPLE: *It takes many years to **qualify** as a doctor.*

4 Choose the correct alternative in the following sentences.

1 The job situation *slowly gets/is slowly getting* better.
2 I *only occasionally go/am only occasionally going* to the theatre.
3 You *don't believe/aren't believing* him, do you?
4 I *stay/am staying* with Paul for a few days.
5 Ask him to give me a call, when you *see/are seeing* him.
6 I *probably play/am probably playing* football tonight.

5 For questions 1–15 read the text and decide which answer **A**, **B**, **C** or **D** best fits each space. Circle your answer. There is an example at the beginning (0)

0 **A** plays **B** contests **C** sports **D** encounters

A SPORTING DISASTER

I never really enjoyed (0) .... at school. I remember when I played football. I was always put in (1) ...., but I used to get bored and read a book. Then when the other side (2) .... the rest of my (3) .... would shout at me. Later on I tried tennis, which wasn't much better. I used to have this habit of dropping the (4) .... each time I went to hit the ball. The worst thing was when I actually won a (5) .... – I was so pleased that I ran and tried to jump over the (6) .... but caught my foot on it, fell and broke my arm.
My latest attempt to get (7) .... was when I tried boxing at a local gym. I'll never forget my first (8) .... I climbed into the (9) .... and the bell went for the start of the first (10) .... I just shut my eyes and swung my fist. Unfortunately, I hit the (11) .... and not my (12) .... Needless to say that was the end of my boxing career. Next I decided to take up mountaineering. I (13) .... a holiday in the Himalayas with two old school friends. On our first climb I managed to slip and found myself hanging on the end of a rope half way up a mountain. All my friends could do was to call out to me to (14) .... until the rescue party arrived. I guess I'll never learn. I (15) .... wanting to try out other sports even though I know I'll never be a champion!

1	**A** net	**B** goal	**C** ring	**D** square
2	**A** scored	**B** pointed	**C** served	**D** drew
3	**A** group	**B** selection	**C** team	**D** club
4	**A** bat	**B** racket	**C** club	**D** stick
5	**A** play	**B** game	**C** race	**D** fight
6	**A** fence	**B** line	**C** net	**D** web
7	**A** strong	**B** well	**C** slim	**D** fit
8	**A** fight	**B** game	**C** match	**D** play
9	**A** court	**B** ring	**C** pitch	**D** square
10	**A** set	**B** half	**C** round	**D** game
11	**A** arbitrator	**B** referee	**C** judge	**D** umpire
12	**A** opponent	**B** enemy	**C** partner	**D** contestant
13	**A** booked	**B** ordered	**C** paid	**D** bought
14	**A** keep on	**B** hold on	**C** go on	**D** carry on
15	**A** keep on	**B** hold on	**C** get on	**D** hang on

UNIT

3 Nearest and dearest

Speaking

🔊 **1** Fill in the gaps in the following poem with the words in the box. Then listen and check your answers.

> twin (x 2) same trick out pain win sick
> again blame shout sin

MY SISTER

My younger sister is a (1) _pain_ ,
She's so naughty again and (2) _agin_ .
Every morning is the (3) _same_ ,
And what is worse I get the (4) _blame_ .
It is so sad, I just can't (5) _win_ ,
'Cos after all she is my (6) _twin_ !!

My Dad says, 'I'll sort her (7) _out_ ,'
But all he does is shout and (8) _shout_ .
But shouting doesn't do the (9) _trick_ ,
It isn't fair, it makes me (10) _sick_ .
It's such a crime, 'Oh! What a (11) _sin_ ,'
Please, oh please DON'T HAVE A (12) _twin_ !!

2 Discuss what the advantages/disadvantages are of:

a) being an only child.
b) having brothers and sisters.
c) being a twin.

Reading

1 Read the following article and decide what you think is the most appropriate title.

a) Twins reunited after a lifetime apart.
b) Twin sisters trapped in a single mind. ✗
c) Bringing up twins – the parents' story.

1 AT FIRST IT'S HARD TO BELIEVE. They speak in unison, walk in step, dress identically to the last button and match each other mouthful for mouthful at the dinner table. But this is no trick with mirrors. This is everyday East London, where everyone knows Greta and Freda Chaplin, the identical twins.

2 The twins do everything together. Whether they are out shopping or doing the housework they mirror each other's actions and mannerisms down to the finest detail. To vacuum the floor both twins grasp the handle of the hoover at the same time as they guide it slowly around the carpet together. If they make tea, both their hands are on the bottle as they pour the milk. Listening to them talk is like hearing one person with a slight echo a split second later. If someone gives them a bar of soap in different colours, they will cut theirs in two and swap a half. They have two black coats, but one came with green buttons and one black. They swapped the buttons around so that each twin had two green and two black buttons on each coat. The sisters themselves say that they feel like one person, not two. Sometimes it's almost as though they inhabit the same mind.

3 The sisters, now 48, live in a flat in Hackney, East London. They are a familiar sight in the area, where they are often seen out shopping together in their long clothes and waist-length hair. Some people are frightened of their strange telepathic bond, others laugh at them. The twins realise this and don't like it, so they avoid crowds. They rely a great deal on the protection and friendship of Jack Davenport who has been like a father to them. 'Sometimes it's as if you're seeing double,' he says. 'If we go out shopping, they automatically buy the same thing in the same colour at the same price, although it might be from a different counter. They do everything at the same time – clean their teeth, eat, drink. If they're having fish and chips, they will pick a chip up at the same time.'

2 Now read the article again and decide if the following statements are True or False. Make a note of the part of the text which helps you decide.

1 Greta and Freda live in England. *yes*
2 They speak nearly at the same time. *yes*
3 They feel the need to look exactly the same.
4 Local people are generally very kind and supportive *no* towards the twins.
5 Their father's name is Jack. *no*
6 Their mother tried to help them grow up with their *no* own identities.
7 They have different characters. *yes*
8 Dr Bryan isn't surprised by the idea of telepathy *yes* between Greta and Freda.
9 Dr Bryan is concerned with the psychological aspects of multiple births. *yes*

3 Find words or phrases in the text with the following meanings.

1 at the same time *(para. 1)* *unison*
2 to hold tightly *(para. 2)* *to grasp*
3 a very short time *(para. 2)* *split second*
4 to exchange *(para. 2)* *swapped*
5 part of your body, above your hips *(para. 3)* *waist*
6 a flat surface in a shop where you go to be served *(para. 3)* *counter*
7 to keep together *(para. 4)* *to stick each other*
8 to agree that something is true *(para. 5)* *admit*
9 to become angry suddenly *(para. 5)* *to temper*
10 part of a woman's body where a baby develops before it is born *(para. 6)* *womb*
11 certain, sure *(para. 6)* *bound to be*
12 anxiety, pressure *(para. 7)* *emotional stress*

4 Discuss the following questions.

1 Do you think the writer of the article:

a) dislikes the twins?
b) feels sorry for the twins?
c) admires the twins?

Why?

2 What do you feel about the twins? Do you know any twins? Are they like the twins in the article?

Little is known about the childhood of the sisters, except that they grew up on a housing estate in York. From babies their mother treated them as one and encouraged their dependence on each other. Everything in their life was identical down to the twin dolls they played with. 'She told us always to stick to each other,' say Freda and Greta in unison. 'She said when you go to the shops always ask for two of something and if they've only got one, don't take it.' ▸ 4

As Jack Davenport remarks, 'They do have different personalities although they won't admit it. Greta is the softer, more sensible one. Freda is the one who tends to dominate her sister and lose her temper more quickly. In the last few years they have become quieter and much more intelligent company. All they want is love, friendship and understanding, which they have never had.' ▸ 5

Dr Elizabeth Bryan, Director of the Multiple Births Foundation says, 'These two are an extreme case, but I'm quite sure there is often telepathy between twins. If you shared the womb and your life together, there is bound to be.' ▸ 6

Having dealt with more than 3,000 sets of twins, she says, 'My concern is to help parents with the emotional stress of having two babies or more at the same time. The mother of Freda and Greta Chaplin tried to bring them up as a single child and didn't give them the chance ever to be separated. So they never had the opportunity to develop as individuals.' ▸ 7

Vocabulary: phrasal verbs (family)

1 Listen to sentences that contain the following phrasal verbs and make a note of what you think each verb means.

1 to grow up
2 to bring (someone) up *education*
3 to look after : *take care*
4 to get on (with someone) *positive*
5 to look up to (someone) *imitate = admire, respect*
6 to take after (someone) *hide*
7 to get up to (something)
8 to tell (someone) off *instruction : to be conver*

2 Use some of the phrasal verbs to describe yourself and your own family situation.

EXAMPLE: *When I was about nine, I used to **get up to** all sorts of things. Once I ...*

from *Today* newspaper

Exam focus

Paper 3 Use of English: Part 4 (error correction)

About the exam: In Paper 3, Part 4 you read a text containing errors and decide if each line is correct or whether there is an extra word that should not be there.

Procedure

1 Read the text all the way through.
2 Look at each line. If it is correct, put a tick (✓) at the end of the line. If there is an extra word, circle it and write it at the end of the line.
3 Remember that the extra words are often grammatical words e.g. prepositions (*in, on, at,* etc.), articles (*the, a, an*), pronouns (*it, that, what,* etc.), auxiliary verbs (*do, will, am,* etc.) and determiners (*some, much,* etc.)
4 In the actual exam you then transfer your answers to boxes on a separate answer sheet.

	MY FAMILY	
00	We are the same as the most families.	*the*
0	There are four children altogether.	✓
1	My brother Pete is quite a bit younger than I am	
2	We are look pretty similar, but he's a little	
3	shorter and slimmer. He isn't as careful with the	
4	money as I am and generally spends it on without	
5	thinking. We play squash together from a time to	∨
6	time, but I'm much worse than he is. He can to run	
7	a lot more quickly than I can. I get on very well	
8	with my sister Sarah, but I am a lot more	∪
9	sociable than she is. She really prefers having	∪
10	her head in a book than to being with people. She is	
11	probably the most intelligent of all of us. I am	∨
12	think Kate she is the nicest and most-easy going	∨
13	person in the all family. I would say she is	∪
14	generally a much more happier person than Sarah.	
15	And me? Well, I'm a pretty happy most of the time too.	

Grammar: making comparisons

1 Look again at the Use of English text and complete the following rules about making comparisons.

COMPARISONS

One-syllable adjectives

a) The comparative and superlative of one-syllable adjectives e.g. *young (line 1)* are generally made by ...er...........

b) An exception is adjectives which end with a vowel plus a consonant e.g. *slim (line 3)* in which case you
.........mer...........

c) Another exception is adjectives which end with -e e.g. *nice (line 12)*, in which case you ......
................st...........

d) There are a number of one-syllable adjectives which have irregular comparatives and superlatives, including ......worst...........

Two and three-syllable adjectives

e) The comparative and superlative of two and three-syllable adjectives e.g. *sociable (line 9)* and *intelligent (line 11)* are generally made by ....
...............most...........

f) However, the comparative and superlative of two-syllable adjectives ending in -y e.g. *happy (line 14)* are generally made by ......ier...........

Extra information

g) Use *as ... as* to compare things which are ....
......similar...........
and *not as ... as* to compare things which are ....
.........different...........

h) Put *a bit/a little* before the comparative to show there is ....little.......... difference.

i) Put *a lot/much/far/a great deal* before the comparative to show there is ......big........... difference.

j) To make the comparative and superlative of adverbs e.g. *quickly*, you generally use ....
.........more quickly...........

Grammar reference p.164 (4)

2 Look at the pictures and decide which of the following sentences are true.

Wayne
Chuck
Floyd

1 Floyd isn't quite as tall as Chuck. F
2 Floyd isn't nearly as tall as Chuck. T
3 Floyd is as tall as Chuck. F
4 Chuck isn't as tall as Wayne. F
5 Chuck is much taller than Wayne. F
6 Chuck is a bit taller than Wayne. T

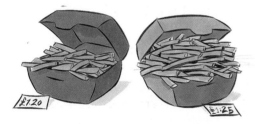

£1.20   £1.25

7 There aren't nearly as many french fries in the red box as in the blue box. T
8 There are slightly fewer french fries in the blue box than in the red box. F
9 There are a lot more french fries in the blue box than in the red box. T
10 The french fries in the red box are far more expensive than those in the blue box. F
11 The french fries in the red box are a little less expensive than those in the blue box. T

3 Each of the following pairs of sentences should mean approximately the same. However, in every second sentence there is a word missing. Decide what the missing word is in each case.

1 My father is the hardest-working person I know.
   No one I know works as hard my father.
2 I've never met such an intelligent person.
   She is most intelligent person I've ever met.
3 We don't have nearly as much money as they do.
   They have lot more money than we do.

4 Simon is much older than I am.
   I am nearly as old as Simon.
5 I can't play tennis as well as she can.
   She plays tennis better I can.
6 Last time the ticket wasn't quite as expensive.
   Last time the ticket was a little expensive.

4 Work in a group with two other students. Student A and Student B should choose one of the alternatives from the list below to 'sell' to Student C.

Student A	Student B
1 a holiday in England	a holiday in the USA
2 a motorbike	a sportscar
3 an evening at a local disco	an evening at a local restaurant
4 a book	a film (of the same story)

Student A and Student B should each try to convince Student C that what they are 'selling' is better than what the other person is 'selling'. Use appropriate language for making comparisons. Student C will finally decide which is the best.

Before you start, listen to an example and decide who you think is the better 'salesperson'.

5 Below are some world records. Look at the pictures and decide what each world record is for. Then compare your ideas with other students.

1 55.8 cm   4 1,009,152,000
2 35m 55cm   5 8.61 seconds
3 92 hours

HIC....HIC...HIC....

29

Pronunciation: /ʌ/

1 Which of the words in the box have the sound /ʌ/ (as in *son*)?

mother   uncle   nephew   cousin   company
bank   money   love   drunk   trouble   drank
enough   young   blood   won   Monday   cup
home   cough   shut   butter   much   London

2 Listen and make a note of the words above that you hear. Then turn to page 199 and look at the sentences you heard. Try saying them with good pronunciation.

Vocabulary: describing people (1)

1 Look at the following relations and decide which ones:

1 can be either male *or* female.
2 cannot be related to you by blood.

stepmother   twin   niece   sister-in-law   nephew
great-grandfather   half-sister   uncle   cousin

2

1 Look at the adjectives for describing people and match each one to the definitions 1–14 opposite.

a) hard-working
b) generous
c) stubborn
d) self-confident
e) reliable
f) loyal
g) strict
h) open-minded
i) thoughtful
j) naughty
k) attractive
l) sensitive
m) modest
n) ambitious

2 Try to think of one person you know who is like each adjective. Tell a partner who it is and give examples of their behaviour.

EXAMPLE: *My brother's very **hard-working**. He sometimes doesn't get home from the office until midnight.*

3 Work in a group with other students and think of an opposite for each adjective. Use a dictionary where necessary.

1 *adj* **1** showing that you are thinking deeply **2** paying attention to the feelings of other people

2 *adj* willing to give money, help, and kindness

3 *adj* having a strong desire to be successful, powerful, or rich

4 *adj* willing to consider new ideas and opinions

5 *adj* determined and having a strong will

6 *adj* severe in demanding obedience to rules of behaviour

7 *adj* **1** that may be trusted; dependable **2** that you can trust to perform well at all times

8 *adj* behaving badly, or not obeying a parent, teacher, or set of rules (used of children)

9 *adj* having a belief in one's own value and abilities

10 *adj* **1** pretty or HANDSOME (used of a person) **2** pleasant to look at

11 *adj* faithful to people, places, or things

12 *adj* having or expressing a lower opinion of your own abilities than you deserve (a word used to express approval)

13 *adj* showing delicate feelings or judgement

14 *adj* dedicating a lot of time and energy to work

3 Describe the different members of your family to a partner. Compare yourself with the members of your family using appropriate language for describing people and making comparisons.

> **Watch Out!** *sensible/sensitive*
>
> 1 He's a rather *sensible/sensitive* child. He gets very upset if people get angry.
> 2 Be *sensible/sensitive* and put on some warm clothes. It's freezing!
>
> Which is the correct alternative in each sentence?

(handwritten notes at top)
EM 21 Ex. 1+2
EM 21 Hòng 1+2
CB 30 Ex 2+1
CB 30 watch out.
CB: 34 Voc 3

Listening: man's best friend

1 Listen to part of a radio programme about pets. Decide which of the situations in the pictures above is not mentioned.

2 Listen again and decide if the vet Jane Herriot would agree with the following statements. Write 'Yes' or 'No' in the box next to each statement and be ready to explain your answers.

1 Pet owners have to be prepared to look after their pets for up to twenty years. _yes_
2 If your home is 'puppy-proof' you can relax and let the puppy play on its own. _no_
3 You shouldn't let your puppy chew everything he wants to chew. _yes_
4 Puppies need to be disciplined in the same way by everyone in the family. _no_
5 You should gently smack a puppy for doing something wrong. _No_
6 You can keep a puppy in a small space provided you take it for walks. _yes_
7 Puppies are often naughty because they don't have anything to do. _yes_

3 Do you agree with Jane Herriot's advice?

Writing: drafting and redrafting

1 These photographs and slogans aim to make people think about pets and their rights. Which would be most effective in your country?

2 Read the following question which asks you to write an article.

> An international magazine for young people who keep pets is concerned about the health and safety of animals bought as presents. The editor has asked you to write an article offering advice to people about choosing suitable pets and looking after them properly.

- Work with a partner and decide on an interesting title for your article, note down ideas and divide them into paragraphs.
- Write a first draft of the article together in 120–180 words. Use informal language.
- Exchange articles with another pair of students. Read their article and mark parts that you do not understand and where you would like some more information. Return the article.
- Rewrite your article with your partner, responding to the comments of other students.
- Go through your final version and check carefully for mistakes of grammar, spelling, punctuation, word order and vocabulary.

Reading

1 Read the following opening paragraphs to an article. What are the two families in the photos below going to do to make themselves very well-known?

Open House

*Families Reveal Their
Real-Life Secrets To Millions*

1 Thanks to the <u>telly</u>, we all know how the rich and famous live. But who knows what our friends and neighbours get up to behind closed doors?

For the first time, the inside secrets of four ordinary families are revealed in Sunday's *Frame the family*. In this 30-minute special the families open their hearts and homes using a camcorder to record the essential ingredients of their daily lives.

At times it's more like watching a video nasty! Huge rows, dad's unpleasant habits and secretly filmed confessions make
10 the show a uniquely revealing documentary.

Here, two families who took part, the Chiappis and the Gibsons, introduce themselves and give us a taste of things to come in the programme.

the Chiappis

the Gibsons

2 Look at the photos of the two families and talk about how you imagine them to be. Think about the following questions:

- How do the various brothers and sisters get on?
- What jobs do the parents do?
- Are the parents strict with their children?
- Are they a very close family?

3 Now read about the two families and check if your ideas were correct.

The Chiappi Family

Loud laughter and even louder arguments can be heard from the Chiappis' house. Italian-born Luciano, his wife Diane and three daughters Enza, 18, Daniela, 15, and Claudia, 13, changed nothing for the camera to reveal themselves as a fiery but
20 fiercely loyal family.

'There was one point when I wished the camera had been turned off,' admits Daniela. 'Claudia and I had a massive <u>row</u>. I was really angry and forgot Enza was filming. I was worried about it because I didn't want to be seen as hot-tempered and horrible.'

At that, the rest of the family <u>yell</u>, 'But you are hot-tempered and horrible!' and
30 the laughter and shouting begin again.

In the middle of it all is Luciano, 48, a garage owner. The four women admit they gang up on him. 'He can be a real pain in the neck! He's often <u>grumpy</u> and thinks he's never wrong,' says his 42-year-old wife Diane, a teacher. 'Everything we've shot is very true to life, except Luciano and I <u>fall out</u> much more than you see on the film.'
40 Claudia, who does a wicked impression of her dad, says, 'His jokes are really bad and he tells them a hundred times. Ever since we've been filming he has said, "You must talk to my agent first." and he still thinks it's funny!'

The girls kept the programme a secret from their dad until the very last moment. 'The irritating part is they didn't ask me, they have no respect. It's always the
50 same,' he <u>moans</u>.

The whole family is in for some surprises when the film is shown – they've all said privately what they think of the others.

'Sometimes it all became annoying when you didn't want to be filmed,' says Enza. 'But the best bit was finding out what irritated dad – long hairs in the plug hole!'

The Gibson Family

60 When 13-year-old Mark Gibson and 15-year-old sister, Suzanna volunteered their family for the programme, the television team knew they were going to have some fun.

'My family's mad, absolutely crazy,' says Suzanna seriously. 'I'm the sensible one,' she insists as dad Jack, 42, and mum Pauline, 38, burst into laughter as they listen to their daughter.

70 Jack, a Geography teacher, and Pauline, a doctor's receptionist, agree with their children's opinion of them. Pauline says, 'The most ridiculous things make us laugh – especially other people's downfalls. Our friends are amazed that we're letting complete strangers see our home-life by doing this. But I can't see why not. We've got nothing to be ashamed of.'

80 Jack, who once lived in a tree-house for a month in aid of charity, adds with a grin: 'Anyway, the kids and teachers at work already know I'm crazy, so it makes no difference to me.'

The fun-loving family obviously had a fantastic time with their camcorder. 'At first we really tried to be on our best behaviour and we even tidied up the house a bit,' laughs Pauline. 'But that 90 only lasted a week, it was impossible to keep up.'

Water fights in the garden, when everything – including the camera – got completely drenched, were a regular feature of the hours of tape the Gibsons made. Mark loved the recording they made of an outing to the local zoo, while Suzanna hated the film her mother secretly took of her as she was doing her 100 aerobic exercises in front of the bedroom mirror. Suzanna retaliated by lying in wait at 7.30 a.m. for her mum to come out of the shower. The family doesn't know which bits of film will actually make it to the screen until the programme is shown on television. But Mark's quite certain that the bit he took of his mum and dad getting ready to go 110 to a party one night will be there.

'They're worse than teenagers, they take absolutely ages to get ready,' he complains. 'Dad stands there trying to decide what tie to wear and Mum spends hours putting on her make-up!'

4 Now read about the two families again and answer the following questions.

1 In which family did two of the children not always enjoy being watched by the camera?
2 Which husband and wife argue a lot?
3 Which father likes to try and make people laugh?
4 Which family seemed to really enjoy the whole experience?
5 Which family sounds particularly noisy?
6 Which daughter used the camera to get revenge on her mother?
7 Which husband and wife take a long time getting ready to go out?
8 Which father isn't treated the way he would like by the rest of the family?

5 Look at the words in the table which come from the text.

1 Decide what part of speech (noun, adjective or verb) each word is as they appear in the article.
2 Look at the suggested meaning of each word and decide if it is appropriate in the context. Two of the meanings are incorrect.

Word	Part of speech	Meaning
telly (*line 1*)	noun	television
row (*line 24*)	noun	noisy argument
yell (*line 28*)	verb	shout, cry out loudly
grumpy (*line 34*)	noun	in a good mood
fall out (*line 38*)	verb	quarrel, argue
moan (*line 50*)	verb	complain, grumble
downfall (*line 75*)	noun	bad luck, misfortune
grin (*line 82*)	noun	wide smile
keep up (*line 91*)	verb	continue to do something
drench (*line 94*)	adject	break

6 Discuss the following questions.

1 Which family do you like the sound of most? Why?
2 Are either of the two families similar to your family? How?
3 How would you feel about your family being filmed for a programme like *Frame the family*?
4 What parts of your family life would you want/not want recorded?

from *TV Times* magazine

Vocabulary: describing people (2)

1 Enza Chiappi is showing some photos of her family to her new boyfriend. The photo they are talking about was taken in the same room as the one that goes with the article on page 32, but there are eight differences between the two photos. Look at the photo of the Chiappi family again, listen to the conversation and make a note of the differences.

2 Now listen again and decide which of the following words and expressions are mentioned in the conversation.

Age
She/he ...

is about (nineteen)
has just turned (sixteen)
is in her/his early/mid/late (forties)
is (quite) young/middle-aged/old

Hair
She/he ...

Length
is (going) (a bit) bald
has got short/shoulder-length/long hair
Style
has got curly/straight hair

Build
She/he is ...

Size
thin   slim   wiry   stocky
well-built   overweight
Height
short   of medium height   tall

Face
She/he has got ...

a beard   a moustache
(long) eyelashes
a round/long face
a (pointed) chin

Body marks
a scar

Accessories
She/he is wearing .../has got ...

an earring
glasses   sunglasses
a (silk) scarf   (leather) gloves
a belt
a (gold) chain
a ring

Attitude
She/he looks ...

annoyed
bored
depressed
excited
as if she/he is having fun

3 Now put these words and expressions in the correct columns in the table.

1 (thin/thick) eyebrows
2 a fringe
3 a ponytail
4 a tattoo
5 contact lenses
6 high cheek-bones
7 wears it in a bun
8 teens
9 freckles
10 pleased with herself
11 plump
12 fed-up
13 frail
14 getting on
15 wavy
16 wrinkles

4 Look again at the photo of the Gibson family and write a description of the people using words and expressions in the table.

5 Work with a partner. Student A should look at the picture on page 199 and Student B should look at the picture on page 204. There are ten differences between the two pictures. Describe the people in your picture and find the differences.

1 For questions 1–8 complete the second sentence so that it has a similar meaning to the first sentence, using the word given. **Do not change the word given.** You must use between two and five words, including the given word.

1 Could you take care of our cat while we are on holiday?

after   *to look after*

Would you mind .... our cat while we are on holiday?

2 My father lived in the country throughout his childhood.

brought   *was brought up*

My father .... in the country.

3 Their daughter is an adult now.

has   *has grown*

Their daughter .... up now.

4 I have a good relationship with my two younger sisters.

well   *get on well with*

I .... my two younger sisters.

5 The teacher was angry with us for being late.

off   *put off*

The teacher .... for being late.

6 He is very like his father in character and appearance.

takes   *after*

He .... his father in character and appearance.

7 He had always admired his Aunt Sandra.

looked   *up to*

He had always .... his Aunt Sandra.

8 I'm sure the twins will be doing something naughty while we're out.

getting   *getting up to*

I'm sure the twins will be .... something while we're out.

2 Compare three of the following things. Write a short paragraph for each using as many words and expressions for making comparisons as possible.

1 Two similar shops that you know well.
2 Two people that you know well.
3 Two pop groups/singers that you know well.
4 Two towns/countries that you know well.
5 Two computer games that you know well.
6 Your house/flat and somebody else's house/flat.

3 Choose one adjective to describe each of the following people.

a) Once Hans has decided to do something, it's impossible to make him change his mind.
b) Tom is very keen to do well in his job. He wants to get to the top of the company by the time he is thirty.   *hard worker*
c) Anna is not fixed in her opinions. She is always ready to consider new ideas.   *open mind*
d) Anita is the sort of person that if she says she will do something, you know she will do it.   *loyal*
e) Once you are a friend of Paul's, you are a friend for life.
f) Maria never does any work. She just sits around doing nothing all day.   *lazy*

4 A man and woman were seen running away from a post office which had just been robbed. This is the report that an eye-witness wrote for the police. Fill in the gaps with an appropriate word from the box. You do not need to use all the words.

at	looking	moustache	well-built	as much
like	contact lenses	wavy	lot	bald	in
wearing	putting	looked	ponytail	sunglasses

DATE: 18/3/96

CRIME: Robbery of Mare Street Post Office

WITNESS: M. Stewart

I was just getting out of my car, when I saw these two people, a man and a woman, running fast down the other side of the street from me. They were being chased by one or two people who ran out of the post office. The man was (1) *well-built* taller than the woman. He was wearing black (2) *wearing* and he had a long (3) *moustache*. He was carrying a red leather bag. He had long black hair, a beard and a (4) *moustache*. He had on a green anorak with badges on the sleeves. He was quite (5) .... and muscular. The woman was quite small and very slim, but she could run just as fast (6) .... the man. She had (7) *wavy* shoulder-length hair and was probably (8) .... her late teens. She was (9) *wearing* a dark blue T-shirt and jeans. They both (10) *looked* quite scared.

35

4 Seeing is believing

Speaking

Look at the paintings and discuss the following questions.

1 Which of the paintings is the original?
2 Which one do you prefer ?
3 What do you know about the original painting?
4 What do you know about the artist?

Reading

1 Read the following article through quickly to answer these questions.

1 Has the 'Mona Lisa' ever been stolen? *yes*
2 Is the painting in the Louvre the original? *yes/not sure*

2 Now read the article again and underline the most suitable heading below for each of the numbered paragraphs.

0 Are all the da Vincis by da Vinci? /Who was Leonardo da Vinci?
1 A mysterious theft/Who was the *Mona Lisa*?
2 A dishonest craftsman/The *Mona Lisa* comes home
3 An international conspiracy/Why Valfierno had to wait
4 A successful conspiracy – a fake *Mona Lisa*?/The mystery solved
5 Museum directors with an interest in science/Would *Mona Lisa* pass a scientific test?

Will the real Mona Lisa please stand up?

(0 ———)

The paintings of renaissance scientist, inventor and musician Leonardo da Vinci have always attracted controversy. Only 14 works have ever been attributed to him and experts have questioned the authenticity of several. Not even such a famous painting as the *Mona Lisa* is above suspicion. It is neither signed nor dated and no record of subsequent payment to Leonardo has ever been found.

(1 ———)

The painting, believed to be a portrait of the wife of a Florentine merchant, is dated at about 1502. It has been on public display in the Louvre since 1804. Now housed in a bullet-proof glass case, it has always been surrounded by tight security. Even so, on 24 August 1911, it was stolen. Initial leads came to nothing and no clues to the thief's motives or the whereabouts of the picture materialised for fifteen months. At one point Picasso, then relatively unknown, came under suspicion, but there was no evidence to suggest that he did anything more serious than 'borrow' some neglected tribal pieces from the museum.

(2 ———)

In November 1913, Florentine art dealer Alfredo Geri received a letter from someone claiming they had the *Mona Lisa*. The writer of the letter was prepared to sell it back to Italy for 500,000 lire. Geri contacted the director of the Uffizi museum in Florence, who arranged a meeting with the person who had written to Geri. This person turned out to be an Italian carpenter, Vincenzo Peruggia, who had been commissioned by the Louvre to make the painting's protective wooden box. He had been able to steal the famous work of art because he knew the museum's routine so well. The *Mona Lisa* he produced was proclaimed genuine by the Uffizi and sent back to Paris. The big question was why did Peruggia wait so long before trying to sell the painting?

(3 ———)

One explanation is that he was an accomplice of the international criminal the Marques de Valfierno, who had copies made of the *Mona Lisa* while it was still in the Louvre. Once the theft was announced, Valfierno went to America where he sold 'the original *Mona Lisa*' six times over to wealthy collectors for two million dollars. Peruggia was left with the original painting and realising that Valfierno was never going to contact him again, attempted to make some money by selling it. As for the American collectors, they couldn't complain for fear of revealing their involvement in the crime. Intriguingly a number of 'original *Mona Lisas*' have since turned up in America.

(4 ———)

But there is another theory. Shortly after the theft, Parisian art dealer Eduard Jonas claimed he was in possession of the original *Mona Lisa*. He subsequently changed his story under threat of being charged with its theft and declared it a fake. Later, however, a British conman, Jack Dean, insisted that he had helped Peruggia steal the painting, but substituted a copy for the original before Peruggia took it to Italy. Dean claimed to have sold the original to a Paris art dealer. If Dean's story is true, and the Jonas incident gives it some support, then the painting now in the Louvre, surrounded by impregnable security systems and seen by thousands of visitors a day, is a forgery.

(5 ———)

So, is there any way of knowing for certain? It would seem that there is. A method known as 'neutron activation analysis' has been used on a number of occasions to establish the authenticity of works of art. It involves bombarding the painting with neutrons so as to identify chemical elements in the paint. It can be used to determine exactly when a painting was produced since chemical elements in even tiny traces of paint vary according to the period of painting. If the directors of the Louvre chose to, they could put the painting's neutrons to the test and perhaps the real *Mona Lisa* would at last stand up.

from *Focus* magazine

Speaking

1 Discuss the following questions:

1 Do you know of any other famous cases of forgery?
2 How important is it for works of art to be genuine?

2 Imagine that the Louvre has decided to hold an enquiry into the authenticity of the *Mona Lisa*. You are going to present evidence to the enquiry. You should find information in the text to support your case. Decide which of these two positions you are going to defend:

- The *Mona Lisa* in the Louvre is the original work and was painted by Leonardo da Vinci.
- The *Mona Lisa* in the Louvre was not painted by Leonardo da Vinci.

Present your case to the enquiry.

Vocabulary: science and technology

1 Work with a partner and make a list of all the useful information that a dictionary can give you.

2 Look at the dictionary entries below from the *Longman Active Study Dictionary of English* to see if they give you more or less information than you have in your list.

3 Now fill in the gaps in the following sentences with an appropriate word from the dictionary entries.

1 Please try and be *realistic* . We have no chance of arriving by 8 p.m.

2 This is an incredible discovery. It is going to *revolutionise* the way we treat our patients.

3 I'm afraid there's been a small explosion in the *laboratory* and it can't be used at the moment.

4 If you mix these two *chemicals* together, you will *discover* a very nasty smell.

5 I suppose, *theory* speaking it's possible, but it will never work in practice!

6 There have been some important *theory* in the search for a cure for cancer.

7 I think the dishwasher is the best *invention* ever!

8 We need to increase the rate of *development* of this new drug. Demand is very high. *production*

4 Look again at the words you used to fill in the gaps. Check how many syllables each word has in natural speech and where the main stress falls. Then say the words, with good pronunciation, to a partner.

EXAMPLE: *realistic: 4 syllables - re . a . 'lis . tic*

---

chem·i·cal /'kemɪkəl/ *n* any substance used in or produced by chemistry
chem·is·try /'kemɪ̯stri/ *n* [U] **1** the study of the substances which make up the universe and the way in which they change and combine with each other: *She's got a degree in chemistry.*

develop /dɪ'veləp/ *v* [I] **1** to grow: *The fighting could easily develop* **into** *a full-scale war.* | *This flower developed from a tiny seed.* **2** [T] to improve `something or make it grow: *a campaign to develop the local economy*
de·vel·op·ment /dɪ'veləpmənt/ *n* **1** [C] a new event: *There has been an important new development in the political situation.* **2** [C] a new invention, or an improvement to an existing machine or process: *recent developments in the treatment of cancer*

theo·ry /'θɪəri/ *n* **theories 1** [C] an explanation for something which is reasonable or scientifically acceptable, but which has not yet been proved to be true: *Darwin's theory of evolution* | *The detective's theory is that the murderer was well known to the victim.* **2** [U] the general principles for the study of an art or science as opposed to practical skill in it: *musical theory* | *There will be two chemistry exams: one on theory and one will be practical.* **theoretical** /θɪə'retɪkəl/ *adj: theoretical science* | *a theoretical possibility* –**theoretically** /-kli/ *adv: Theoretically it's my job, but in fact I don't do it.*

dis·cov·er /dɪs'kʌvə/ *v* to find or learn about something for the first time: *Columbus discovered America in 1492.* | *The stolen goods were discovered in their garage.*
dis·cov·ery /dɪs'kʌvəri/ *n* **discoveries 1** [U] the action of finding something: *The discovery of oil on land made the family rich.* **2** [C] something that is found out: *He made an important archaeological discovery.*

la·bor·a·tory /lə'bɒrətri || 'læbrətɔːri/ *n* **laboratories** (also **lab** *infml*) a building or room which contains scientific apparatus and in which a scientist works

real /rɪəl/ *adj* **1** actually existing and not just imagined: *The new system has real advantages ...* **2** not false or artifical; GENUINE: *real gold/real leather*
re·a·lis·tic /rɪə'lɪstɪk/ *adj* **1** judging and dealng with situations in a sensible practical way because you realize which things are possible: *It's not realistic to expect my parents to lend us any more money.*

in·vent /ɪn'vent/ *v* [T] **1** to make up, think of, or produce something for the first time: *Alexander Graham Bell invented the telephone in 1876.* **2** to make up something unreal or untrue: *The whole story was invented.* | *I tried to invent an excuse.*
in·ven·tion /ɪn'venʃən/ *v* **1** [U] the act of inventing something: *The invention of the telephone was the start of modern telecommunications systems.* **2** [C] something that has been invented: *The telephone is a wonderful invention.*
in·ven·tor /ɪn'ventə/ *n* a person who invents something new

pro·duce /prə'djuːs || 'duːs/ *v* **produced, producing** [T] **1** to have as a result or effect: *Gordon's jokes produced a great deal of laughter.* **2** to make something, especially in large quantities: *Gas can be produced from coal.* | *The factory produces 500 cars a week.* | **3** to grow or supply: *Canada produces good wheat.*
prod·uct /'prɒdʌkt || 'prɑː-/ *n* **1** something that is produced or made somewhere: *a new range of kitchen products* -see PRODUCTION (USAGE). **2** the result of experiences or certain situations: *Criminals are sometimes the product of bad homes.*
pro·duc·tion /prə'dʌkʃən/ *n* **1** [U] the act of producing something, especially for sale: *This factory specializes in the production of larger cars.* **2** the amount of something which is produced: *Oil production is falling world-wide.*

rev·o·lu·tion /ˌrevə'luːʃən/ *n* **1** [C;U] great social change, especially the changing of a ruler or political system by force: *the Russian revolution.* **2** [C] a complete change in ways of thinking or acting: *The invention of the aeroplane caused a revolution in travel and communication.*
rev·o·lu·tion·a·ry[1] /ˌrevə'luːʃənəri || -ʃəneri/ *adj* **1** connected with revolution (1): *a revolutionary leader* | *revolutionary ideas*
rev·o·lu·tion·ize /ˌrevə'luːʃənaɪz/ (also **revolutionise** *BrE*) *v* **revolutionized, revolutionizing** [T] to cause a complete change: *The discovery of the new drug has revolutionized the treatment of many diseases.*

Grammar: *like*

1   The two people below have just been to see the *Mona Lisa* at the Louvre. Look at what they say and answer the following questions.

1   Who was impressed? Who wasn't?
2   What is the meaning of *like* in each case?

> She was so real. I felt like her eyes were following me around the room.

> Oh no, she was so stiff and posed. It was like looking at a waxwork dummy.

2   Look at the following sentences with *like* and decide which ones you think are correct. Correct those sentences in which you think there is an error.

1   What's the weather like in Lisbon today?
2   My brother is the same age like me.
3   I am just like my father.
4   He is look like a banker.
5   What are you like doing at the weekends?
6   I like to get up very early on Sunday mornings.
7   That sounds like the postman.
8   Let's do something fun, like going ice-skating.
9   Would you like me making some tea?
10   I'll go and buy some bread if you like.

Grammar reference p.177 (19.1)

Watch Out! *like to do/like doing*

- Gavin *likes getting up* early because it's so quiet.
- Pete *likes to get up* early so he can get to work before the rush hour starts.

Who **enjoys** getting up early? Who **chooses** to get up early, but may not particularly enjoy it?

3

1   Make questions for the following answers using *like*.

a)   Playing football and seeing my friends.
b)   About 7.30 a.m. so that I can use the bathroom before my brother gets up!
c)   She's very funny. She makes me laugh all the time. That's why I like her.
d)   The weather forecast on TV said that it's going to be warm and sunny.
e)   It's quite big with plenty of cinemas and places to go in the evening. The only problem is that there is quite a lot of pollution.
f)   Just like me, except I have long hair and he has very short hair.

2   Now ask a partner the same questions.

4   Imagine that your sister has just shown you a photo of her new boyfriend (the man in white below).

1   What do you think he does?
2   What kind of family do you think he has?
3   What do you think he is like?
4   What do you think he likes doing in his free time?

Exam focus

Paper 4 Listening: Part 3 (multiple matching)

About the exam: In Paper 4, Part 3 you hear five short extracts which are related in some way. The extracts can be monologues, or pairs or groups of speakers interacting. You match sentences or prompts to each of the extracts. There is one extra prompt that does not go with any of the extracts. You hear the extracts twice.

Procedure

1 Read the prompts before you listen and underline key words.
2 When you hear the extracts the first time, focus on listening for links between the extracts and the prompts and match as many of the prompts as you can.
3 When you hear the extracts the second time, check your answers and match any prompts you couldn't match the first time.

You will hear five people talking about lies they have told. For questions **1–5** choose which of the sentences **A–F** applies to each of the speakers. Use the letters only once. There is one extra letter which you do not need to use.

A didn't want to hurt someone's feelings.

B feels lots of people tell similar lies.

C has decided never to lie again as a result.

D didn't report a crime.

E was put in a difficult position by a friend.

F pretended to know more than s/he did.

Speaker ☒ 1 F
Speaker E 2 A
Speaker A 3 E
Speaker 4 D
Speaker B 5 B

Speaking

1 Discuss the following questions.

1 What do you think about the behaviour of the people who told lies in the listening extracts? Would you have done the same thing in each situation or not?

2 a) Do you ever tell lies? If so, in what situations?
   b) Is it the same to lie by not saying anything as it is to lie by saying something?
   c) Are you a 'good' or a 'bad' liar (is it obvious or not to other people)?
   d) Do you generally know when other people are telling lies?
   e) Can the truth ever be a bad thing?
   f) What is a 'white lie'? In what situations might you tell a white lie?

2 Work in a group with three or four other students. Think of a strange or funny experience which happened to you, either real or imaginary, and tell the other members of the group your story. The other students should listen and decide whether you are lying or telling the truth. Then listen to the other students tell their stories.

Vocabulary: phrasal verbs (*take*)

- *They were completely **taken in** and told me to take it easy.*

1 What do you think the phrasal verb in **bold** taken from the last listening extract means?

2 Match a phrasal verb with *take* in Column A with its correct meaning in Column B.

A	B
1 You need to *take* a few days *off* work.	a) to imitate another person to make people laugh
2 I'm thinking of *taking up* golf to get some exercise.	b) to occupy space or time
	c) to employ
3 He's very good at *taking off* famous politicians.	d) to suddenly increase, to do well
4 I really should *take on* one or two more waiters. The restaurant is so busy.	e) to have a holiday or a change
5 This table *takes up* to much room in the kitchen. Lets put it somewhere else.	f) to take control
	g) to start a new hobby
6 Sales of the new BMW have *taken off*.	
7 He's so bossy. Whenever I try and work with him, he just *takes over*.	

3 Now write a response for each of the following sentences using the phrasal verb in brackets.

EXAMPLE: Has there been much interest in that new computer game? *(take off)*
Oh yes, it's really taken off in the last month!

1 I feel terribly overweight at the moment. *(take up)*
2 How is your new secretary getting on? *(take over)*
3 I'm very tired and fed up at work just now. *(take off)*
4 Why have you stopped playing football on Saturdays? *(take up)*
5 Have there been any changes at work while I've been away? *(take on)*
6 Did you realise that he wasn't really a policeman? *(take in)*
7 Why is Mike being kept behind after class? *(take off)*

Watch Out! *actually*

1 A: Hi, Suzanne! How are you?
  B: *Actually*, my name is Susan!
2 Peter was in the living room, but I don't know where he is *actually*.

In which sentence is *actually* used correctly? What should the speaker have said instead of *actually* in the incorrect sentence?

Grammar: narrative tenses

1 Read the first part of the story opposite and answer the following questions.

1 What did the people of the USA think was happening?
2 What do you think was actually happening?

2 Look at the first part of the story again. Find examples of the Past Simple, Past Continuous and Past Perfect tenses and underline them.

3 Which tense is used to refer to:

1 an action which happened before another past action?
2 a finished (single or repeated) action or situation in the past?
3 an action in progress at a definite time in the past?

Grammar reference p.176 (17.5/17.6/17.7)

War of the Worlds?

PART 1
A few minutes after eight o'clock on the night of Sunday, October 30, 1938, a sombre voice interrupted a radio broadcast to warn Americans, 'Ladies and gentlemen, I have a grave announcement to make …'

The words that followed, beamed out in a programme networked across the USA, caused remarkable scenes of panic. For the announcement was that the Martians had landed in North America and were moving across the country at great speed. Nothing seemed able to stop them. All resistance was useless. The USA was being taken over by aliens from outer space.

4 Now read the rest of the story and answer these questions:

1 What was actually happening?
2 Why were so many people listening to CBS at that time?
3 What made the programme so convincing?
4 How did people react to 'the President's' warning?
5 What was the effect of the broadcast on Orson Welles' career?

41

War of the Worlds?

PART 2

This announcement was in fact part of a radio play, but one so realistic that most people who heard it took it for the real thing.

The programme had started undramatically enough. At 8 p.m. an announcer (1) .... (*say*), 'The Columbia Broadcasting System presents Orson Welles and his Mercury Theatre of the Air in *War of the Worlds* by H.G. Wells.' But by chance, at the same time on the main rival network a music programme (2) .... (*begin*) featuring a completely unknown singer. By ten past eight bored listeners were turning their dials to see if there was anything better on CBS. This is what they (3) .... (*hear*).

'Ladies and gentlemen, I have an important announcement to make. The strange object which fell in New Jersey earlier this evening was not a meteorite. Incredible as it may seem, it (4) .... (*contain*) strange beings who are believed to be part of an army from the planet Mars.'

Soft music (5) .... (*follow*). A subtle touch to get people anxious. What (6) .... (*go on*)?

The announcer (7) .... (*come*) on again. There was a nervy, panicky tone to his voice. He said the situation (8) .... (*change*) rapidly. The Martians, hideous, leathery-skinned creatures, (9) .... (*take over*) most of New Jersey already and (10) .... (*move*) quickly into neighbouring states. Army and police units (11) .... (*race*) to stop them.

There was more music, more urgent announcements, chilling silences. People were glued to their sets. One of Welles' actors (12) .... (*pretend*) to be the President of the United States and warned the American people against the dangers of panic. Despite this there (13) .... (*be*) terrible scenes of panic in New Jersey that evening. Everyone (14) .... (*try*) to leave and the roads were filled with cars racing for the hills. Families (15) .... (*flee*) from their homes with wet towels over their heads believing this would save them from the nauseous space gases the radio (16) .... (*tell*) them about. The panic had started.

After it was all over, Welles, already a well-known actor at the age of 24, was fiercely criticised for throwing half the USA into terror. Dozens of people took legal action against CBS, but in the end the complaints were all withdrawn and, instead of taking Welles' show off the air, CBS bosses congratulated themselves for having hired the most talked-about actor in America.

5 Read the text again and fill in the gaps with the correct form of the verb in brackets.

6 Discuss the following questions.

1 Do you think something like this could ever happen in your country? Why?/Why not?
2 Do you think that there is intelligent life on other planets in our universe? If so, what do you think it is like?
3 Do you believe that people have actually seen UFOs?
4 What other evidence is there that life exists on other planets?

One person in the group should summarise and report back the main views of the group to the class.

Scene from the film 'War of the Worlds'

EM: Writing exercise. 1+2 page 32
+ Read p. 176-

Squirrel

7

1 Divide into two groups. Students from Group A should complete Joke A by filling in the gaps with the correct form of the verbs in the box. Students from Group B look at Joke B on page 200 and do the same.

tell	call	go	feel	never be	ask
finish	do	stare	come	hop	put

I was having a drink in my local pub the other day when to everybody's amazement this pink and purple spotted kangaroo (1) _came_ through the door, hopped straight up to the bar and onto one of the bar stools.

The barman, who (2) _done_ his best not to show how astonished he was, (3) _went_ over and asked him what he wanted to drink. The kangaroo (4) _put_ a twenty pound note down on the bar and said he'd have a pint of beer. The barman served him and the kangaroo began to drink his pint. All the other customers (5) _felt_ in disbelief.

As soon as the kangaroo (6) _finished_ his pint, he (7) _asked_ the barman how much he owed him. The barman was almost certain that the kangaroo (8) _had never been_ in a pub before and couldn't possibly have any idea of the price of a pint of beer so he (9) _told_ him he owed twenty pounds. The kangaroo handed over the money and jumped down from his stool.

As he (10) _hopped_ towards the door of the pub, the barman, who (11) _felt_ a bit guilty about overcharging him so much, (12)............ out to him: 'See you again some time! We don't get many pink and purple spotted kangaroos drinking in this pub, you know.'

'I'm not surprised,' said the kangaroo, 'considering that you charge twenty pounds for a pint!'

2 Now tell a student from the other group your joke using appropriate narrative tenses.

Listening: extracts

1 Listen to five short extracts and decide which one:

A involves a joke. ✗
B is part of a discussion about visitors from outer space. _B_
C takes place in a school. ✗
D involves a policeman.
E takes place in a hotel.

2 Now listen again and choose the correct alternative for each extract in turn.

1 You hear this conversation in a school. Who is speaking? _B_
  A two pupils
  B two teachers ✗
  C two parents

2 You hear someone complaining to a hotel receptionist.
  The receptionist is: _B_
  A rude.
  B helpful.
  C confused.

3 You hear a boy telling his friends a joke. The boy in the joke speaks to his teacher because he:
  A has been punished unfairly.
  B is worried his teacher will be angry.
  C has lost his homework.

4 You hear a woman talking to a policeman in the street. She wants the policeman to:
  A let her do something. ✗ _A_
  B give her some information.
  C get her car.

5 You hear two people having a conversation about UFOs.
  The man:
  A agrees with the woman completely.
  B disagrees with her completely. ✗ _B_
  C doesn't seem interested in what she says.

Writing: narrative

In Paper 2 of the exam you may be asked to write a short story. You will probably need to write this in the past. The key elements for this are:

- correct use of past tenses
- linking expressions
- interesting and varied vocabulary
- imagination!

1   Read the following story and put the different parts in the correct order. Then compare your answers with a partner and say which words helped you to decide.

A They included maps with distant stars which were not known to astronomers at that time, but which have since been discovered.

B Few people believed the Lawsons until some astronomers were shown the pictures the Lawsons had drawn of the inside of the spaceship.

C Suddenly[1], an enormous[2] spaceship with flashing lights landed right in front of their car and a strange[3], glowing figure got out.

D They say that they were well-treated and that the aliens just wanted to find out about human beings.

E After that[4], the Lawsons claim they were taken aboard the spaceship and given a series of tests.

F Bill and Betty Lawson had been driving along a lonely road in New Hampshire when an amazing thing happened.

G In the end, the Lawsons were left on the same road unharmed but thirty kilometres further on.

Watch Out! after/afterwards/after that

1   I'm going swimming and ~~after/afterwards/after that~~ I will probably go home.
2   ~~After/Afterwards/After that~~ I go swimming, I will probably go home.

Which alternatives are possible in each sentence?

2   The following words and phrases can help to make your narrative writing more interesting and clearer to read. Decide if they are similar to words [1], [2], [3], or [4] in the story in Exercise 1.

a) gigantic
b) following this
c) weird   *in instant*
d) all of a sudden
e) afterwards
f) without warning
g) odd
h) huge

i) out of the blue
j) vast
k) massive
l) some time later
m) from out of nowhere
n) after a while
o) peculiar

3   *E m 93 34 next Tuesday*

1   Read the following question which asks you to write a short story.

> You have decided to enter a short story competition. The competition rules say that the story must begin or end with the following words:
>
> *They left Planet Earth surprised and rather disappointed by what they had found.*
>
> Write your story for the competition.

2   Now work with a partner and write the story together in 120–180 words. Follow this procedure:

- First decide whether you want to begin or end your story with the words provided.
- Then write a series of questions such as: *Where did they come from? Why did they come to Earth?*
- Next make notes to answer your questions. Arrange your notes in paragraphs.
- Now write your story. Try to include appropriate linking expressions e.g. *then, next* and interesting vocabulary e.g. *all of a sudden.*
- Finally check your work very carefully, particularly for errors with narrative tenses.

1 Fill in the gaps in the following text with the correct form of the words in capitals.

I always wanted to be a great (1) ....
I had these dreams of discovering a (2) ....
new drug that would save the lives of hundreds of
people. Unfortunately, I was never very good at
(3) .... at school and I kept producing
these horrible smells and the teacher used to get
very cross with me.

    After a while, I decided I would become an
(4) .... and design an amazing new
(5) .... which would become a household
name. My parents were quite encouraging, but told
me to be a little more (6) .... and not
quite so (7) .... A few weeks later I had
a brilliant idea for a pen that, at least
(8) ...., would write upside down. To my
(9) .... a friend of mine pointed out that
it was not a new (10) ....

SCIENCE
REVOLUTION

CHEMIST

INVENT
PRODUCE

REAL
AMBITION

THEORY
DISAPPOINT
DISCOVER

2 Put the words in the following sentences in order. The first word in each sentence has been underlined.

1 year off much you have time <u>how</u> taken this?
2 things really to soon going <u>I</u> off think are take.
3 on staff moment <u>we</u> any just can't more take the at.
4 time football on too much Saturdays takes <u>playing</u> up.
5 Bill tennis so <u>why</u> after many up has taken again years?
6 money taken gave I before been the <u>I</u> realised in had him I.
7 well off amazing how is history <u>it</u> he teacher take can his.
8 I'm take <u>could</u> you while over lunch me from at?

3 Read the following sentences and choose the correct tense.

1 I *was doing/did* my homework when I *heard/had heard* someone knock loudly on the door.
2 We *didn't see/weren't seeing* Paul because nobody *had told/was telling* us he was there.
3 Louise *painted/was painting* the bathroom at the same time as I *was cleaning/had cleaned* the kitchen.
4 I suddenly *was realising/realised* that I *left/had left* my wallet at home.
5 I *was having/had* a shower, *ate/had eaten* my breakfast and *was going/went* to work.
6 Everyone *had stood/was standing* around talking when she *walked/had walked* into the room.

4 You have been asked to write a story for a magazine called 'Crimes of the century' ending with the words:

'The necklace Julia wore around her neck with such pride was, in fact, a worthless fake.'

5 Talk about these photographs. They show people doing research. Compare and contrast the photographs saying what kind of research you think would be more interesting to do.

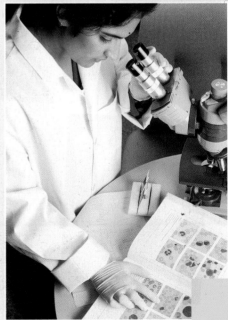

All you need is love

Speaking

1 Look at these photos of famous singers. Do you recognise them? What do you know about them? What famous songs have they sung?

A

B

C

D

E

F

G

H

2 Discuss the following questions.

1 What kinds of music do you like?
2 Do you have any favourite singers/musicians/groups at the moment? Why do you like them?
3 Do you ever go to see them in concert?
4 Do you ever watch pop videos? What makes a 'good' pop video?
5 Do you play/Have you ever played any musical instruments? Which ones? Do you/Did you enjoy playing them? Are there any instruments that you would like to learn?

Listening: song

1 You are going to hear a song. As you listen think about the following questions.

1 Which of the singers in the photos is it?
2 What is the singer singing about?

2 Look at the words of the song opposite and fill in the gaps with an appropriate word from the box. Then listen again and check your answers.

blue	gift	world	funny	show	simple	roof
kind	sculptor	live	sweetest	hide	cross	

3 Discuss the following questions about the song.

1 What *feeling* is he talking about? *(line 2)*
2 What can't he *hide*? *(line 3)*
3 What word is missing in *line 4*?
4 Why does he say 'No' in *line 8*?
5 What is another word for *potions* in *line 9*?
6 Why does he say *I hope you don't mind* in *line 15*?
7 Why is he *cross* in *line 19*?
8 What do you think *turned on* in *line 21* means?
9 ... *these things I do (line 22)*: what things is he talking about?
10 What does *they* refer to in *line 23*?

Your Song by Elton John

1   It's a little bit (1) ....,
    This feeling inside,
    I'm not one of those who can easily (2) ....,
    Don't have much money,
5   But boy if I did,
    I'd buy a big house where we both could (3) ....

    If I was a (4) ....,
    But then again 'No',
    Or a man who makes potions in a travelling (5) ....,
10 I know it's not much, but it's the best I can do,
    My (6) .... is my song and this one's for you.

    Chorus
    And you can tell everybody this is your song,
    It may be quite (7) ...., but now that it's done,
15 I hope you don't mind, I hope you don't mind,
    That I put down in words,
    How wonderful life is while you're in the (8) ....

    I sat on the (9) .... and kicked off the moss,
    Well, a few of the verses, well, they've got me quite (10) ....
20 But the sun's been quite (11) .... while I wrote this song,
    It's for people like you that keep it turned on.
    So excuse me forgetting, but these things I do,
    You see I've forgotten if they're green or they're (12) ....,
    Anyway, the thing is, what I really mean,
25 Yours are the (13) .... eyes I've ever seen.

    Chorus

Vocabulary:
phrasal verbs (*down*)

1 Read the following general meanings of *down* when used in phrasal verbs and then match each meaning to one of the pairs of sentences below.

1 destruction, bringing to the ground
2 reduction, decreasing
3 stopping, completion
4 writing, recording

a) I *put down* in words how wonderful life is ...   to write
    Could you *take down* this letter as I dictate, please?

b) Will you *slow down*? You're   decrease reduce
    going too fast.
    You must *cut down* on the amount of chocolate you eat.

c) I know he's in there. We'll have to *break* the door *down*.
    Lots of trees *came down* in last night's storm.   bring some down

d) I'm afraid John is going to be late. His car has *broken down*.
    She waited for the laughter to *die down* before continuing.

2 Imagine the context for each of the sentences and decide who is speaking and what they are speaking about.

3 Now add the following sentences to the appropriate pair of sentences above.

1 If we *cut* that tree *down*, we'll let a lot more light in here.
2 We will have to *close* the mine *down*. There just isn't the demand for coal anymore.
3 Have you finished *getting* all the details *down*?
4 I think the price of bread will *go down* soon.

47

Reading

Wuthering Heights is the story of two families: the Earnshaws and the Lintons. Cathy Earnshaw spends much of her childhood playing on the wild Yorkshire moors with Heathcliff, a boy her father adopts. When Mr Earnshaw dies, his son and heir, Hindley, treats Heathcliff as a servant and Cathy begins to spend most of her time with Edgar Linton, a young man who lives on a neighbouring farm.

1 Read the extract from Wuthering Heights below and decide who the people in the pictures are.

2 Discuss the following questions.

1 What is the secret Catherine tells Nelly?
2 What is Nelly's reaction to Catherine's secret?
3 What is the difference between Cathy's love for Edgar and Heathcliff?
4 Who do you think she should marry and why?

3 Can you think of some adjectives that could be used to describe the characters of a) Cathy and b) Nelly? Underline parts of the extract that support your answers.

1 Later that same evening, Catherine came to find me in the kitchen. I thought I was alone, but I later realised that Heathcliff was there, too. He was sitting behind a high-backed seat out of my sight.

Catherine sat silent for a while, and I saw a tear or two fall from her cheek.

'Oh, dear,' she cried at last. 'I'm very unhappy!'

'A pity,' said I. 'You're hard to please. So many friends and so few cares, and you can't be satisfied.'

10 'Nelly, will you keep a secret for me?' she asked.

'Is it worth keeping?'

'Yes, and it worries me. I want to know what I should do. Today, Edgar Linton has asked me to marry him, and I've accepted him, Nelly. Be quick and say whether I did right.'

'There are many things to consider before that question can be answered properly,' I answered. 'First, do you love Edgar?'

'Who can help it? Of course I do,' she said.

20 'Why do you love him?'

'Nonsense, I do – that's enough.'

22 'It is not: you must tell me why.'

'Well, because he is handsome, and pleasant to be with.'

'Bad,' I said.

'And because he is young and cheerful.'

'Bad, still.'

'And because he loves me.'

'Better.'

30 'And he will be rich, and I would like to be the greatest woman in the neighbourhood.'

'Worst of all. Now say how you love him.'

'I love the ground under his feet, and the air over his head and everything he touches, and every word he says. I love all his looks and all his actions, and him entirely and completely.'

'Then what are you unhappy about, Catherine?' I asked. 'Your brother Hindley will be pleased.

Mr and Mrs Linton will not object, I think. You will
40 escape from a disorderly, comfortless home into a wealthy, comfortable ordered one, And you love Edgar, and he loves you. All seems smooth and easy. Where is the difficulty?'

'Here! And here!' replied Catherine, striking one hand on her forehead and the other on her breast. 'In my head and in my heart, I'm certain I'm wrong. I can't explain clearly but I'll give you an idea of how I feel. I oughtn't to marry Edgar Linton. If my brother had not brought Heathcliff so low I
50 wouldn't have thought of it. It would shame me to marry Heathcliff now, so he shall never know how I love him; and that's not because he's handsome, Nelly, but because he's more myself than I am. Whatever our beings are made of, his and mine are the same, and Linton's is as different as ice from fire.'

Before she finished speaking, I became aware of Heathcliff's presence. I turned my head, and saw him rise from his seat and leave noiselessly. He had
60 heard Catherine say she would be ashamed to marry him, and he stayed to hear no more. Catherine noticed nothing.

'My love for Linton is like the trees in the woods: time will change it, I'm well aware, as winter changes the trees. My love for Heathcliff is like the rocks beneath: it gives little delight but is necessary. Nelly, I am Heathcliff! He's always, always in my mind: not as a pleasure, but as my own being. We can never be separated.'

70 Catherine paused. I was out of patience with her foolishness.

'If I can make any sense out of your nonsense, Miss,' I said, 'you know nothing of the duties of marriage. But trouble me with no more secrets: I'll not promise to keep them.'

'Will you keep this one?' she asked.

'I'll not promise.'

H: ex5 to 21.11.02
P 50 speaking Ex 2.
CB : speaking Ex 4 ⇒ Wich bank would you like to read
and why ?
Ex page 52 ⇒ 1 + 2

UNIT 5   All you need is love

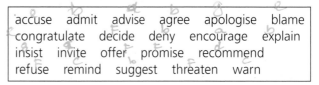

Grammar: reported speech

1 Look at the following examples of reported speech and find their direct speech equivalent in the text from *Wuthering Heights*.

1 She said she was very unhappy.
2 She said that that day Edgar Linton had asked her to marry him.
3 I asked her why she loved him.
4 I told her she had to tell me why.
5 She said she loved him because he loved her.
6 She said they could never be separated.
7 She asked if I would promise to keep that secret, but I said I wouldn't.

2 Compare the reported speech and direct speech forms from Exercise 1 and answer the following questions.

1 What changes are made each time?

2 What rules about changing direct speech to reported speech can you make based on these examples? Think about:

- tenses of verbs e.g. Past Simple, etc.
- modals e.g. *will*, *might*, etc.
- questions
- time and place words e.g. *today*, *here*, etc.

3 Now turn to page 173 and check your ideas against Grammar reference 15.2/15.4.

3

1 Listen to a conversation between two friends. What is Tom's problem?

2 Now listen to the conversation again and write a summary of what you hear using reported speech.

    EXAMPLE: *Mike saw Tom and **asked him how he was**. Tom **said** ...*

3 Compare what you have written in reported speech with a partner.

Watch Out! *to suggest*

He suggested { *going*
that they go
that they went
~~*them to go*~~
that they should go } *to an Italian restaurant.*

One of the above patterns is not possible. Which is it?

Reporting verbs

4 Match the verbs in the box to a pattern below according to how they are used in reported speech.

> accuse   admit   advise   agree   apologise   blame
> congratulate   decide   deny   encourage   explain
> insist   invite   offer   promise   recommend
> refuse   remind   suggest   threaten   warn

a) verb + object + infinitive e.g. *He asked me to go.*
b) verb + (that) e.g. *She said (that) he had to go.*
c) verb + object + (that) e.g. *He told us (that) he had to go.*
d) verb + gerund e.g. *He admitted stealing her bag.*
e) verb + object + preposition + gerund e.g. *He accused me of stealing the money.*
f) verb + infinitive e.g. *He decided to lend her the money.*
g) verb + preposition + gerund e.g. *He insisted on lending her the money.*

5 Report the following statements using one of the reporting verbs above.

1 'I'm so sorry that I was late.'
2 'Don't touch that chair. It's just been painted!'
3 'I will do my homework after the film, honestly!'
4 'Why don't we go to the beach for a swim?'
5 'I'm *not* going to the party.'
6 '*You* stole that money.'
7 'Don't forget to get Paula a birthday present.'
8 'I'll take you to the airport if you like.'
9 'Yes, it's true. I did lie about my age.'
10 'I'll tell a teacher if you don't put it back.'

6 Work in small groups and write a short story in 120–180 words. The story must:

- be on the theme of love.
- use a mixture of direct and reported speech, including at least five of the verbs in Exercise 4.
- include reference to each of the following objects:

Speaking

1 Discuss the following questions.

1 What is the best book you have read recently? Who was it by? What was it about? Why did you particularly like it?
2 Have you read any books or graded readers in English?

2 Now look at these back cover blurbs taken from various readers and match them with the following book titles.

1 *Brave New World* (Aldous Huxley)
2 *A Passage to India* (E.M. Forster)
3 *Crime Never Pays*
4 *Rebecca* (Daphne du Maurier)
5 *Pygmalion* (Bernard Shaw)

3 Discuss which of the books you think would be suitable for:

1 someone who likes mysteries and solving problems
2 someone who likes reading about love and relationships
3 someone who is interested in political issues
4 someone who is interested in language and accent
5 someone who is interested in cross-cultural differences

4 Put the books in order according to which ones you would be most/least interested in reading. Compare your order with other students. Is it the same or different? Explain the reasons for your order.

A

MURDER: the unlawful, intentional killing of a human being. A terrible crime.

But murder stories are always fascinating. Who did it? And how? Or why? Was it murder at all, or just an unfortunate accident? Who will triumph, the murderer or the detective? This collection contains a wide range of murder stories, from the astute detections of the famous Sherlock Holmes, to the chilling psychology of Ruth Rendell.

B

AFTER THE DEATH of his beautiful wife, Rebecca, Maxim de Winter goes to Monte Carlo to recover. There he marries a quiet and ordinary young woman who is very different from his first wife. Maxim takes her back to England – to Manderley, his lovely country house.

The new Mrs de Winter finds that at Manderley Rebecca is still in everyone's thoughts – including Maxim's – and she begins to feel that she will never be able to equal Rebecca as a wife or as mistress of Manderley.

Then one day a discovery is made – and the young Mrs de Winter begins to understand why Rebecca is still so important to all those at Manderley.

C

'You see this creature with her kerbstone English: the English that will keep her in the gutter to the end of her days. Well, sir, in three months I could pass that girl off as a duchess at an ambassador's garden party.'

❀ ❀ ❀ ❀

Can Professor Henry Higgins *really* turn flower-girl Eliza Doolittle into a lady?

D

East meets West in this intriguing story. Or does it? Why should Miss Quested accuse Dr Aziz of assaulting her on an outing to the Marabar Caves? How can Dr Aziz defend himself against such an unfair charge?

Will the trial cause a bloody battle between the Indians lined up behind Dr Aziz and the British community solidly behind Miss Quested?

E

ALL human values have changed. What in the past were seen as virtues have been wiped out. Family life has disappeared, human beings are produced in bottles instead of being born in the natural manner. People do not suffer; but they have no ideas of their own, their lives are planned for them from start to finish, and they know nothing of the passions, the joys and sorrows, the triumphs or the defeats of the great figures of the past. In spite of the light and often amusing way this book is written, here is a warning to us all to think carefully about the way the world is developing before it is too late.

Writing: background reading texts

1

In Paper 2 of the exam, Question 5 will refer to various set books. There will be one or two general questions which you can answer by referring to one of these books. You may be asked to write your answer in the form of a composition, an article, a report or a letter.

Here is a procedure to follow when reading a set text:

- Read the book once all the way through to get a general idea of the story and the main characters.

- Explain the basic story to another student (in English!).

- Read the book again, more carefully this time. As you go through each chapter, underline key words which you do not know the meaning of and look them up in your dictionary.

- Read the book one last time and make notes in a notebook under headings.

  EXAMPLE: **Characters Relationships Places Events**

  You may want to add other headings depending on the content of the particular book.

- Make a list of questions that you might be asked about your book and discuss them with other students.

2 When you have done all of the above, write an answer to one of the following questions in 120–180 words.

> 1 What do you think is the most important event that takes place in the book you have read? Write an account of it and why it is important for a student who has not yet read the book.
>
> 2 Who do you think is the most interesting person in the book you have read? Write a report for your school magazine, explaining why this person is interesting and how she/he contributes to the story as a whole.

Vocabulary: ways of talking

1

1 Complete the following table on the use of *say, tell* and *speak*.

	say	tell	speak
a lie	✗	✔	✗
'Yes'	✓	✗	✗
English			✗
a story		✗	
something	✗	✗	
loudly			✗
me his name		✗	

2 Translate the verbs into your language. Do they go with the same words and phrases as in English?

2

1 Read the following short text and decide if it comes from:

a) a newspaper article.
b) a diary.
c) a letter to a friend.

I went to a party the other night at Jo's. Do you remember I was telling you about her the other day. She's Paul's best friend. It was great. I got (1) .... to these really interesting people. We started (2) .... various things and I really felt they were on my wavelength. One guy (3) .... me he had done the same course (Spanish) that I want to do at university but dropped out after a year. I (4) .... him why. He (5) .... that they never actually (6) .... much Spanish on the course, and that most of the time they (7) .... in English about Spanish literature.

2 Now choose the correct alternative to fill each gap.

1 **A** saying   **B** telling   **C** chatting
2 **A** speaking   **B** discussing   **C** talking
3 **A** told   **B** asked   **C** said
4 **A** discussed   **B** told   **C** asked
5 **A** said   **B** spoke   **C** told
6 **A** told   **B** discussed   **C** spoke
7 **A** said   **B** talked   **C** told

Use of English

1 Look at the picture below and describe what you can see in as much detail as possible. Think about:

- what year it might be
- where it might have been taken
- who the people are

2 Fill in the gaps in the following text with the words in the box. You will need to use three more words that are not in the box.

was	being	still	that	to (x 2)	has	when	will	be	their

Sweethearts claim share of picture profits

by ALISON JAMES in Paris

TWO lovers steal a kiss on a busy Paris street, oblivious to everything around them, including a photographer. Forty-two years on, the same pair stand in the same spot, (1)................... very much in love. At least, Denise and Jean-Louis Lavergne claim they are the lovers in the world's most romantic picture taken (2)................... a spring morning in 1950. Photographer Robert Doisneau, 80, says otherwise. The dispute over 'The Kiss by the Hotel de Ville' will now (3)................... settled in court. The Lavergnes are demanding £50,000 plus a share of the millions the famous shot (4)................... made for Doisneau and his picture agency Rapho, since it (5)................... made into a poster in the 1980s.

Denise, 64, (6)................... runs a small Paris printing company with her 66-year-old husband, said, 'It was a romantic time, we were young, engaged, so in love and oblivious to the people around us. We didn't even see that our picture was (7)................... taken. We got married on July 8 that year.'

It was only (8)................... they saw the picture on the cover of a magazine – on (9)................... 38th wedding anniversary – that they realised their kiss (10)................... been captured forever. They tracked down Doisneau and met him in 1990. 'He was very friendly and told us other people, but no couples, had come forward claiming (11)................... be in his picture.'

Last night Doisneau's lawyer Julien Hay said he had proof (12)................... models posed for the picture. He said the photographer humoured the Lavergnes (13)................... let them believe they were the romantic subjects. 'They (14)................... not get a franc,' he added.

from *Today* newspaper

Handwritten notes at top: H. Wk / CB: 55·57 program / EM 35 / 36 / 37 / 38 / H2

Exam focus

Paper 5 Speaking: Part 2 (individual long turn)

About the exam: In Paper 5, Part 2 each candidate is shown two theme-related photographs. Both candidates speak about the photographs on their own. They are asked to compare and contrast them, to comment on them and to give some kind of personal reaction. Each candidate has about a minute to do this while the other candidate listens. The other candidate then has a chance to comment briefly on the photographs as well.

Procedure

Your Long Turn:

Look at the photographs and answer the examiner's question. You do not have to describe the photographs in detail. Begin by saying what the photographs have in common. Then say something about one of the photographs and go on to say in what way the other photograph is different. Do this two or three times, commenting on a different aspect of the photographs each time.

The Other Candidate's Turn:

Look at the photographs and listen carefully. Do not say anything. When the other candidate has finished, answer the question the examiner asks you.

1 Look at the photographs above. Which of these sentences describe the photographs and which compare or contrast them? Mark them D (describe) or C & C (compare and contrast). Underline the words or phrases which are used to compare or contrast the photographs.

1 I can see a little girl holding some flowers.
2 In the first photograph I can see a group of women, whereas the second photograph shows a group of men.
3 The women in the first photograph are eating strawberries.
4 The women in the first photograph are inside a restaurant, but in the second photograph the men are outside a pub.
5 They're both photographs of weddings.
6 In the church wedding, on the other hand, the bride is wearing white and the groom is dressed in a very formal suit.

2 Now listen to two students doing Paper 5, Part 2 with these photographs. Which of the sentences above do they use?

3 Your teacher will now tell you how to roleplay Paper 5, Part 2 using the photographs on this page and p. 206.

Vocabulary: love and marriage

1 Explain the difference between the following pairs of words.

1 to go out with someone/to live with someone
2 to be infatuated/to fall in love
3 to get engaged/to get married
4 to get pregnant/to have a baby
5 to have an anniversary/to have a birthday
6 to have rows/to have discussions
7 to chat/to flirt
8 to get a divorce/to split up

2 Look at the words in the box and discuss:

1 the meaning of each one.
2 the significance of each one when people get married.

> a wedding   a registry office   a church   the aisle
> a vicar   the bride   the bridegroom   the best man
> the bridesmaids   the ring   the reception
> the organist   the choir   a bouquet   a veil
> a honeymoon

Listening: Do you take this man?

1 You are going to hear five people talking about weddings. For each of the extracts 1–5 choose a title from the list (**A–F**) below. There is one extra title you don't need to use.

A A wedding on … and in the water
B Almost too late to change your mind
C A very special place … for us
D Two for the price of one
E Late for her own wedding
F Don't walk down the aisle with your pets

Extract		1
Extract		2
Extract		3
Extract		4
Extract		5

2 Listen again. This time match a statement (A–F) with each speaker (1–5). There is one statement you don't need to use.

A The speaker didn't know what was going to happen.
B The speaker had to persuade someone else to cooperate.
C The speaker did not approve of the wedding ceremony.
D The speaker didn't wear traditional clothes.
E The speaker regrets not making a decision earlier.
F The speaker was happy to have some strangers at the wedding.

Speaker		1
Speaker		2
Speaker		3
Speaker		4
Speaker		5

Speaking

Discuss the following questions.

1 What happens when people get married in your country? Are there any special activities or customs?
2 Describe the last wedding that you went to. Whose wedding was it? Who was there? What happened?

Paper 3: Part 1 (multiple choice cloze)

1 For questions **1–15** read the text below and decide which answer **A, B, C** or **D** best fits each space. Circle your answer.

AN UNHAPPY HOLIDAY

Julia and James had a church wedding in the early spring. For their honeymoon they went on a (1) .... in the Greek islands. It was a very modern (2) .... and there was even a swimming pool on one of the (3) .... . They had an enormous (4) .... with a bathroom and a bedroom. Julia was a bit (5) .... about travelling by ship because she'd seen the film *Titanic* a few weeks before. She wanted to (6) .... that there were enough lifejackets and lifeboats before they left the port just in case anything (7) .... wrong.

For some reason James found this very (8) .... and they started to (9) .... the most terrible rows on the very first day. Julia could hardly believe that this was the same man she had (10) .... in love with a year before. He had never shown any sign of being so (11) .... when they were just going (12) .... together. She began to (13) .... ever having married him.

To make matters even worse, James started to (14) .... with some of the other young women on board. He danced with one of these women all evening on the last night and that made Julia decide that the only solution was to split (15) .... with James and start her life all over again.

1 **A** voyage	**B** cruise	**C** travel	**D** journey
2 **A** ferry	**B** tanker	**C** liner	**D** yacht
3 **A** decks	**B** docks	**C** storeys	**D** floors
4 **A** compartment	**B** flat	**C** room	**D** cabin
5 **A** sensitive	**B** nervous	**C** fed up	**D** overcome
6 **A** prove	**B** confirm	**C** secure	**D** check
7 **A** did	**B** made	**C** had	**D** went
8 **A** irritation	**B** irritated	**C** irritating	**D** irritate
9 **A** fight	**B** do	**C** make	**D** have
10 **A** felt	**B** fallen	**C** found	**D** fault
11 **A** impatient	**B** unconscious	**C** surprising	**D** thrilling
12 **A** away	**B** over	**C** through	**D** out
13 **A** repent	**B** regret	**C** relieve	**D** respect
14 **A** flit	**B** flight	**C** flirt	**D** float
15 **A** away	**B** out	**C** up	**D** apart

2 Write questions for the following answers.

1 Teresa? She'll be twenty-four next birthday.
2 Quite like me, actually. She's rather shy when you first meet her, but once you get to know her she's very friendly.
3 A boyfriend? Yes, his name's Nelson. He's from Brazil.
4 She studies journalism and works part-time in a boutique.
5 She goes swimming a lot and plays the violin with a local orchestra.

Paper 3: Part 2 (open cloze)

3 For questions **1–15** read the text below and think of the word which best fits each space. Use only **one** word in each space. There is an example at the beginning **(0)**.

SPORTS

Though they are very different in (0) *all* sorts of ways cricket and baseball are also quite similar.
(1) .... they are both played with very hard balls, some of the players have to wear
(2) .... to protect their hands and to help
(3) .... catch the ball. Golfers wear them too, but (4) .... need them to stop their hands slipping on the (5) ....

In racket sports (6) .... tennis, squash and badminton a good grip is essential as well
(7) .... strength, speed, stamina and, in the case of modern tennis, height. Tall players have a tremendous advantage when they serve because they can hit the ball at (8) .... great speed that their opponents are lucky to get the ball back over the
(9) .... It's (10) .... important to keep your cool. Lots of players lose concentration if a linesman says a ball they have returned is
(11) .... Occasionally the (12) .... will overrule the decision and say that the ball was in after all.

There's not often any doubt whether someone (13) .... scored a (14) .... or not in football, but players sometimes disagree (15) .... the referee over penalties.

4

1 Match a prefix in Column A with a word in Column B. Use each prefix and word once only.

EXAMPLE: *il + legal > illegal*

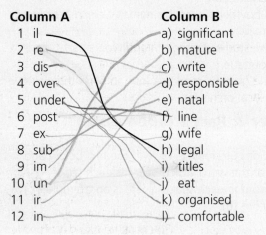

Column A	Column B
1 il	a) significant
2 re	b) mature
3 dis	c) write
4 over	d) responsible
5 under	e) natal
6 post	f) line
7 ex	g) wife
8 sub	h) legal
9 im	i) titles
10 un	j) eat
11 ir	k) organised
12 in	l) comfortable

2 Now fill in the gaps in the following sentences with an appropriate word formed in 1 above.

a) You wouldn't be so .... if you had a diary and wrote down all the things you have to do.

b) This letter is very badly written. I'm afraid you'll have to .... it.

c) I prefer to see American films in English with .... in my own language.

d) If you ov................. like that, you'll get indigestion.

e) This sofa is really .... It makes my back ache.

f) In most countries it is ....*illegal*.... to open a bank account in a false name.

g) It was very .... of you to go out and leave your younger brothers and sisters alone in the house.

h) After you've read the book once straight through, read it again and .... some of the words you want to look up in your dictionary.

i) He has been divorced for ten years now, but he still has a good relationship with his ....

j) She really is very .... – she always gets upset when she doesn't get her own way.

Paper 3: Part 3 (key word transformation)

5 For questions **1–10**, complete the second sentence so that it has a similar meaning to the first sentence, using the word given. **Do not change the word given.** You must use between two and five words, including the word given. Here is an example **(0)**.

Example:
(0) The photocopier broke down three days ago.
order
The photocopier *has been out of order* for three days.

1 Nobody in our class is as good at basketball as I am.
player
I am .... in our class.

2 My older brother is a social worker in one of the big hospitals.
works
My older brother .... in one of the big hospitals.

3 My friends left before I arrived at the meeting point.
when
My friends .... at the meeting point.

4 'Alright, I stole the money. I admit it,' she said.
that
She admitted .... the money.

5 Susan plays the piano better than Jacky.
as
Jacky doesn't play .... Susan.

6 Badminton and tennis are similar in some ways.
like
Badminton .... in some ways.

7 'Would you like to stay for dinner?' she asked.
invited
She .... for dinner.

8 The Nigerian beat the Moroccan by 2.5 seconds.
faster
The Nigerian ran .... the Moroccan.

9 'What's the time?' he asked.
tell
He asked me .... the time.

10 Are you saying I'm lying?
accusing
Are you .... lying?

Paper 3: Part 4 (error correction)

6 For questions **1–15** read the text below and look carefully at each line. Some of the lines are correct and some have a word which should not be there. If a line is correct, put a (✔) at the end of it. If there is a word that should not be there, circle it and write the word at the end of the line. There are two examples at the beginning (**0** and **00**).

A BIG WIN

0	I was absolutely delighted when I found out my sister and I	✔
00	had (to) won a big prize in the national lottery. But when I	to
1	tried to find out the ticket, I started to worry. I had	out
2	thrown away a lot of the old bus tickets and receipts just a	✔
3	few days before and I had nearly thrown it away the lottery	
4	ticket as well. Luckily I have realised just in time and put	
5	it away safely. Now that I knew our lucky number was the	that
6	winning number the problem was that I couldn't remember	
7	exactly where did I put it. I was looking through the papers	did
8	on my desk when I remembered it had been a very windy	
9	the night before it. Some of my papers had blown off the	it
10	desk and I was very relieved when I found the ticket amongst	very
11	them on the floor. I checked the numbers carefully in the paper	
12	and immediately phoned to my sister to tell her the good	to
13	news. She could hardly believe it how lucky we had been	
14	and just kept asking me if I was sure I did had the right number.	did
15	We met in that evening to decide how to spend the money.	

Paper 3: Part 5 (word formation)

7 For questions **1–10** read the text below. Use the word in capitals at the end of each line to form a word that fits in the space in the same line. There is an example at the beginning (**0**).

ADVERTISING

Many people find their work rather **(0)** *boring*	BORE
I get a lot of **(1)** .... from my job. Advertising	SATISFY
can be very **(2)** .... because you have to think of	CREATE
new ways to attract people's **(3)** .... . The best	ATTEND
way to do this is by surprising them. **(4)**.... is	FAMILIAR
boring and people soon get fed up with an **(5)**	ADVERTISE
they have seen many times before. **(6)** .... they	CONSCIOUS
want to be shocked. Apart from **(7)** .... , the other	ORIGINAL
really important **(8)** .... of a good campaign is	CHARACTER
(9) .... . After all if people don't remember what	MEMORABLE
was being advertised, they won't buy the **(10)**	PRODUCE

8 Fill in the gaps in the following sentences with an appropriate particle (*in, at, through*, etc.) or verb in the correct form.

1 I was feeling very unfit so I decided to take .... aerobics.
2 Sorry we're late. The car .... down on the way.
3 He tells really funny jokes and makes us all laugh by taking .... our dad.
4 .... down! You're driving much too fast.
5 Mobile phones have really taken .... here. Everyone seems to have one.
6 It took several days for the fire to .... down after it had been burning for so long.
7 We'll have to get rid of that old sofa. It takes .... too much space and it's very uncomfortable.
8 I think it's terrible the way they've cut .... all the lovely trees in this street.
9 Whenever she joins in our games, she just takes .... and starts telling us all what to do.
10 That new supermarket is taking .... over one hundred people to work as cashiers.
11 My boss threatened to sack me if I .... on making mistakes.
12 Her parents died when she was ten and she .... up by her aunt.

For linked Paper 5 practice, see pages 187–189.

6 It's all in the mind

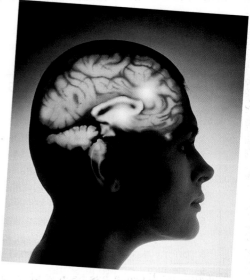

Reading

1 You are going to read an article about the brain and intelligence. Before you read, discuss the following questions.

1 What is 'intelligence'?

2 Is an 'intelligent' person someone who:

- is good at passing exams?
- is imaginative?
- gets what she/he wants in life?
- understands new ideas quickly?
- has a good memory?
- deals with people well?
- is sensible?
- reads a lot?
- is good at crosswords?

2 The following words all appear in the article. Match each one with its correct definition on the right.

1	brain	a)	a natural form of sugar found in fruit
2	myth	b)	the bone of your head which encloses your brain
3	IQ	c)	a measure of how clever someone is
4	skull	d)	a tool with a narrow blade at one end, used to put screws into something or remove them
5	addicted	e)	the organ in the top part of your head which controls thought, feeling and physical activity
6	glucose	f)	instructions for cooking a particular dish
7	screwdriver	g)	a false story which many people may believe
8	mental	h)	unable to stop taking or using something
9	recipe	i)	concerned with the brain or thinking

3 Read the article quickly and decide which one of the following subjects it does *not* refer to.

a) improving your brain power
b) men and women
c) psychological illness
d) brain weight
e) old age
f) the physical needs of the brain

4 Read the article again and choose the most suitable heading from the list below for each numbered part of the article. The first one has been done for you.

A A horrifying history.
B Bloodthirsty.
C Is bigger better?
D Make your brain work.
E How much do we know?
F The battle of the sexes.
G The super computer.

5 Make a note of two things you did not know before reading the article which you found interesting. Tell a partner.

6 If you would like to try some IQ puzzles to develop your mental agility, turn to page 200.

The Mind Machine?

(0 — E —)

Although intelligence has been studied, and the brain has been studied, there is little understanding of how the brain works to produce intelligence. This has something to do with the fact that the brain contains around 100 billion cells (about the number of stars in the Milky Way).

(1 ———)

One of the continuing myths about the relationship between intelligence and the brain is that the brains of very clever people are somehow physically different from those of ordinary people. At the beginning of the century an American scientist called E.A. Spitzka produced a list of the weights of the brains of important, well-known men. The heaviest brain on the list was that of Turgenev, the Russian novelist, at 2000g. However, the brain of another great genius, Walt Whitman, weighed only 1282g.

(2 ———)

There are no significant differences between the intelligence levels of males and females. However, girls under seven score a little higher than boys in IQ tests and the highest IQ recorded is that of Marylin vos Savant at 230. However, men and women do differ in the way they think. Generally, women are more skilled verbally and men do better on visual-spatial tasks.

Interestingly, the fibres which join the two halves of the brain have been found to be larger in women than in men. This supports the theory that women can change from 'practical' to 'emotional' thinking more quickly than men.

(3 ———)

People with mental problems have often been treated extremely badly. Two hundred years ago, the mentally ill were swung around in revolving chairs, or holes were drilled in their skulls to release evil spirits. From the 1930s, the mentally ill were subjected to electric shock therapy and lobotomy – the removal of part of their brain. In the 1960s and 70s, thousands of people were given drugs to cope with anxiety and then became addicted to them.

(4 ———)

The brain needs ten times as much blood as other organs of the body, as it can't store glucose for later use. This is different to muscles and other organs and although the adult brain makes up only two per cent of the body weight, its oxygen consumption is twenty per cent of the body's total.

(5 ———)

There are similarities between brains and computers. Computers can do complicated calculations at incredible speeds. But they work in a fixed way, because they can't make memory associations. If we need a screwdriver and there isn't one, we will think laterally and use a knife or coin instead. Computers can't do this. In fact, it is claimed that when it comes to seeing, moving and reacting to stimuli, no computer can compete with even the brain power of a fly.

(6 ———)

Most of our mental processes are deeply formed habits. Challenging your brain to do things differently helps it develop. Try changing routines as often as you can: take a bus instead of going by car, sit in a different chair. An extreme but useful exercise is to read something upside down – you can actually feel your brain at work.

Exercise more. Good health and fitness levels give you overall improved energy which leads to better concentration.

Cooking is a good all-round mental exercise. It needs mathematical, organisational and scientific skills as well as challenging memory and creative ability. Use recipes at first and then learn to guess amounts, combinations, reactions of ingredients and timing.

Do puzzles and play games. Teach yourself to work out codes and expand your vocabulary at the same time.

from *Esquire* magazine

Vocabulary: word formation

1 Look back at the article on the brain and find the following words.

1 the noun from *intelligent (part 0)*
2 a verb from *different (part 2)*
3 the noun from *similar (part 5)*
4 a noun from *to calculate (part 5)*
5 the positive adjective from *useless (part 6)*
6 the noun from *healthy (part 6)*
7 the noun from *energetic (part 6)*
8 the adjective from *science (part 6)*

2 Mark where the main stress falls in the pairs of words in Exercise 1. In which pairs is it the same and in which pairs is it different?

EXAMPLE: *in'telligent, in'telligence (same)*

3 Now complete the following sentences with the correct form of the word in brackets. Use your dictionary if necessary.

1 My mother was such an .... person, always busy, always in a hurry. (ENERGY)
2 I made a stupid .... and so things didn't turn out as planned. (CALCULATE)
3 I'd like to do it .... this time. I hope you don't mind. (DIFFERENT)
4 There is one important .... between Sean and Katie. They both really enjoy discussing politics. (SIMILAR)
5 If you ate more ...., you wouldn't have all these problems with your skin. (HEALTH)
6 I want to be an important .... when I grow up. (SCIENCE)
7 It's almost impossible to actually measure .... (INTELLIGENT)
8 He's .... at mending things. I'll just have to do it myself. (USE)

Speaking

1 Discuss the following questions.

1 What do you think is the purpose of going to school? Is it to make you more intelligent? Is it to learn information? Is it to pass exams? Is it to develop social skills when dealing with others?
2 How successful are the schools you have been to in achieving these aims?

2 What are the five most important characteristics that make:

a) your ideal teacher?
b) an ideal student?

List the characteristics in order of importance.

Vocabulary: education

1 Fill in the gaps in the following sentences with the words in the box.

playground   truant   cheat   heart   correct
term   give   absent   hard   degree   break
university   headmaster   report   board

1 Our teachers .... our homework in the evening and .... it out the next day.
2 My brother tried to .... in the exam, but he was caught and sent to the ....
3 I like to play football in the .... with my friends during the lunch ....
4 She got a very good school .... because she worked so .... this ....
5 I'd like to go to .... when I finish school and do a .... in Economics.
6 The teacher wrote the rules on the .... and told us to learn them by ....
7 Were you .... for a good reason yesterday or were you playing .... ?

2 Read the following text and choose the correct alternative in each case.

I started school when I was five and I went to the local (1) ~~nursery~~/primary school. I liked it very much; the (2) classes/~~lessons~~ were small and the (3) teachers/~~professors~~ were very friendly. At eleven I changed and went to (4) ~~sixth form college~~/secondary school. Things didn't go so well here. I hated studying (5) subjects/~~courses~~ like Biology and Physics and I got terrible (6) ~~points~~/marks in tests. My parents tried to (7) teach/~~learn~~ me the things I didn't understand, but it was no good. I used to get very worried about my end-of-year exams and one year, even though I spent a lot of time (8) revising/~~reviewing~~, I knew I wouldn't (9) pass/~~succeed~~. In the end I was right – I (10) failed/~~missed~~ all the exams and had to (11) retake/~~remake~~ them all a few months later. That was the worst year of my school life, but it didn't stop me having a good (12) ~~course~~/career as an engineer.

> **Watch Out!** take/pass/fail
>
> 1 He *passed* the exam.
> 2 He *took* the exam.
> 3 He *failed* the exam.
>
> What did he do first? Which is a good result? Which is a bad result?

3 Read the following sentences and match each phrasal verb in *italics* to a meaning below.

1 Please *speak up*! We can't hear you at the back.
2 If you don't know what it means, *look* it *up* in a dictionary.
3 Why do you always *pick on* me? It's just not fair!
4 Paul is having problems *keeping up* with the other children in his class.
5 You need to try and *get across* your ideas better.
6 He *catches on* very quickly. You never have to explain anything twice.
7 I'll *let* you *off* this time, but I don't want to catch you two fighting again.
8 I can't *work out* how to do this maths problem.
9 He *picked up* a lot of Italian by just chatting to people in cafés.

a) learn	f) talk more loudly
b) not punish	g) find information in a reference book
c) understand	
d) treat badly	h) communicate
e) calculate	i) maintain the same level

4 Think about the different schools you have been to in the past or which you go to now and discuss the following questions.

1 How did/do you feel about each of them? Did/do you enjoy them?
2 What would you (have) change(d) about your school in order to improve it?
3 Were/Are they single-sex or mixed? Do you think it is better to have single-sex or mixed schools?
4 Were/Are they strict?
5 Did/Do you have any special friends?
6 Did/Do you play any sports/musical instruments at school?
7 Did/Do you have any teachers or subjects that you especially like(d)/dislike(d)?
8 How often did/do you have to take exams? How did/do you feel about exams? Did/Do you enjoy them/hate them/get nervous about them?

Listening: exam fever

1 You are going to hear three students talking about exams. Listen and answer the following questions.

1 Which person doesn't mind exams?
2 Which person doesn't like exams?
3 Which person doesn't give his/her opinion?

2 Now listen again and decide which of the students (1, 2 or 3) talk about the following things.

a) oral exams	d) writing speed
b) coursework	e) revising for exams
c) competitive exams	f) failing exams

3 Make a note of what each student says about the above points.

[handwritten notes: CB:60 Voc Ex 1 EM: 44 / CB:54 Ex 1+2 EM:45 voc. 1+2 / CB 64 Ex. 1]

Function: giving opinions, agreeing/disagreeing

1

1 Look at the following ways of giving opinions and fill in the gaps.

> I think (that)
> .... my opinion
> .... my point of view
> As .... as I'm concerned
> } exams are a good thing.

2 Mark where you think the main stress usually falls in the expressions on the left.

3 Now listen to someone saying the sentences and check that you put the stress in the right place.

2

1 Put the following ways of agreeing and disagreeing in order from strong agreement to strong disagreement. Decide which two are similar in strength.

a) I don't really agree.
b) I completely agree.
c) I agree up to a point, but ...
d) I couldn't agree more.
e) I don't agree at all.
f) That's right.

2 Listen to the phrases being used in conversation and check your answers. Then say the sentences/phrases imitating the pronunciation of the people you heard.

Watch Out! *agree*

● I'm sorry, but I am not agree with you.

What's the mistake in this sentence?

---

3 Work with a partner and briefly give your opinion about each of the following. Your partner should say if she/he agrees or disagrees and why.

1 the weather at the moment
2 smacking young children
3 banning smoking in restaurants
4 the need to look after the environment
5 the quality of the programmes on TV

4 Work in a group with other students and discuss whether you agree or disagree with the following statements. Give reasons.

1 Exams are not an accurate measure of a person's ability.
2 A mixture of exams and coursework is a good idea.
3 You should repeat a school year if you fail your exams.
4 You should be told the questions a little time before you go into the exam.
5 Exams should involve an oral and a written part.
6 Competitive exams are a good idea.

Writing: article

In Paper 2 you may be asked to give your opinion on a particular question. Here is an example of the type of question you may have:

> An international young people's magazine is investigating the question:
>
> *Should students only be judged by their results in end-of-year exams?*
>
> Write a short article for the magazine on this topic, based on your own experience.

1 You are going to read a sample answer to this question, but first look at the following sentences and say what the names are of the different punctuation marks.

> How do you spell 'competitive'?
>
> "It's time to stop writing," she said.
>
> Stop throwing those paper-clips!

2 Now look at the following sample answer to the question above.

1 In the first and second paragraphs there are ten mistakes of punctuation. Find and correct them.
2 In the third paragraph there is no punctuation. Rewrite it, putting in the correct punctuation as necessary.

More and more in my country, student achievement is being based on a mixture of continuous assessment, and end-of-year exams, some people claim that this is leading to lower standards in schools', but I don't believe this is true.

In my opinion, it is much fairer to allow the work students do during their school year to count towards their final result for various reasons. Firstly, it is possible to have a bad day when you take your exams, and not show your true ability secondly, exams don't encourage real learning as students just memorise lots of information for the exam and then immediately forget it all, as well as this, it is much more realistic to spend time thinking about a question or problem, discussing it with other people and researching it in books. This is, of course something you cannot do in an exam.

In conclusion then, i believe that we should make coursework an increasingly important part of students' final marks. This will give a fairer and more accurate picture of each students' real ability.

3 Now read the sample answer again and decide:

1 what the purpose of each paragraph is.
2 if you agree in general with the views of the person who wrote it.

4 You are going to write your own answer either to the question preceding Exercise 1 or the one below in 120–180 words.

You should follow this procedure:

- Work with a partner and think of ideas to include.
- Organise your ideas into sensible paragraphs.
- Write a rough draft.
- Read through the draft and make sure you have included appropriate linking expressions.
- Check your punctuation.
- Show the draft to another student and ask them if everything is clear and easy to understand. If not, discuss how you might reword it.
- Write a final version.

> An international young people's magazine is investigating the view that:
>
> *There is no point in making students repeat a school year if they fail their exams.*
>
> Write a short article for the magazine on this topic, based on your own experience.

Grammar: gerunds and infinitives

1 Look at the following sentences and decide which are grammatically correct and which are not. Correct those which you think are wrong.

1 He decided planning his first break. *to plan*
2 I like to study with friends. *studying*
3 I hate revising for exams.
4 She wants buying a good dictionary. *to buy*
5 He promised to work all night.
6 He keeps failing his exams. It's terrible. ✓
7 Have you considered to leave school at sixteen? *leaving*
8 Simon admitted cheating in the exam.
9 He began to answer the question without making a plan.

2 Look at the verbs in Exercise 1 that are underlined and how they are used. Then put each of them into one of the following categories.

Verbs + infinitive (with *to*)	Verbs + -*ing* form	Verbs + infinitive or -*ing* form

Grammar reference p.167 (7)

3 Here are some more verbs. Make sure that you understand the meaning of each one and then put them in the correct category above.

agree arrange avoid can't stand choose
continue deny enjoy expect fail hope
intend manage mind offer plan prefer
pretend promise refuse remember seem
stop suggest try

act
lie

Watch Out! *to mind*

A: Would you mind closing the window?
B: No, not at all.

Is B happy to close the window?

---

4 Look at these pairs of sentences and decide if there is a significant difference in meaning. If you think there is a difference, say what it is.

1 She stopped to have lunch.
  She stopped having lunch.

2 I'd like to have a coffee at 11a.m.
  I like to have a coffee at 11a.m.

3 I began to read that book last night.
  I began reading that book last night.

4 I remembered to lock the front door.
  I remembered locking the front door.

5 She prefers working in the evenings.
  She prefers to work in the evenings.

6 He tried learning ten new words every day.
  He tried to learn ten new words every day.

5 Look at the words in Columns A, B and C and write five complete sentences using one word from each column.

EXAMPLE: *She agreed to marry her boyfriend.*

A		B		C
admit	agree	buy	give	elephant
arrange	avoid	go	have	boss
begin	continue	kill	like	boyfriend
decide	deny	marry	start	business
offer	refuse	stay	steal	new Rolls Royce
suggest	try	wash	school	

6 Now look back at all the verbs that you put into categories in Exercises 2 and 3 and invent a story as a class. The story begins:

It had been a very exciting day for George ...

Each student should add one new sentence which includes one of the verbs you have studied. Each verb can only be used once.

CB 68-69
CB 67
CB 63
EM 46

1 What words are being defined in each of the following sentences?

1 A child who misses school without a good reason.
2 The qualification you get if you succeed at university.
3 The school year is divided into three of these.
4 The type of school for children between three and five years old.
5 A phrasal verb which means 'to learn'.
6 To try and see another student's answers during an exam.
7 A phrasal verb which means 'not to punish'.

2 Write a short description of your experience of school like the one in Vocabulary Exercise 2, page 61.

3 For questions 1–10 read the text below. Use the word given in capitals at the end of each line to form a word that fits in the space in the same line. There is an example at the beginning (0).

NOT FIT, BUT SMART

In my family we don't worry about (0) *fitness*.   **FIT**
I suppose you could say I'm rather (1) ....   **HEALTH**
I only eat junk food and I never do any exercise.
I'm not very (2) .... and I'm completely   **ENERGY**
(3) .... at sports. My two sisters are not   **USE**
(4) .... to me when it comes to leading   **SIMILAR**
active lives. Neither of them has played any
kind of sport since (5) .... What they lack   **CHILD**
in sporting ability, they make up for in (6) ....   **INTELLIGENT**
They are two of the (7) .... people I know.   **CLEVER**
One of them works as a research (8) ....   **SCIENCE**
and the other designs electronic equipment
like (9) .... and mobile phones. They have   **CALCULATE**
both done extremely well in what are very
(10) .... professions.   **COMPETE**

---

4 Punctuate the following sentences.

1 we need eggs tomatoes and some rice
2 how do you say teacher in italian
3 do you think hes good looking she asked
4 first of all in my opinion we should ban smoking in all public places
5 sarah has lived in argentina since she was a child
6 don't give him the gun she screamed

5 For questions 1–10, complete the second sentence so that it has a similar meaning to the first sentence, using the word given. **Do not change the word given.** You must use between two and five words, including the word given.

1 'I'll send you a postcard from Greece,' he said.
   promised
   He .... a postcard from Greece.
2 Could you possibly help me with this box?
   mind
   Would .... with this box?
3 'I won't speak to Tom,' she said.
   refused
   She .... to Tom.
4 'I have never seen the woman before,' he said.
   denied
   He .... the woman before.
5 'Yes, I think we should invite Sue to the party too,' she said.
   agreed
   She .... invite Sue to the party.
6 Have you thought about getting a holiday job this summer?
   considered
   Have you .... a holiday job this summer?
7 'We'll look after your cat while you're away if you like,' he said.
   offered
   He .... our cat while we were away.
8 You shouldn't give them the impression you don't want the job.
   avoid
   You should .... them the impression you don't want the job.
9 'OK. I've been going out with another girl,' he said.
   admitted
   He .... out with another girl.
10 I am fairly sure I will pass all my exams this year.
   expect
   I .... all my exams this year.

Listening: the psychology of fame

1 You are going to hear a radio programme about psychology and fame. Before you listen, discuss the following questions:

1 Look at the photographs and describe what is happening in each one. How would you feel if you were in these situations?
2 In what ways would being famous change your life?
3 What does it take to become famous?

2 Listen to the programme to see how many of your ideas were mentioned.

3 Listen again and for questions 1–7 decide whether the statements are True or False.

1 Olga and Simon agree that famous people were often unhappy as children.
2 Simon thinks that talent is as important as motivation in achieving fame.
3 Olga thinks that famous people are more likely to take drugs.
4 Simon and Olga disagree about the role of the star's manager.
5 Simon says that many stars enjoy behaving badly.
6 Simon thinks the media are very interested in rock music.
7 Olga thinks that most stars like being the focus of media attention all the time.

4 Have you ever met a famous person? What would you do if you saw a famous person walking along your street?

Writing

1 Look at the following writing task and underline any key words.

Imagine that you have had a chance encounter with a famous person you admire. Write an e-mail message to a friend describing what happened.

2 Will you write in a formal or informal style? Why?
3 Look at the advice on writing a narrative on page 44.
4 Write your e-mail message.
5 Check it carefully for spelling and grammar mistakes.

Use of English

1 Work with a partner and describe what you can see in the photos opposite.

2 Read the text below to find out where the photos were taken.

3 Read the text again and fill in the gaps with an appropriate word. Seven of the words you need are in the box below.

the	enough	to	on	with
had	by			

Madame Tussaud's is London's

(1) .... visited tourist attraction, with over two and a half million visitors a year. There are over 400 models (2) .... display. Each one is worth £20,000, so security is tight. However, (3) .... the monitors and eagle-eyed staff, visitors can't resist picking up souvenirs and someone even went off (4) .... Marie Antoinette's head.

Making the wax models is a highly skilled and lengthy process. From start to finish (5) .... takes months of work for the artists and craftsmen who combine to produce the final figure. All the waxworks are life-size replicas of the real person, down to the last detail. Even Michael Jackson's inside trouser leg (6) .... been measured and recorded. This is considered highly classified information, of course.

Stuart Williamson, a sculptor here for fifteen years, says, '(7) .... they come to the museum or we go to them. We went to Buckingham Palace to do the Royal Family and the Neverland Ranch for Jackson. They sit on a turntable where they (8) .... measured and photographed from every angle possible.

I then sculpt the clay, trying to get a feel for their personality, which is (9) .... important as what they look like.'

The most nerve-racking part of the job can be when the real person meets their wax double. Bob Geldof thought that he wasn't scruffy (10) .... and proceeded to ruffle his twin's hair. The Dalai Lama thought the whole thing was hilariously funny.

Clothes for the models are often chosen (11) .... the famous themselves. Madame Tussaud's has the only exact replica of Princess Diana's wedding dress. Sometimes clothes (12) .... given to the museum. John Haigh, the acid bath murderer, donated his suit (13) .... day before he was executed. And when comedian, Lenny Henry, revisited Madame Tussaud's, he was horrified to see his wax double wearing his favourite pink suit – he (14) .... been looking for it for two years.

The public's fascination with fame and fortune means Madame Tussaud's will continue to be a popular venue for many years (15) .... come. ∎

Looking good

Speaking

1 Look at the photos and discuss the following questions.

1 What do you think of the styles in the photos?
2 What decades do you think they come from (the 1920s, the 1930s, etc.)?

A

B

C D

E

2 You are going to hear a famous song. Listen and answer these questions.

1 Which photo would you associate with this type of music?
2 What do you think the title of the song is?

3 Listen to the song again and put the lines of the verses in the correct order. You have been given the first line of each verse.

Verse 1
Well, you can do anything
But don't you step on my blue suede shoes
Two for the show
Now go, cat, go
Well, it's one for the money *(1)*
But stay off my blue suede shoes
Three to get ready

Verse 2
And don't you step on my blue suede shoes
Step on my face
But uh-huh honey lay off* them shoes
Slander** my name all over the place
But stay off my blue suede shoes
Well, do anything that you want to do
Let's go, cats
Well, you can knock me down *(1)*
Well, you can do anything

*lay off = don't touch
**to slander = to say bad things about

4 Discuss the following questions.

1 What kind of clothes do you generally wear to school or work/to go out with friends in the evening/around the house at weekends?
2 Do you prefer any particular kind of clothes?
3 Do you have a piece of clothing that you particularly like wearing?

Vocabulary: clothes

1 Put the words in the box below into one of the following categories.

Types of clothes	Types of shoe	Accessories	Patterns

belt sandals jacket anorak pullover skirt cardigan trainers
plain slippers brooch T-shirt vest tights socks shorts
Wellington boots earrings bow-tie waistcoat striped suit
raincoat bracelet checked blouse dress high-heeled shoes
dungarees sweatshirt leggings pyjamas braces scarf

2 Describe some of the items above to a partner, who should tell you their names.

EXAMPLE: A: *You wear it around your neck to keep warm or to look nice.*
          B: *A scarf.*

3 Look around the class. Can you name what the other students are wearing?

Watch Out! *suit/fit/go with*

1 This coat doesn't *fit/suit/go with* you. It's the wrong colour.
2 The tie doesn't *fit/suit/go with* this shirt. It needs to be plain.
3 The sweater doesn't *fit/suit/go with* me. I need a larger size.

What is the correct alternative in each sentence?

4 Work with a partner.

Student A: look at the pictures opposite. They are in a jumbled order. Listen to Student B describe each picture and then number them according to the description you hear.

Student B: look at the pictures on page 201. Say the number of the picture and then describe it for Student A.

Grammar: *can, could, may, might*

1 Complete the second sentence in each of the following pairs so that it has a similar meaning to the first.

1 a) But we could be losing our ability to laugh.
   b) But it is possible (that) we ...
2 a) Laughter can even provide a kind of pain relief.
   b) Laughter is even able ...
3 a) Those who had listened to the humorous tape could tolerate the discomfort for much longer.
   b) Those who had listened to the humorous tape were ...
4 a) Anyone may attend the workshop.
   b) Anyone is allowed ...

2 Rephrase each of the following sentences using *possible, allowed* or *able to*.

1 You could be right.
2 You may go now if you wish.
3 They might be in the kitchen.
4 You can't smoke in here.
5 He might be home late tonight.
6 It could rain this evening.
7 I can swim.
8 Paul may know the answer.
9 He can't still be at the office.
10 I could play the piano when I was much younger.

3 Look at these pictures of everyday objects taken from strange angles and say what you think they could/might be.

4 Comment on your ability in relation to the following things. Say if you can/can't do them, when you began to learn how to do them, how you learnt to do them and how well you can do them now.

1 cook   4 speak French
2 drive   5 swim
3 play a musical instrument   6 paint

5 Work with a partner and roleplay the following situation. One of you is Student A and the other is Student B. You should use *can, could, may, might* as much as possible.

Student A: your teenage daughter/son has asked you if she/he can have a party in your house/flat. You have said 'Yes' but now must discuss the 'rules', that is what is allowed and what is not allowed. Think about the following questions:

– How many people will come?
– What food and drink will there be?
– How loud will the music be?
– Where will people stay overnight?
– Which rooms will be used?
– Who will tidy up afterwards?

In general you are a little nervous about the idea because last time a number of things were broken and your neighbours complained about the noise.

Student B: you have asked if you can have a party at home and your parents have agreed. Your mother/ father wants to discuss now how it is going to be organised. You have a horrible feeling that they are going to make so many rules that it won't be any fun at all. Try and get your parents to go out, so you can organise it how you want.

1 Fill in the gaps in the following text with an appropriate word. You have been given the number of missing letters in each case.

40 years in bed – with flu

A DOCTOR taking over a local practice visited a 74-year-old woman (1) – – – had been bedridden for 40 years. He wasn't (2) – – – – to find anything wrong with her. He discovered that the doctor before him (3) – – – ordered the woman to bed because she had influenza and had told (4) – – – not to get up again until he returned. Unfortunately, he had forgotten (5) – – return.

Within a (6) – – – days, the 34-year-old single woman had recovered. But she remained in her sickroom waiting for (7) – – – doctor's visit. Several weeks went by and he still did not call. By then the patient had discovered that she enjoyed (8) – – – – – looked after so much that she refused to move.

At first she (9) – – – nursed by her mother. But when the old woman died, a brother-in-law took over. Finally, a new doctor to the area paid a routine call to (10) – – – patient's home in Taunton, Devon, and examined the woman, now (11) – – – – 74 and still determined to keep to her bed. It took seven months (12) – – sympathetic encouragement before the old lady was persuaded (13) – – leave her bed, but happily she was on her feet again (14) – – – three fairly active years before her death (15) – – the age of 77.

2 Choose the correct alternative in the following sentences.

1 He *used to/would* be very good at art when he was at school.
2 She *would/was used to* come up to my room before I went to sleep and tell me stories.
3 I can't *be/get* used to working on the night shift.
4 I *am used/used* to the weather now. I've been here for nearly a year.
5 We didn't use to *spend/spending* all our time working.
6 She *could/was able* play the piano very well when she was your age.
7 They *can/might* be away for the weekend, but I'm not sure.
8 You *may/might* leave now if you wish.
9 They *can't/couldn't* come over to see us until next Thursday.
10 *Could/May* you open the window a little?

3 Fill in the gaps in the following sentences with a correct particle (*up, in, out,* etc.).

1 She never gave .... hope that he would come back one day.
2 I couldn't decide whether to keep the money he left me or give it ....
3 He gave .... an air of importance as if he really knew he was special.

4 Under no circumstances will we give .... to threats.
5 Could you give .... the exam papers, please?
6 His hands were shaking and this gave .... how nervous he was.
7 Did you give me .... that book I lent you the other day?

4 Write a description of a famous person. Then read it out to the rest of your class and see if they can guess who you are describing.

5 Work with a partner and revise the phrasal verbs you have learnt so far. Look back at pages 17, 27, 40, 47, 61 and 81.

● Write five sentences, using phrasal verbs you have learnt.
● Then write the sentences again without the phrasal verbs but keeping the same meaning. (Underline the words which could be replaced by a phrasal verb.)
● Show the second set of sentences to another pair of students and see if they can rewrite them, this time using phrasal verbs.

EXAMPLE:

Pair A – I <u>stopped</u> eating chocolate a month ago.
Pair B – I **gave up** eating chocolate a month ago.

Vocabulary: phrasal verbs (*put*)

● *We decided to go back to one of the Shiplake islands, and **put up** there for the night.*

1   Match each of the following sentences to a correct response below.

1   So what couldn't you *put up with*?
2   I'm afraid he's going to have to be *put down*.
3   Didn't you *put* any money *by*?
4   I hated the way you *put* me *down* at the party this evening.
5   Do you think you could *put* me *through* to the Managing Director?
6   I think we should *put* prices *up* again.
7   Why don't we *put* it *off* for a couple of months?
8   Could you *put* me *up* for a couple of nights?
9   How quickly can you *put* that fire *out*?

a)   Are you joking? We only just had enough to live!
b)   I'm really sorry, but we just don't have room.
c)   I'm terribly sorry, but he's in the middle of a meeting.
d)   I don't know. It depends how far it has already spread.
e)   The way he never came home. He was always in the bar with his friends.
f)   Our wedding! How could you suggest such a thing?
g)   I only said you were being a bit silly.
h)   Are you sure? But he's only broken a leg.
i)   But if we do, we'll lose all our regular customers.

2   Now decide what the meaning of the phrasal verb is in each sentence.

3   Choose one of the pairs of sentences from Exercise 1 and continue the conversation.

EXAMPLE:
A: **Could you put me up for a couple of nights?**
B: **I'm really sorry, but we just don't have room.**
A: *But I can't afford to stay in a hotel.*
B: *Well, I could give my brother a ring. He lives quite close.*
A: *Would you? That would be really kind! ...*

Vocabulary: food and cooking

1   Decide which is the odd one out in each of the following groups of words.

1   parsley/peas/thyme/basil
2   a wooden spoon/a penknife/a ladle/a spatula
3   to roast/to grate/to bake/to fry
4   a cooker/an oven/a cook/a grill
5   to slice/to chop/to roll/to cut
6   a frying pan/a saucepan/a sieve/a pressure cooker
7   to mix/to sprinkle/to stir/to whisk
8   sweet/sour/sharp/hard
9   a bowl/a plate/a course/a dish
10 tough/rare/medium/well-done
11 a starter/a second helping/a main course/a dessert
12 to crack/to fold/to scramble/to boil

2   Think of other words to add to some of the groups in Exercise 1.

'I'm sorry, sir, but you did ask for the chef's speciality.'

3   Fill in the gaps in the following sentences with an appropriate word from one of the word groups in Exercise 1. You may need to change the form of the words you use.

1   I'd like a .... egg for breakfast with some bread and butter.
2   Could I have my steak very ...., practically uncooked, please?
3   .... some chopped herbs on top of the pasta before serving.
4   Leave the meat in the .... for at least two hours to make sure it is properly cooked.
5   Put the rice in the .... and shake it to get rid of all the water.
6   They .... their own bread. It's absolutely delicious.

4 Discuss the following questions.

1 Do you enjoy eating meat? If so, what kinds of meat do you like? How do you like them cooked? How do you like your steak done? If you don't like meat, explain why and say what kinds of food you do particularly like to eat.
2 What are your favourite desserts?
3 How well can you cook? Do you enjoy cooking? Why?/Why not?

> **Watch Out!** *lay/lie*
>
> 1 Could you *lay* the table for lunch please?
> 2 I think I'll go and *lie* on the bed for an hour.
> 3 He *lied* in the sun and read a book.
> 4 I can't understand why he *lied* to me. He normally tells the truth.
>
> Which of these sentences is not correct?

5 You are going to mime some actions to a partner, who should try to guess what you are doing. Student A should look on page 202 for a list of things to mime, and Student B should look on page 205.

Exam focus

Paper 4 Listening: Part 2 (note taking/blank filling)

About the exam: In Paper 4, Part 2 you hear either a monologue or a conversation. You have to answer ten questions. These take the form of gapped notes, questions or statements. You have to listen and write down the missing word(s) in each gap.

Procedure
1 Look at the questions and try to work out what kind of information you will need to listen for to fill each gap.
2 The first time you listen fill as many of the gaps as you can. **REMEMBER** you don't need to write a complete sentence, just two or three words, a date or a name.
3 The second time you listen, concentrate on gaps you missed the first time.

You will hear a radio documentary about the history of the pizza. For questions **1–10**, complete the sentences.

The people who invented pizza were
[1   ]
The earliest pizzas were [2   ] with a crust.
The first pizzeria opened in Naples
in [3   ]
Raffaele Esposita made a pizza in honour of Marguerita Teresa Giovanii, the [4   ]
The first pizzeria in the United States was founded in
[5   ]
Pizza topped with pepperoni sausage is the most popular variety in [6   ]
Australians like pizzas topped with [7   ]
The crust of the pizza, the tomato topping and the cheese represent three major [8   ]
Pizzas are quite nutritious because they contain
[9   ] and calcium.
The Naples Pizza Association wants to regulate what people can [10   ] of a pizza.

Listening: an addict's story

1   You are going to hear an extract from a radio programme. Listen and answer the following questions.

1   What is Lawrence's problem?
2   Is he better now?

2   Now listen to the extract again and decide if the following statements are True or False.

1   The presenter at first doesn't think Lawrence is so different from anybody else.
2   Lawrence would only buy food, tapes, clothes or dolls' houses.
3   Lawrence found the experience of buying in this way very exciting.
4   Lawrence never received his bank statements.
5   The presenter is shocked by how serious Lawrence's problem became.
6   Lawrence believes his behaviour was a way of compensating for what he didn't get as a child.
7   Lawrence's wife left him.
8   Lawrence got professional help.
9   Marlene got a new job to try and pay some of the bills.
10 They sold a lot of the things that Lawrence had bought to help get money.

Vocabulary: shopping

1   Match each of the following statements to a shop below in which you might hear it being said.

1   I only bought these last week and already the heel has come off.
2   Could I have a dozen red roses, please?
3   Do you have anything to help with a sore throat and runny nose?
4   A large, brown loaf and a couple of jam doughnuts, please.
5   I'd like to send this first class – and do you have any of those special airmail letters?
6   I'm afraid this check-out is only for customers with fewer than ten items.
7   Could you give me a couple of those avocados and a pound of the mushrooms, please?

a) a florist's   e) a supermarket
b) a greengrocer's   f) a post office
c) a baker's   g) a shoe shop
d) a chemist's

2   Complete the missing words in the following sentences. You have been given the correct number of letters in each case.

1   There are always good bar—————— in the January sa———.
2   I had to qu——— for ages, but the food is very good va——— in that shop.
3   I'm afraid these trousers are too lo——— around the waist. Do you have a slightly smaller si—— ?
4   Do you know, I think the shop assi————— gave me £1 too much cha——— .
5   I'm afraid we can't give you a ref——— if you don't have your original rec————.
6   How much do you cha——— to have things deli—————— ?
7   Oh, that colour really su——— you. It mat———— your eyes.
8   Did you see on the la——— that this shirt is made of si—— and has to be handwashed?
9   I'm sorry, we don't have any in st——— at the moment, but there are a number on or———. They should be here next week.
10 Oh no! I've lost my wal——— and it's got all my cre——— cards in it.
11 If anything goes wr———, all parts and labour are fully covered by the one-year guar—————— .

3   Discuss the following questions.

1   What are your favourite shops?
2   When was the last time you really enjoyed going shopping? What did you buy?
3   Have you ever had any bad experiences while shopping? (For example, have you ever had to complain?) If so, what happened?

Listening: a complaint

1 You are going to hear a conversation between a shop assistant and someone making a complaint. Listen and put the following pictures in the order in which they are referred to.

2 Now listen again and answer the following questions.

1 What does a) the customer b) the shop assistant say about each of the pictures above?
2 How does the shop assistant react to the customer's complaint?
   a) He sympathises with the customer.
   b) He is rude and impatient with the customer.
   c) He suggests that the customer may be responsible for the problems.

3 Look at these incomplete sentences from the conversation between the customer and the shop assistant and try to remember who said each one. Then listen to the complete sentences and fill in the missing words.

1 I see. .... matter?
2 But you should .... bought it.
3 That's ridiculous. But anyway .... thing.
4 Well, you know it's .... for ten hours.
5 Look, it says here .... undetectable by other people.
6 We've certainly never .... before.
7 Well, I suppose .... model.
8 Well, if I............... .... receipt.

Speaking

1 Work with a partner and roleplay the situation you heard above, using your own words and/or some of the expressions from Listening Exercise 3.

2 Now roleplay two of the following situations, taking it in turns to be the person who is complaining.

a) You have just had a disgusting meal at an expensive restaurant. When you tried to complain, the waiter was rude to you. You have asked to speak to the manager.
b) You bought a new coat from a local shop. Soon after, you discovered that there is a tear under one of the arms and that two of the buttons have fallen off. You have taken it back to the shop.
c) You have just arrived at a hotel on holiday. Your room is not how it was described in the brochure. For example, there is no view of the sea and there is no bath, only a shower. Also, the sheets on the bed do not appear to have been changed since the last guest. You have gone down to reception.
d) You bought a board game from a shop. You gave it to a friend as a present but, very embarrassingly, some of the pieces and cards are missing. You have taken it back to the shop.

Writing: a letter of complaint

1 In Paper 2 you may be asked to write a more formal letter, for example a letter of complaint. Look at the following phrases/sentences and decide which ones you would normally expect to find in an informal letter and which you might find in a more formal letter. Mark them **I** (informal) or **F** (formal).

1 Dear Mr Jenkins,
2 Lots of love, Pierre.
3 See you on the 20th. I can't wait!
4 I am writing with reference to a purchase I recently made in your store.
5 I look forward to receiving a reply at your earliest convenience.
6 Yours sincerely, Maria Gonzales.
7 It was really great to hear from you after such a long time.
8 Thank you for your letter of 15 September.

2 Mike Harding, the customer who complained in the conversation you heard on page 95, was not happy about what happened in the shop, so he decided to write a letter to the Manager. Complete the middle part of the letter continuing with the formal style you can see at the beginning and end.

Dear Sir/Madam,

I am writing to complain about a personal stereo that I bought from your shop last week and also about the treatment I received from one of the staff there.

When I got home, and took it out of its box, I was not very pleased to find

So, I am sure you will understand why I feel so annoyed and frustrated by the whole incident. I look forward to hearing from you in the very near future, either to offer me a complete refund or to exchange the original personal stereo for one which is actually in a decent condition.

Yours faithfully,

M.Harding

3

1 You are going to write a letter of complaint as a follow-up to one of the situations you roleplayed on page 95. Before you write the letter, match up the two halves of the following sentences.

1 When I came to the main course, I found	a) that we couldn't actually play the game.
2 To my horror, the first time I wore it	b) that all the pieces were there.
3 I was shocked at the difference between the standard of the rooms in the hotel	c) I found a tear under one of the arms.
4 At the time the shop assistant assured me	d) by anyone in all my life.
5 I have never been spoken to so rudely	e) that all the vegetables were stone cold.
6 Even more embarrassing was when	f) but in fact I was facing out on to a motorway.
7 I had been promised a view of the sea,	g) compared to how they were described in the brochure.
8 My friend's children were extremely disappointed	h) two of the buttons came off as I was in the middle of a formal dinner.

2 Now write your letter of complaint in 120–180 words. You may use some of the phrases from Mike Harding's letter or from the sentences above.

1 Look at this picture of a kitchen and name all the items you can see.

2 Look at the following pairs of words and decide what the difference is between them.

a) a ladle/a spatula
b) to fry/to boil
c) a bowl/a plate
d) a cooker/an oven
e) well-done/tough
f) tight/loose
g) a bargain/a sale
h) to suit/to fit
i) a receipt/a recipe

3 Fill in the gaps in each of the following sentences with an appropriate particle (*up, out, down,* etc.).

1 I can't believe it. The price of bread has gone .... again.
2 I can't put up .... his rudeness any longer!
3 My cat got very old and in the end he had to be put ....
4 Put that cigarette .... Can't you see this is a No-Smoking area?
5 If the weather doesn't change, we'll have to put the match .... until next Saturday.
6 I try and put about £25 .... every month in a special savings account.
7 I can't stand the way he's always putting her .... He thinks he's so clever.
8 She said she was going to put me .... to the Customer Services Department, but then I got cut off.
9 Come and stay with us. We can put you .... for as long as you like.

4 For questions 1–15, read the text below and think of the word which best fits each space. Use only one word in each space.

I had some important business to do in (1) .... United States last week and I flew out last Monday. It was all a (2) .... of a disaster. On (3) .... news before I went I heard that the weather was going to be bad so I took (4) .... of warm clothes. This meant that I had four (5) .... of luggage apart from my briefcase but only three of them appeared and I had to wait two days before the (6) .... bag was delivered to my hotel.

The first evening I wanted to go out to dinner so I asked the hotel receptionist for some (7) .... about local restaurants. He recommended one in the same street and I decided to take his (8) .... I ordered their speciality: (9) .... whole roast chicken with a garlic sauce. When the waiter brought my meal he somehow managed to spill some of the sauce on my favourite (10) .... of trousers leaving a terrible stain. The food tasted awful so I decided to go back to the hotel and go to (11) ....

About an hour later I woke up with (12) .... terrible headache and hardly got any sleep for the rest of the night. In the morning I got into the shower intending to wash (13) .... hair only to discover that there was no hot water. I rushed off to my meeting but when I got there I was told it had been cancelled because the president of the company was ill in bed with (14) .... cold. It had all been a (15) .... of time.

U N I T

10 How to make a fortune

Reading

1 Look at the photographs and the headline of the article. Answer these questions:

1 Who do you think these men are?
2 What is the relationship between them?
3 How do you think they have become so rich?

2 Now read the article to check your ideas. Which other man is important in their story? Why?

3 The following sentences have been removed from the article. Read it again and put each sentence in the correct numbered gap. There is one extra sentence that you do not need to use.

A But it was already clear that Hans would play the leading role in the company.

B I decided it should also be pressed together at the other end.

C However, it seems that the reality could be rather different.

D I was very angry and still feel very sad about it.'

E Yet although clearly among the world's most successful businessmen, they pride themselves on their secrecy.

F Now aged 78, he recalls the day Ruben Rausing came to him.

G I think that Ruben Rausing realised its potential immediately.

H So, he began questioning his wife about the method she used.

Leaders of the Pak

The incredible rise of the Rausing billionaires

Gad and Hans Rausing are among the richest men in Britain, their wealth surpassing even that of the Queen. These Swedish brothers, who came to Britain in 1983 have made their millions from one product – TetraPak, the aluminium and plastic laminated container for milk and fruit juice found all over the world.

One evening, near Christmas 1944, a young Swedish economist called Ruben Rausing was watching his wife Elisabeth making sausages in the small kitchen of their home in the university town of Lund, Sweden.

He was impressed by the manner in which the sausages were contained in a skin and kept fresh by pressing shut each end. **(1 ———)** Their conversation that evening was to lead to the invention that would revolutionise lives throughout the world, and make the couple – and their family – billionaires.

For Ruben was to apply the principle to milk, inventing the low-cost, germ-free packaging system which he called

TetraPak – a roll of cardboard twisted to make a pocket and sealed into a rectangular carton. Today if you buy milk or orange juice at virtually any supermarket from Dublin to Peking it will have come from Rausing's idea that day in his kitchen.

This is the legend of TetraPak. **(2 ———)** It is certainly true that Ruben realised the huge potential if a form of germ-free sealed packaging could be found for household items such as milk. But the alternative version of the story suggests that at this point he approached Erik Wallenberg, a young research scientist working for his company. Wallenberg claims that he is in fact the person who designed the first TetraPak, working from an idea originated by Ruben.

(3 ———) Rausing told him that he had bought a herd of cows which needed milking, and wanted a container made to package the milk.

'I was under a lot of pressure to find a solution,' Wallenberg said, 'but strangely it was while I was at home with flu that I came up with the idea of the tetrahedron-shaped milk package.'

Rolling up a piece of paper to demonstrate the process, he continued. 'I made up my mind that a cylinder – a tube – should be made and that it should be pressed together at one end. **(4 ———)** However, to avoid getting a flat cushion-like package which could contain only a small amount of liquid, I decided to make the second pressing together in a plane at right angles to the first one ... that is simply how the TetraPak was born. I went back to the laboratory and we began testing.'

Wallenberg said Ruben had early doubts about the possible success of the idea, 'but we tested it by putting water inside for several days and, when there was no leakage, he was convinced. **(5 ———)** He bought the patent and all rights from me for 3,000 kronor (a little less than £300), which to some people was a half a year's wages at that time. Obviously, at the time those in the company knew of my work but after a while another story began to emerge of the invention – that it had all been the work of Mr Ruben Rausing. **(6 ———)**

Whatever is the reality, by 1952 the first TetraPak containers were being successfully produced, and in a few years Ruben had built up a huge business.

By the late Fifties, all three of Ruben's sons had joined their father within the company. **(7 ———)**

'He was,' says Wallenberg, 'extremely able and, like his father, single-minded. He only seemed to have one interest and that was to make money.'

Despite their enormous wealth, today both Hans and Gad live modestly, and as far as Hans is personally concerned, in a recent interview he admitted, 'I have no idea how much money I have. You can't measure money in lists.'

Grammar: relative clauses and pronouns

1 Here is some important information on defining relative clauses. Read it and then do the exercise which follows.

DEFINING RELATIVE CLAUSES

a) *He is the man who designed the first TetraPak.* The underlined part of this sentence is a **defining relative clause** and is essential to the meaning of the sentence.

b) *The person (who) I spoke to had red hair.* In this case **who** can be left out because it refers to the object of the verb 'speak', that is I spoke to *the person.*

c) *Have you got the money which I lent you?* **Which** is used to refer to things and places.

d) **Who** and **which** can both be replaced by **that**.

e) **Whom** is possible (instead of **who**) when it is the object of the verb in the relative clause. However, it is not very often used in informal English. For example, it would be much more natural to say **Who** *are you going to the party* **with**? than **With whom** *are you going to the party?*

f) *This is the house* **where** *I was born.* **Where** is used to refer to places.

g) *Are you the person* **whose** *car is blocking my drive?* **Whose** indicates possession.

h) Commas are not used to separate the clause.

Grammar reference p.173 (14)

Join a clause in Column A to a clause in Column B with an appropriate relative pronoun to make a complete sentence. Use each clause once only.

A	B
1 We went to the Italian restaurant	a) dog was barking all night.
2 Where's the book	b) I first met Andrew.
3 They are the people	c) had the biggest screen.
4 Could you tell me the nearest place	d) stole my bag.
5 That boy is the thief	e) has noticed my new haircut.
6 The disco over there is	f) I picked from the garden.
7 I bought the TV	g) they sell stamps?
8 You are the only person	h) you said you would lend me?
9 These are the flowers	i) they have fantastic pizzas.

Speaking

Imagine the following situation. A language school in London is offering two scholarships. All applicants are invited to write in and explain their situation. The scholarship includes three months of English courses, all food and accommodation and some pocket money. You and a partner have been given the task of selecting the two most deserving candidates. Read the list of candidates below and decide on the two who you think should be awarded the scholarship. You should be prepared to give reasons why.

First look at page 62 to remind yourself of the language of giving opinions and agreeing/disagreeing.

Ioanna comes from Greece. She is a teacher of English and already quite fluent. She wants to make her English perfect and is interested in being involved in the training of other English teachers.

Wang I-Hua comes from a small town in the south of China. She has never been outside her town, but has always dreamed of travelling. This would be the chance of a lifetime.

Mehmet is a very clever student who is brilliant at science, but keeps failing the English part of his university entrance exam. His teachers have written a letter supporting his case.

Carmen is a Spanish nurse working for a small charity. She is about to go out to a part of Africa currently suffering from disease and famine where English is widely spoken. She will work in a village hospital with local people.

Christiane is an excellent primary school teacher who has been told she must start teaching English to her pupils as well as everything else. At the moment she has no ability in English.

Javier is a refugee living in London. He can't go back to his country because of the political problems there. He is with his wife and two young children. He is having problems finding a job because of his English.

Wojtek is a young man from Poland who would like to set up an import-export business, but needs to improve his English to do so.

Writing: an application

In Paper 2 you may be asked to write an application. In this type of writing task you will often need to give information about yourself and say why you would be good for a certain thing, for example a scholarship or a job. The style of writing will be similar to that of a more formal letter.

1 Here is part of the application form for the scholarship on page 102 which one of the applicants has completed. Which of the applicants is it from?

Describe your reasons for wanting the scholarship and what you intend doing when you finish the course.

I arrived in London ago three months with my wife and two children young. Since then I very hard have tried to get a job (in my country I was a lawyer). However, isn't very good my English and I think this is the reason why I yet haven't found a job. I seem always to have problems when I have to speak at interviews. I am sure that if I could improve my English spoken, I would to get a job be able and my family support.

I have done my best to improve my English since I arrived. I have studied books of grammar and listened to the radio, but to meet people so that I can practise my speaking it is quite difficult. I think that having regular classes of language would really help me and as soon as possible I am very keen to start. I know what a reputation good has your school and very grateful I would be if seriously you would consider my application.

2 The applicant who wrote this has a problem with word order in English. Read the text again and correct all the word order mistakes that you can find.

3 Now write an application for the above scholarship. You can either take the part of one of the other applicants or you can apply yourself.

Vocabulary: numbers

1 Work with a partner. Take it in turns to say each of the numbers in the pyramid, starting at the top. Then make your own number pyramid for your partner to say.

58
958
7,958
47,958
647,958
3,647,958
13,647,958

2 Match the following numbers to a description on the right.

a) ¼	1	a speed
b) 0.25	2	a weight
c) 3–0	3	a telephone number
d) 40–15	4	a decimal
e) 0171 491 2598	5	a date
f) 30/6/95	6	a percentage
g) 1 m 65 cm	7	a temperature
h) 85 kg	8	a height
i) 78%	9	a price
j) 32°C	10	a fraction
k) 85 mph	11	a score (in football)
l) £14.05	12	a score (in tennis)

3 How do you pronounce the numbers on the left? Listen and check your answers.

4 Work with a partner. Student A should look at the questions on page 202 and Student B at the questions on page 205. Ask your partner the questions and make a note of the answers. Then answer the questions your partner will ask you.

Watch Out! '0'

How many different ways can '0' be said?
Think about: football, tennis, telephone numbers, decimal numbers, etc.

Exam focus

Paper 3 Use of English: Part 1 (multiple choice cloze)

About the exam: In Paper 3, Part 1 you read a text with fifteen gaps. You choose one word or phrase from a set of four (A, B, C, D) to fill a gap in the text.

Procedure

1 Read the text all the way through.
2 Read the text again and look at the words on either side of each gap. Then look at the alternatives.
3 Decide which alternative best fits each gap.
4 Leave any gaps you are unsure of and come back to them at the end.
5 In the actual exam you will have to mark your answers on the separate answer sheet.

BURIED TREASURE

We know a good deal about the history of coins. The first coins were issued in the ancient kingdom of Lydia, probably by King Croesus, in the **(1)** .... seventh century BC. The first Greek drachmas were not far behind and before **(2)** .... coins were being used throughout the Mediterranean. Soon they had caught **(3)** .... all over the developed world.

We know so much about the history of coins because there are still a lot of them around. Before the **(4)** .... of banks people often buried coins for **(5)** .... keeping, sometimes so thoroughly that centuries passed before they were found again.

Coins often have a tale to **(6)** .... They provide us with what are sometimes the only **(7)** .... we have of the rulers of the past, giving us what amounts **(8)** .... a gallery in miniature of the great and powerful. By tracing the distribution of buried coins we can **(9)** .... at a record of the territories these people controlled or influenced and of the trade **(10)** .... they made with other nations. For example, Roman coins have **(11)** .... up as far away as India and ancient Greek silver coins have been found in Italy, North Africa and **(12)** ....

As the fortunes of these city states varied so did the **(13)** .... of the metals they used in their coins. Gold, silver, copper and brass have, in times of hardship, been mixed with other less **(14)** .... metals or have been replaced altogether by nickel, iron and even cardboard and leather. Though these materials are not so durable, it seems that coins themselves are here to **(15)** ....

1 **A** late	**B** end	**C** final	**D** finish
2 **A** soon	**B** long	**C** after	**D** early
3 **A** up	**B** out	**C** on	**D** through
4 **A** days	**B** weeks	**C** years	**D** times
5 **A** secure	**B** safe	**C** certain	**D** guarded
6 **A** say	**B** narrate	**C** tell	**D** count
7 **A** views	**B** visions	**C** portraits	**D** profiles
8 **A** at	**B** as	**C** to	**D** up
9 **A** reach	**B** arrive	**C** get	**D** come
10 **A** connections	**B** ties	**C** bonds	**D** links
11 **A** come	**B** put	**C** got	**D** turned
12 **A** far	**B** away	**C** beyond	**D** distant
13 **A** purity	**B** concentration	**C** intensity	**D** strength
14 **A** worthwhile	**B** valuable	**C** worthy	**D** valid
15 **A** remains	**B** stop	**C** last	**D** stay

Paper 3: Part 1 (multiple choice cloze)

1 For questions **1–15** read the text below and decide which answer **A, B, C** or **D** best fits each space. Circle your answer.

A SUCCESSFUL OPERATION

When the doctor told my mother that I (1) .... have to have a minor operation, she was surprised because I didn't (2) .... a fuss at all. I was actually quite excited about going into hospital. I imagined how interested all my classmates would be when they heard why I was (3) .... from school.

I had a whole day just to get used to (4) .... in hospital before the operation and I spent my time talking to the other (5) .... and watching TV. I was a bit scared when they came to take me from the children's (6) .... to the operating (7) .... . The doctor gave me a(n) (8) .... and told me to count to ten. I didn't get as far as three before I fell asleep.

When I woke up back in my bed, my stomach felt very (9) .... . A nurse told me it would take a couple of weeks for the wound to (10) .... , but that I would be able to get up and walk around in a couple of days. She took my (11) .... to make sure that I didn't have a fever and I went off to sleep again. When I woke up a few hours later, there was a boy I hadn't seen before in the next bed. He was about the same age (12) .... me. He'd fallen off his bicycle while trying to (13) .... up with his older brother who was riding very fast. He had (14) .... his left leg. It was going to take him a lot longer to (15) .... than me.

---

1 **A** will	**B** do	**C** would	**D** am
2 **A** make	**B** do	**C** get	**D** have
3 **A** dismissed	**B** allowed	**C** permitted	**D** absent
4 **A** being	**B** be	**C** was	**D** am
5 **A** customers	**B** clients	**C** students	**D** patients
6 **A** compartment	**B** ward	**C** section	**D** division
7 **A** theatre	**B** room	**C** place	**D** hall
8 **A** puncture	**B** injection	**C** syringe	**D** stab
9 **A** hurt	**B** damaged	**C** injured	**D** sore
10 **A** cure	**B** recover	**C** heal	**D** fix
11 **A** heat	**B** climate	**C** temperature	**D** thermometer
12 **A** like	**B** that	**C** than	**D** as
13 **A** get	**B** make	**C** put	**D** keep
14 **A** ruptured	**B** broken	**C** smashed	**D** crunched
15 **A** recover	**B** heal	**C** cure	**D** better

2 There are mistakes with verb tenses in the following sentences. Find the mistakes and write the sentences out again correctly in your notebook.

1 When I leave school, I am looking for a job in a hotel.
2 I think I go to bed now. I'm very tired.
3 I promise I phone you tonight.
4 I can't come this Tuesday because I'll play volleyball.
5 If I will see her, I will give her your love.
6 Are you making my bed for me this morning? I'm too tired.

Paper 3: Part 2 (open cloze)

3 For questions **1–15** read the text below and think of the word which best fits each space. There is an example at the beginning **(0)**.

THE JOY OF COOKING

Cooking is fun once you know (0) *how* to do it. The easiest (1) .... to learn is to borrow (2) .... basic cookery books from the local library or from a friend and (3) .... experimenting. Spend a couple of hours reading through the (4) .... until you find one that you think sounds tasty.

(5) .... a list of the necessary ingredients and check the fridge and cupboards to (6) .... sure you have (7) .... you need. There is nothing worse (8) .... starting to cook a meal and then realising you don't have (9) .... essential like lemons or breadcrumbs. It is really (10) .... to check that you have all the basic equipment like cheese graters and knives as well. The recipes in most cookery books have been tested many (11) .... so the instructions (12) .... be accurate and clear. Read them through carefully and assemble all the things you (13) .... need.

Another thing, (14) .... a lot of people forget unfortunately, is that cleaning up as you go along makes cooking easier. My mother, (15) .... was a superb cook, always said, 'The best meals come from a tidy kitchen.'

Paper 3: Part 3 (key word transformation)

4 For questions **1–10**, complete the second sentence so that it has a similar meaning to the first sentence, using the word given. **Do not change the word given.** You must use between two and five words, including the word given. Here is an example **(0)**.

Example:

(0) My brother is too young to drive a car.

not

My brother *is not old enough to* drive a car.

1   I tried as hard as I could, but I still didn't pass.
    best
    I ...., but I still didn't pass.

2   My parents met in 1970.
    since
    My parents .... 1970.

3   I don't share your opinion about military service.
    agree
    I .... you about military service.

4   He has too much free time since he retired.
    hands
    He has too much .... since he retired.

5   Driving on the left will always feel strange to me.
    get
    I don't think I will ever .... on the left.

6   Can you calculate the answers to these sums?
    work
    Can you .... the answers to these sums?

7   She said she wouldn't tell anyone about what happened.
    not
    She promised .... anyone about what happened.

8   The operator had trouble connecting me to the sales department.
    through
    The operator had trouble .... to the sales department.

9   I lived in London as a child, but I don't anymore.
    used
    I .... in London as a child.

10 Could you possibly share your book with me?
    mind
    Would you .... your book with me?

5 There are mistakes of grammar or vocabulary in the following sentences. Find the mistakes and write the sentences out correctly in your notebook.

1   A: Could I borrow your dictionary?
    B: Yes, of course you might.
2   Her parents gave a party when they heard she had successfully taken all her exams.
3   My family lived in the city since 1963.
4   You lie the table while I finish cooking the dinner.
5   He gained a really big prize in the National Lottery.
6   I have finished school two years ago.
7   I'm sorry. I am not agree with you.
8   You ought take up jogging.
9   In my point of view, spending a lot of money on expensive clothes is stupid.
10 You really should to go and see that film. It's fantastic.

6 Fill in the gaps in the following sentences with an appropriate word. The first two letters of each word have been given to help you..

1   I fell over in the pl.......... at school today and hu.......... my leg
2   The he.......... telephoned my parents when he caught me ch.......... in the final exam.
3   We were lucky enough to get seats in the front ro.......... so we could see all the members of the gr.......... really well.
4   I didn't enjoy that book at all. I thought the pl.......... was too simple and the ch.......... were really artificial.
5   He must have just got up because he was still wearing his py.......... and sl.......... .
6   If you've got such a high te.........., I don't understand why the doctor didn't give you a pr.......... for some antibiotics.
7   Most of the cuts have he.......... since the accident, but she's still got some nasty br.......... on her face.
8   Would you like your eggs sc.........., bo.......... or fr.......... ?
9   Po.......... the sauce over the cauliflower and sp.......... some gr.......... cheese on top.
10 That dress really su.......... you and it was such a ba.......... at only £20.
11 The shop as.......... said they would or.......... a pair of those jeans in my si.......... .
12 Good morning. I'd like to wi.......... some money from my ac.........., but I seem to have left my ch.......... book at home.

Paper 3: Part 4 (error correction)

7 For questions **1–15** read the text below and look carefully at each line. Some of the lines are correct, and some have a word that should not be there. If a line is correct, put a (✔) at the end of it. If there is a word that should not be there, circle it and write the word at the end of the line. There are two examples at the beginning (**0** and **00**).

	THIS YEAR'S FASHIONS	
0	This summer's fashions should brighten up your wardrobe.	✔
00	Most of the designers have introduced ⓣⓗⓔ brilliant colours	**the**
1	to their collections. There are dresses in bright pinks,	
2	yellows and oranges with matching short-sleeved jackets.	
3	Many women will have be wearing wide striped trousers in all	
4	the colours of the rainbow with matching blouses. You're going	
5	probably asking what do you will wear on your feet this	
6	season. Well, the answer is the very highest of high-heels.	
7	And if you are someone who would likes to be comfortable,	
8	there are also some very attractive flat sandals for to wear	
9	in the evening. The emphasis in this season's men's fashions it	
10	is on style and comfort. Cool fabrics like cotton and linen	
11	are popular with all the designers. There is a wide variety they	
12	of suits for more formal than occasions, as well as	
13	dungarees and T-shirts for casual wear. And hats are back.	
14	Men and women will be wearing hats just like the ones our	
15	grandparents got used to wear in the forties and fifties.	

Paper 3: Part 5 (word formation)

8 For questions **1–10** read the text below. Use the word given in capitals at the end of each line to form a word that fits in the space in the same line. There is an example at the beginning (**0**).

AMATEUR ATHLETICS	
Events like city marathons are (**0**) _increasingly_ popular.	**INCREASE**
You don't have to be a (**1**) .... person to take	**COMPETE**
part in (**2**) .... , though you do need to be fairly	**ATHLETE**
(**3**) .... and reasonably fit. You can build up fitness	**ENERGY**
by jogging. It's not the (**4**) .... that matters, but how	**DISTANT**
long you jog for. You can improve your (**5**)	**PERFORM**
gradually over a period of weeks. In (**6**) .... for a	**PREPARE**
long race like a marathon it's (**7**) .... to run more	**NECESSARY**
than a couple of kilometres most days. (**8**)	**SUCCESS**
marathon runners work on the (**9**) .... aspects of	**PSYCHOLOGY**
running long races. Mental (**10**) .... is just as	**STRONG**
important as being physically fit.	

9 Replace the underlined words and phrases with an appropriate phrasal verb in the correct form.

1 Philip couldn't <u>maintain the same level as</u> the other students in his class.
2 I just won't <u>tolerate</u> his bad behaviour any more.
3 I think we should <u>postpone</u> the party until everyone gets back from their holidays.
4 I'm sure I <u>returned</u> your sweater.
5 Tina, could you help me <u>distribute</u> the books?
6 He <u>revealed</u> his feelings when he blushed at the sound of her name.
7 Could you <u>raise your voice</u> a bit? We can't hear you at the back of the room.
8 You really must <u>stop</u> smoking – it's so bad for your health.
9 They always <u>provide me with accommodation</u> when I'm in Sydney.
10 He said 'no' at first, but in the end he <u>relented</u> and said we could go to the party.
11 Profits are down – I'm afraid we're going to have to <u>increase</u> our prices.
12 She doesn't earn much, but she still manages to <u>save</u> a little money each month.

For linked Paper 5 practice, see pages 190–192

Reading

1 Describe what you can see in the pictures.

2 Check that you know the meaning of the following words. Use a dictionary where necessary.

a meteor   dust   to dye   a sand dune
a gust   an earthquake   to wrestle
a tornado   a storm

A

B

C

3   Divide into two groups, A and B. Group A should look at the text below, Group B should look at the text on page 202. Each group should read through their text and decide what kind of information is missing in each of the numbered gaps. Is it a name, a date, a thing, a distance or something else?

Group A

Weird Weather Facts

■ The study and forecasting of weather is called (**1**) .... because it was once precisely that – the study of meteors. The idea that meteors were formed in the sky from various combinations of earth, water, air and fire, and that they contributed to weather conditions, goes back to the great philosopher and scientist, Aristotle, in the 4th century BC. It was believed in Europe until late in the 17th century.

■ In AD 582, it rained (**3**) .... on Paris. The terrified local people saw this as a sign from Heaven and responded by repenting for their sins. The true cause of the strange event was the 'sirocco',

the wind that sometimes blows from the Sahara across the Mediterranean into Europe. It carries a fine, red dust from the desert interior, and this had (**5**) .... the rain that fell on Paris.

■ On May 29, 1986, twelve schoolchildren in west China were sucked up by a tornado. It put them down again on some sand dunes (**7**) .... km away – completely unharmed.

■ The highest wind speeds ever officially recorded have occurred at the top of Mount Washington in New Hampshire, USA, where gusts have reached 370 km/hour.

■ (**9**) .... believed that the Earth lay on the back of a giant tortoise, and when it shuffled its feet the Earth would quake. One ancient Japanese legend held that the movement of a vast underground (**11**) .... caused

earthquakes; a later account said it was a monster catfish. The ancient Greeks blamed huge giants wrestling underground.

■ An average of (**13**) .... tornadoes strike the United States each year. In April 1974, 148 tornadoes hit thirteen states in just twenty-four hours, leaving (**15**) .... people dead.

■ If you are stuck out in a storm, never shelter under a tall isolated tree. Try to get indoors, or into a car. Get away from metal objects and get rid of any (**17**) .... you are carrying. If you're with other people, spread out. Unfortunately, sometimes even being indoors is no protection. In July (**19**) .... a woman was struck by a bolt that came through the window and hit the metal tea-strainer she was holding. The force of the bolt threw her across the kitchen.

from Reader's Digest *Did you know?*

4   Now decide what questions you need to ask to find out what the missing information is.

5   Finally work with a partner from the other group. Ask your partner the questions, listen to the answers and fill in the gaps in the text with the missing information.

Grammar: the article

1 Read the following rules for when we use the definite article (*the*), the indefinite article (*a/an*) and for when we do not use an article at all (the zero article). Then match each of the examples opposite to one of the rules.

THE ARTICLE

The definite article (*the*) is used:

a) with inventions and species of animals e.g. *When was **the radio** invented?/I think **the whale** may soon be extinct.*

b) with rivers/oceans/seas e.g. ***The Amazon** flows into **the Atlantic Ocean**.*

c) when there is only one of something e.g. ***The sky** is full of stars tonight.*

d) with national groups e.g. ***The British** drink a lot of tea.*

e) with superlatives e.g. *He is **the kindest person** I know.*

f) with particular nouns when it is clear what we are referring to e.g. *Could you pass **the salt**, please?*

g) with previously mentioned nouns e.g. *There is an apple and an orange. I want **the orange**.*

The indefinite article (*a/an*) is used:

h) with jobs e.g. *She is **a doctor**.*

i) with singular countable nouns (mentioned for the first time or when it doesn't matter which one) e.g. *I live in **a small house**./You will need **a ruler** in the exam.*

No article (the zero article) is used:

j) with most streets/villages/towns/cities/countries/ lakes/mountains e.g. *I'm going to **Oxford Street** today./I love living in **Rome**./He comes from **Greece**./When did the first person climb **Mount Everest**?* (For countries/groups of islands in the plural we use *the* e.g. *He was born in **the United States**.*)

k) with uncountable, plural and abstract nouns used in their general sense e.g. *I like **orange juice**./I hate **cities**./**Travel** broadens the mind.*

Grammar reference p.163 (3)

EXAMPLES:

1 It rained 'blood' on Paris.
2 The highest wind speeds ever officially recorded have reached 370 km/hour.
3 The ancient Greeks blamed huge giants wrestling underground.
4 It blows across the Mediterranean into Europe.
5 When it shuffled its feet the Earth would quake.
6 The idea that meteors were formed in the sky goes back to Aristotle.
7 I'd like to be a meteorologist when I grow up.
8 A later account said it was a monster catfish.
9 The elephant is mainly hunted for its tusks.
10 In July 1982 a woman was struck by a bolt. The force of the bolt threw her across the kitchen.
11 In July 1982 a woman was struck by a bolt. The force of the bolt threw her across the kitchen.

2 Fill in the gaps in the following sentences with *a, an, the* or (–) when no article is needed.

1 Could you turn on ....the........ television, please?
2 Watch out! There's ....a...... policeman coming!
3 It's ....the........ best film I have seen in ages.
4 Could I borrow ....a.......... piece of paper to make notes on?
5 Is that ....the....... new carpet you were telling me about?
6 I think that .... young people are much more mature these days.
7 We're going to .... Kenya at Christmas.
8 Would you like to see ....the......... photos I took on holiday?
9 They tell me that .... honesty is the best policy.
10 She said that .... carrots were her favourite vegetable.
11 Sometimes I wish ......the........ telephone had never been invented.
12 Look at .....the......... sea. Isn't it beautiful?
13 Why do you think .....the........ Japanese are so hard working?
14 We went sailing on .... Lake Windermere at the weekend.

3 Look back at some of the compositions you have written to check whether you have made any mistakes with the article. If there are mistakes, make sure you understand why.

4 In the following text *the* is missing ten times and *a/an* is missing twice. Insert them in the correct places.

Dead Sea, which lies between Jordan and Israel, is lowest lake in world. It is about 397 metres below sea level and it contains saltiest water in world. This is because several rivers carrying minerals (including salt) flow into lake, but none flow out of it. Surface water evaporates, but all minerals remain behind. Salt makes it easy for swimmers to float – you can even read book while floating on your back. In fact lake contains six times more salt than ordinary sea water so swimmer's body is six times more buoyant than usual.

Vocabulary: weather

1 Put the words in the box into one of the categories below. Some of the words can go in more than one category. Then decide if the words can be used as nouns, verbs or adjectives.

damp freezing humid breeze drizzle snow
pour boiling hail gale shower warm
chilly cool frost gust sunny mild

• **rain** • **wind** • **heat** • **cold** • **wet**

2 Describe what the weather is typically like in your country:

1 at 6.00 a.m.
2 at 1.00 p.m. } this month
3 at 8.00 p.m.

4 in January.
5 in April.
6 in August.
7 in November.

3 Tell a partner what kinds of weather you love and hate.

4 Look at the idioms in *italics* below and try to work out what they mean. Do you have similar idioms in your own language?

1 I'm feeling a bit *under the weather* today.
2 *Make hay while the sun shines.*
3 *It never rains but it pours.*
4 Don't worry. He'll be *as right as rain* in no time.
5 It's just *a storm in a teacup.*
6 He really *put the wind up me* when he said we might lose our jobs.

5

1 Certain adjectives go with or 'collocate' with certain nouns in English. Decide which of the adjectives on the left collocate with the nouns on the right.

• heavy   a) winter
• strong   b) fog
• hard   c) rain
• thick   d) wind
              e) tea
              f) traffic
              g) smoker
              h) opinion
              i) skin
              j) accent
              k) bed

2 Now choose four combinations which are new to you and make sentences which show that you understand the meaning.

EXAMPLE: *It was such **a strong wind** that my hat blew off.*

113

Pronunciation:
homophones

1 Look at the following pairs/groups of words and decide if all the words are pronounced in the same way or if any are pronounced differently.

1 wind/(to) wind (a watch)
2 weather/whether
3 mist/missed
4 pour/paw/poor
5 won/one
6 there/their/they're
7 bear/bare/beer
8 bird/beard
9 so/sew
10 white/wait/weight
11 hat/hate/height
12 flower/floor/flour
13 wear/where/were/we're
14 hurt/heart
15 court/caught
16 whole/hole
17 won't/want
18 sight/site
19 saw/sore
20 (to) row (a boat)
(a) row (= an argument)
(a) row (= a line of chairs)

2 Listen and check your answers.

3 Listen to the following sentences and then try to say them with good pronunciation.

1 I saw a bear over there.
2 I wonder whether you could pour me a beer, please.
3 I don't want to wear a flower in my hair.
4 I hurt my shoulder yesterday. It's still sore today.
5 We had a bad row last night: He won't speak to me today.
6 Can you tell me your weight and height, please?
7 We caught a rare bird.

Exam focus
Paper 1 Reading: Part 3 (gapped text)

About the exam: In Paper 1, Part 3 you will be asked to read a text from which six or seven sentences (or paragraphs) have been removed and placed in jumbled order after the text. You have to decide from where in the text the sentences (or paragraphs) have been removed. It is important to remember that in the exam one of the extra sentences (or paragraphs) will not be needed.

1 Discuss what you think the best way is to approach this task type. If necessary, look again at the suggested **procedure** on page 23 and say if this is what you do, or whether you have a different way of approaching this task.

2 Look at the photos below and discuss the following questions.

1 Where do you think this place is?
2 What are the objects you can see?

3 Now read the following text and find out if you were right.

Easter Island: A terrible warning

The people of Easter Island crossed the ocean to create a peaceful and prosperous 1000-year civilisation. But then their culture collapsed into war and mass starvation. (0 _H_)

The most isolated piece of inhabited land on the planet is in the South Pacific, 3,765 kilometres west of South America and 2,253 kilometres south-east of the nearest island. Easter Island is famous for its astonishing Stone Age culture – hundreds of enormous stone statues, many of them standing on massive stone platforms. **(1 ———)**

The civilisation that produced these amazing constructions has now nearly died out. Today, Easter Island is a 166-square-kilometre museum to that civilisation. Most researchers believe that the first colonists arrived in the first centuries AD and that Easter Island's stone structures were well developed by the 7th century. The archaeological record suggests a single unbroken culture, so there was probably just one major arrival of people by canoe. **(2 ———)**

Over its three million years of existence before humans came along, Easter Island had developed a balanced ecosystem. **(3 ———)** During this early period, the islanders built simple types of ahu (platform), with small statues either on or in front of them.

The second period of the island's history, from about AD 1000 to 1500, was its golden age. As they became more prosperous, the people devoted great energy to building bigger and better ceremonial platforms and hundreds of large statues. As the population grew, probably reaching between 10,000 and 20,000 in about 1500, the need for land increased. **(4 ———)**

The third and final period saw the tragic collapse of the earlier way of life. The causes of the island's change and decline were complex, but mainly due to one thing – the destruction of large numbers of trees. Starting at least 1,200 years ago, this meant that there were almost no large trees left by the time the Europeans came in the 18th century.

Without these trees, statues could no longer be moved and nor could ocean-going canoes be built. **(5 ———)** Deforestation also caused massive soil erosion, which damaged the island's potential for growing crops.

It is impossible to know exactly what happened on Easter Island as there are no records. What is certain is that the civilisation collapsed because of population growth, together with the decline in food and the great expense of effort on wasteful activities (platform building, statue carving and transportation). Starvation led to raiding and violence – perhaps, even to cannibalism. **(6 ———)** At that time the population was reduced to about 2000, living in poverty in the ruins of their former culture. The Easter Island story provides a model for disaster. The parallel between the ecological disaster on Easter Island (isolated in the Pacific) and what is happening elsewhere on planet Earth (isolated in space) is far too close for comfort.

4 The following sentences have been removed from the text. Read it again and decide in which numbered gap each sentence should go. There is one extra sentence which you do not need to use.

A This natural balance was disturbed by the arrival of voyagers, probably a few dozen Polynesians.

B So the population was cut off from the important protein supply of deep-sea fish.

C But once settled on the island, the colonists were trapped – it became their whole world.

D By 1722, when the first Europeans arrived, it was all over.

E The foreign visitors also brought with them European diseases which devastated the local population

F However, the story of the island is also a warning to us all.

G There is also evidence of a serious decline of the forest.

H It's a lesson we have to learn from.

5 Discuss the following questions.

What, if anything, do you think
a) governments
b) individuals should be doing to protect the environment? Consider the following:

- nuclear power stations
- tropical rainforests
- the ozone layer
- recycling of rubbish
- the quantity of traffic
- pollution
- acid rain

Grammar: modals of deduction/ criticism (past)

1   Decide which of the underlined words below suggest:

1 certainty   3 criticism
2 impossibility 4 possibility

They <u>must</u>
They <u>might/could</u> } have moved the statues on wooden rollers.
They <u>can't</u>

They <u>shouldn't</u> have destroyed the forest.

2   Complete this dialogue with the correct form of the words in brackets. Then practise saying it with a partner.

A: Do you know why Simon didn't come to my party?
B: He must (1).................... *(be/ill)*.
A: Oh no, he can't (2).................... *(be/ill)*. I saw him at school this morning and he was fine.
B: Well, he might (3).................... *(forget/about it)*.
A: No, he can't (4).................... *(do)*. I reminded him about it yesterday morning.
B: Well, he has got an exam tomorrow. He could (5).................... *(stay/at home to work)*.
A: Yes, but he should (6).................... *(tell/me)!*

3   Read this short story about Paul. After each part of the story react to each suggested reason for what happened using *must have*, *might have*, *could have* or *can't have*.

1 Paul left school early at sixteen although he passed his exams.

a) not like his teachers
b) not clever enough

EXAMPLE: He **might have left** school early because he didn't like his teachers.

2 He really didn't want to work in his father's firm, but in the end he did.

a) no other possibilities
b) his father promised him a good job.

3 He met Sophie, a secretary on a very low salary, at work. They started going out together.

a) he was after her money
b) they liked each other
c) she knew he was the boss's son

4 He suddenly decided to leave his job and go abroad without Sophie.

a) he loved her very much
b) she started seeing another man
c) he wasn't enjoying his job

4   Look at the people in these photos and make deductions about who they are, what their relationship is and what happened just before and in the time leading up to the photo. Use *must have/ might have/can't have*.

5   Write down the names of five people you know. Next to their names write down one thing that they have done wrong in your opinion. Then make a sentence using *should (not) have* and give a reason.

EXAMPLE: *Diana - not set her alarm clock.*
*Diana **should have set** her alarm clock last night because she overslept and was late for school.*

Grammar reference p.169 (10.3/10.4/10.7)

Vocabulary: problems/disasters

1 Fill in the gaps in the following sentences with an appropriate word from the box.

> floods earthquake famine drought disease
> emergency refugees aid charity injuries

1 The crops have failed again and .....*famine*..... is widespread.
2 The latest San Francisco ..*earthquake*.. measured 4.5 on the Richter scale.
3 In case of .... break the glass and push the button.
4 Half a million ..*refugees*.. have now crossed the border in an attempt to find food.
5 I never give to ...*charity*........ . I think it should be the government's responsibility.
6 The present government has given more in ....*aid*........ to needy countries than any other in living memory.
7 Many children have suffered terrible ..*injuries*..... as a result of the fighting.
8 A new ...*disease*..... has been discovered which causes partial blindness and skin problems.
9 There has been a ....*drought*...... in certain parts of the country due to the lack of rain.
10 There has been so much rain that some rivers have burst their banks and there have been ....

2 Fill in the gaps in the following sentences with the correct form of the words in brackets.

1 The ......*destruction*........ of the ozone layer is one of the worst things that has happened. (DESTROY)
2 If we don't send food, there will be ..*starvation*.. on a massive scale. (STARVE)
3 We need to find a ..*solution*..... to the problem before things get seriously out of hand. (SOLVE)
4 There was a ..*demonstration*.. of 100,000 in the centre of London today. (DEMONSTRATE)
5 It is shocking that ten per cent of the population live below the ..*poverty*.... line. (POOR)
6 Some of the most beautiful Indian tigers are facing *extinction*.......... . (EXTINCT)
7 If the ..*pollution*..... gets any worse, I'm going to move to the country. (POLLUTE)
8 I believe the ...*survival*..... of the planet is worth fighting for. (SURVIVE)

Listening: Biosphere 2

1 Look at the photo and discuss where you think it was taken.

future village on mars.

 **2** You are going to hear a radio interview which describes an experiment. Listen and decide if in general it has been a success or a failure.

3 Now listen to the interview again and make a note of the significance of the following.

1 £100 million
2 the pigs
3 an oxygen tank
4 sweet potatoes
5 hairdryers
6 goats
7 20 kilos

Speaking

Imagine you were going to live in the Biosphere for two years. Due to lack of space, you can only take the following possessions with you (all the essentials of life will be provided). Say which ones you would take and why.

- two books
- a video film
- a picture/poster
- a game
- two CDs/cassettes/records
- a musical instrument
- three photos
- one other thing

Writing: transactional letter (2)

Read the following exam task and then the sample answer below. Discuss with a partner what the main problem with the answer is. Then work together and rewrite it in a more appropriate way.

You have seen the following advertisement in a magazine. You have always wanted to take part in an expedition like this one, but would like to have more information. Read the advertisement carefully and the notes which you have made below. Then write your letter.

OPERATION SEA WOLF
Chance Of A Lifetime!

If you want to see the world, visit exotic places, make new friends and work hard as part of a team, this could be just the opportunity you've been looking for.

Operation Sea Wolf sets sail on November 15th and currently needs:
- marine biologists/anthropologists/ geologists
- enthusiastic crew members (no previous sailing experience necessary)

The voyage will last for approximately 6 months and will include research into the animal and plant life of Indonesia.

- *any qualifications needed?*
- *cost?*
- *what need to take?*
- *exact date of return?*

Dear Sir/Madam,

I was really thrilled to see your super advertisement in Eco Magazine yesterday. I've always wanted to go on a sea voyage ever since I was little and this looks like it could be my big chance.

There are just a few little points that crossed my mind. First of all, I was just a bit worried that I might need some special qualifications or something. Another thing was that you didn't say if we would have to pay anything and I'm actually a bit short of cash at the moment, you know how it is!

If it was alright with you and I did come, my mum wanted me to ask what I would need to bring but I suppose you have some kind of list, don't you? Oh yes, and the other thing was... when exactly do you think we'll be back because I really fancy doing a Spanish course next summer and I can't book it without knowing when we're getting back.

Well, I can't wait to meet everyone. Do write back soon and let me know what's next!
See you soon,

Dieter

1 Read the text and decide which answer **A, B, C** or **D** best fits each space. Circle your answer.

A MISERABLE HOLIDAY

Unfortunately, when we went on holiday last month we had the worst weather you could possibly imagine. The night we arrived there was a really (1) ..C.. fog and the pilot had to wait until it had cleared before he could land the plane. On the ground, it was absolutely (2) .... The temperature couldn't possibly have been higher than two or three degrees. For the first three days there was (3) ..A..... rain and the first hail (4) ..A....... for twenty years! To make matters worse there were these terrible (5) ..A....... of wind and we heard that there had actually been (6) .... in the mountains that had caused quite a lot of damage. People said it had been one of the (7) .... winters anyone could remember. Suddenly on the fourth day of our holiday the rain changed to (8) ....C. and then there were (9) ..A....... spells with the occasional (10) .... It wasn't what you'd call beach weather but at least it wasn't (11) .... with rain. The last two days were quite (12) .... though there was still a cool (13) .... on the coast and it was really rather (14) ....B. in the evening. The morning we left, believe it or not, the temperature went up to twenty eight degrees and in the coach on the way to the airport we were all absolutely (15) .... !

	A	**B**	**C**	**D**
1	strong	hard	thick	firm
2	boiling	freezing	frozen	cold
3	heavy	thick	huge	strong
4	storm	torment	shower	burst
5	gusts	breezes	showers	currents
6	breezes	winds	gales	drafts
7	heaviest	hardest	strongest	thickest
8	fizzle	dribble	drizzle	trickle
9	sunny	boiling	humid	cool
10	hail	gail	frost	shower
11	drizzling	freezing	boiling	pouring
12	bland	mild	soft	suave
13	gale	gust	current	breeze
14	freezing	cold	boiling	frosty
15	warm	mild	hot	boiling

2 Rewrite the following sentences using the words given so that the meaning stays the same. You will need to use 2–5 words in each case.

1 It wasn't a very good idea for you to sit in the sun for so long.
   should
   You .... in the sun for so long.

2 I'm sure he hasn't gone far because the car is still here.
   can
   He .... far because the car is still here.

3 I think it was possibly the cat which scratched the table.
   might
   The cat .... the table.

4 She was definitely here earlier because she's left her umbrella.
   must
   She .... here earlier because she's left her umbrella.

5 Buying that car was a real mistake.
   should
   We .... that car.

6 There's a chance that he phoned, but I haven't been in.
   could
   He ...., but I haven't been in.

7 There's absolutely no chance that she took the money. I've been with her all the time.
   can
   She .... the money. I've been with her all the time.

8 I'm sure she's gone to play tennis. She's taken her racket.
   must
   She .... to play tennis. She's taken her racket.

12 The great persuaders

Reading

1 Look at the title of the text opposite. How do you imagine this was possible?

2 The following words all appear in the text or the extracted sentences. Match each one with its correct definition on the right. Then think again about your answer to the question in Exercise 1.

1 a conman		a)	a silly or stupid person
2 a fool		b)	someone who buys and sells material which has been used and finished with but which may still have some value
3 a tender		c)	dishonest behaviour which is intended to deceive people, often in order to gain money
4 a bid		d)	easily tricked or persuaded to believe something
5 a scrap merchant		e)	a gift or favour you give someone in a position of power in order to influence or persuade them to do something
6 a bribe		f)	a statement of the price you would charge for doing a job or providing goods
7 gullible		g)	someone who cheats people by telling them things that are not true
8 fraud		h)	an offer to pay a certain price for something that is being sold

3 Now read the text and see if you were right.

Conman who sold the Eiffel Tower – twice!

If there is indeed a fool born every minute, for every fool there seems to be a conman ready to make him a little wiser[1].

Two of the most extraordinary conmen of all time were Count Victor Lustig, an Austrian who worked in the French Ministry of Works, and Daniel Collins, a small-time American criminal. (1 ___)

The count set about arranging the deal by booking a room in a Paris hotel in the spring of 1925 and inviting[2] five businessmen to meet him there. When they arrived, he swore them to secrecy[3], then told them that the Eiffel Tower was in a dangerous[4] condition and would have to be pulled down. (2 ___)

The count explained[5] the hotel meeting and the need for secrecy by saying that his ministry wanted to avoid[6] any public anger over the demolition of such a well-loved national monument.

Within the week, all bids were in and the count accepted that of scrap merchant, André Poisson. The deal was made, and a banker's draft was handed over at a final meeting at which the count introduced[7] his 'secretary', Collins. Then the conmen played their best card. They asked Poisson for a bribe to help the deal go smoothly[8] through official channels. (3 ___) If he had ever had any suspicions[9], they were now put to rest. After all, a demand for a bribe meant that the two men must be from the ministry.

Lustig and Collins were out of the country within 24 hours. (4 ___) Poisson was so ashamed at being taken in that he never reported them to the police.

The count and his partner returned to Paris and repeated[10] the trick. They sold the Eiffel Tower all over again to another gullible scrap merchant. (5 ___) They were never brought to justice, and they never revealed just how much money they had got away with.

from *The World's Greatest Mistakes*, edited by Nigel Blundell

4 Five sentences have been removed from the text. Look at the sentences below and decide which sentence A–F goes in each of the numbered gaps in the text. There is one sentence you do not need to use.

A But they only stayed abroad long enough to realise that the outcry they had expected to follow their fraud had not happened.

B Together they managed to sell the Eiffel Tower – not once, but twice.

C They claimed that the minister himself had asked them to act on his behalf.

D He asked for tenders for the scrap metal contained in the famous landmark.

E This time the man did go to the police and the conmen quickly left the country.

F The dealer agreed willingly and gave the money in cash.

5 Put the numbered words from the text in the following sentences in the correct form.

EXAMPLE: 1 ...**Wisdom**... is not necessarily something which comes with age.

2 Have you had an .... to Sarah's party?
3 Please don't tell anyone that I'm pregnant. It's still a ....
4 There is no .... of anyone finding out.
5 I'm afraid that .... is just not good enough!
6 I'm really sorry we were late, but it was absolutely ....
7 There is a very good .... to this book.
8 I love the way babies' skin is so ....
9 He is being very nice to me. It's making me rather ....
10 I promise there won't be any .... of this behaviour.

Vocabulary: phrasal verbs (get)

● *... they never revealed just how much money they had **got away with**.*

1 Match the phrasal verbs in the following sentences to one of the meanings a)–h).

1 I've been trying to *get through* to you on the telephone all afternoon.
2 If you're unemployed, it's very hard to *get by* on the money the government gives you.
3 Apparently he stole thousands of pounds from the company and *got away with* it for years.

4 It took him a very long time to *get over* the death of his wife.
5 I'm sorry, but I really must *get down to* my English homework.
6 Do you *get on* well *with* your father-in-law?
7 Don't worry. I know how to *get round* my Dad.
8 What are the children *getting up to* now? It's far too quiet.

a) recover
b) make contact
c) start doing seriously
d) have a good relationship with
e) persuade someone to let you do something
f) survive
g) do something naughty or bad
h) avoid being caught and punished

2 Now fill in the gaps in the following sentences with the correct particle (*away, down,* etc.).

1 You won't get ...away... with it, you know. Someone will find out!
2 I'm surprised you and Simon don't get ...on... better. You're so similar in character.
3 Now, don't get ...up to... to anything while I'm out, will you?
4 I've got just enough French to get ...by... on holiday, but that's about it!
5 If you don't get ...down... to writing some postcards soon, the holiday will be over!
6 I know she's disappointed about her exam results, but she'll get ...over... it.
7 If I want an extra day's holiday, I'll have to think of a way of getting ...round... my boss.
8 It's so frustrating. I just can't get ...through... to Brian. The line is constantly engaged.

3 Put the words in the following sentences in order.

1 you sister on why get your don't with?
2 in I've Spanish everyday enough got by situations get to.
3 him to will long illness how take it over this get?
4 always can flowers round her get I buying by her.
5 to away what getting while have been you up have I been?
6 business time get to it to down is.
7 it hurt away he me to going get and is with not.
8 hospital Dr Jones easily I to got phoned and through the.

Grammar: *have to/don't have to/ must/need*

- *'The Eiffel Tower **has to** be pulled down.'*

1   Can you think of any other ways of saying the sentence above without using *have to* but so that it keeps the same meaning?

2   Answer the following questions.

1   Can you put the following sentence into the past?

- *I must tell John about the party.*

2   In which of these two sentences:

   a) does the speaker probably decide for himself?
   b) is the speaker probably told by someone else?

- *I have to take a holiday before the end of May.*
- *I must take a holiday before the end of May.*

3   Which of these sentences are good English and which aren't? Why?

   a) *I've got to give up smoking.*
   b) *I've to give up smoking.*
   c) *I have to give up smoking.*
   d) *I often have to work until 7 o'clock at night.*
   e) *I often have got to work until 7 o'clock at night.*

4   Is there any difference between these sentences?

   a) *You don't have to wait.*
   b) *You needn't wait.*
   c) *You don't need to wait.*
   d) *You mustn't wait.*

5   Is there any difference between these sentences?

   a) *You are not allowed to smoke in here.*
   b) *You can't smoke in here.*
   c) *You don't have to smoke in here.*

6   Did he do his homework?

   a) *You didn't need to do the homework.*
   b) *You needn't have done the homework.*

Grammar reference p.170 (10.5/10.6)

Watch Out!   *supposed to*

1   You *are supposed to* speak English in class.
2   You *are not supposed to* speak Greek in class.

How can we rephrase these sentences using *should*?

---

3   Rewrite the first sentence using the word in **bold** so that the meaning stays the same.

1   It's very important for me to write to my brother.
   must
   I .... to my brother.

2   It wasn't necessary for them to cook so much food.
   need
   They .... cooked so much food.

3   They were forced to do their homework before they went out.
   had
   They .... their homework before they went out.

4   It is not permitted to take photographs in here.
   can
   You .... in here.

5   There was no need for you to come.
   have
   You .... come.

6   You shouldn't talk while the teacher is speaking.
   supposed
   You .... talk while the teacher is speaking.

7   It's necessary for me to work late tonight.
   got
   I .... work late tonight.

8   No one expected you to wait for them.
   need
   You .... to wait for them.

4   Complete the first sentence in each of the following short dialogues using an appropriate form of *(don't) have to, must* or *need*.

1   A: .... do photocopying or filing?
    B: No, I don't. That's not part of my job.

2   A: .... take with me?
    B: Just an umbrella, in case it rains.

3   A: .... come to Martin's party if you don't want to.
    B: Are you sure that's OK, I'd really prefer not to.

4   A: .... hit your brother, it's not kind.
    B: But, Mum, why not? He hit me first!

5   A: Oh, no! It's nine o'clock. I've overslept.
    B: .... get up. It's Saturday, stupid!

6   A: .... wear a seatbelt?
    B: Yes, I'm afraid so. It's the law and anyway it will protect you in an accident with another car.

7   A: .... buy any new shoes.
    B: I think you do. Your old shoes are worn out!

5   Work with a partner. Choose one of the following and say what is necessary and not necessary to do to become excellent at it. Use *have to, don't have to, must* or *need* as appropriate.

- play tennis/piano/chess
- speak a new language
- cook
- drive
- paint

Listening: radio advertisements

1   You are going to hear five different radio advertisements. Listen and decide what each one is advertising.

2   Which advertisement did you think was the best? Why?

Speaking

Homework 14.05.03

1   Discuss what skills and qualities you need to be an effective salesman.

'It's got more special-function keys than you'll find on many of the larger models. It's solar-powered and it even tells you the time in different countries. I'd say that more than makes up for the fact that it doesn't have the number nine!'

2   Imagine that you work for a company that makes ice cream, chocolate bars and frozen foods such as pizzas and chips. The company is about to launch a new product and you have been asked to give a presentation to the sales team telling them all about it, but first you should prepare yourself with some necessary language by doing the following exercises.

A Grammar: modifiers/intensifiers

1   Three of the following sentences are not possible. Decide which ones and why.

a) The film was absolutely incredible. ✓
b) He's a terrific guy. I really like him. ✓
c) The food in that restaurant was <u>very</u> marvellous. ✗
d) John's got a wonderful sense of humour.
e) He's an extremely amazing football player. ✗
f) The number of people at the concert was <u>quite</u> incredible.
g) We had a really great time at Jo's party last night.
h) The special effects in the film were just superb.
i) Her English is really fantastic. She must have lived in an English-speaking country.
j) We saw an absolutely <u>good</u> tennis match on TV this afternoon. ✗

2   Think about the last really good time you had with either your friends or family. Note down some of the key points about it, for example where you went, what you did, why it was so good. Now tell a partner about it. Be very enthusiastic and use some of the modifiers/intensifiers from the sentences in 1.
Grammar reference p.171 (11).

B Writing and speaking: linkers (addition)

1   Look at the following ways of linking two positive or negative points about something. Which ones would you use i) mainly in writing ii) mainly in speaking iii) in both writing and speaking?

- **Not only does** this machine tell you the time, **but** it **also** makes the tea.
- **As well as** tell**ing** you the time, this machine makes the tea.
- **In addition to** tell**ing** you the time, this machine makes the tea.
- This machine tells you the time **and** it makes the tea.
- This machine tells you the time. **Moreover/Furthermore**, it makes the tea.
- This machine tells you the time. **What's more**, it makes the tea.

Grammar reference p.168 (9.1).

3 Use the words and patterns above to link the information in the following sentences.

a) He is very good-looking. He is also very intelligent.
b) The room in the hotel was dirty. It was also cold.
c) They want us to start working half an hour earlier. They also say they can't pay us any more.
d) The weather in Cairo is fantastic. The people are also incredibly friendly.
e) He did all the washing. He ironed all my shirts.
f) The volume control on the personal stereo was faulty. The headphones were very uncomfortable.

4 Now you are ready to prepare your product presentation. You will have to speak for one minute on your product explaining what it is, what special features it has, why it is better than anything else on the market and why it represents good value for money. Remember to use addition linkers to strengthen your arguments. Organise your product presentation like this:

• Describe the new product and why the company has developed it.
• Explain what is new and different about it.
• Convince the sales team that this product is exactly what the customer wants and much better than any similar products already on the market.

Vocabulary: media

1 Fill in the gaps in the following sentences with an appropriate word. You have been given the exact number of letters in each case.

1. Are there any interesting head————— in today's paper?
2. Mike's a journ————— for a local newspaper.
3. The cros————— and the cart———— are the only parts I look at in the paper!
4. Do you know that paper has a circu—————— of over 3 million a day?
5. Did you read the edit————— in the paper today? I agreed with every word it said.
6. I hate the way the papers seem to be so full of gos——— and sca———— these days.
7. What freq————— is the BBC World Service on? Can I get it on my radio?
8. I listen to my local radio sta———— a lot. It has great music and regular news broad—————.
9. Do you know how many television chan———— they have in the United States?
10. The picture on our TV isn't very good. Perhaps we should move the aer———.
11. Give me the rem——— con————! I hate the way you keep changing what we are watching!
12. Let me phone you back. My favourite so—— is just starting and I never miss it.

2 Discuss the following questions.

1. Do you regularly read a newspaper? If so, which one? Why do you like it?
2. Do you often listen to the radio? What stations do you listen to and what kind of programmes?
3. What are your favourite TV programmes? Are there any TV programmes you can't stand? Why?

Exam focus

Paper 5 Speaking (a complete interview)

1 You are going to do a complete Paper 5 interview. First consider the following categories:

- grammar
- vocabulary
- pronunciation
- discourse management
- interactive communication

Which of them do you think are your strong points and which are weak areas in speaking?

2 Now listen to a sample interview and give each candidate a grade for each of the categories listed in Exercise 1: poor/satisfactory/good/excellent. The photos they refer to for Part 2 appear below and the pictures for Part 3 appear on page 204.

3 Now work in groups of four and roleplay an interview, similar to the one you have heard, using the same photos and pictures.

Student A

You are the interlocutor. You should tell the two candidates what to do. Your teacher will give you the instructions for Parts 2 and 3. You will find the questions for Parts 1 and 4 of the interview on page 205.

Student B

You are the assessor. You should refer to the different categories in Exercise 1 for each candidate and give feedback at the end on the strong and weak points of the candidates.

Students C and D

You are both candidates.

After you have finished change roles, so that Students A and B become the candidates.

1

2

3

4

Reading

1   Read the following definitions and discuss what you think a 'television ration box' is. How do you think it works? Who might use it?

ration² *v* [T] **1** to limit someone to a fixed amount of something: *On this diet, you are rationed* **to** *two eggs a week.* **2** to control supplies of something: *The government had to ration petrol during the war.* **ration** sthg ↔ **out** *phr v* (T) to give out supplies in limited amounts: *He rationed out the water to the sailors.*

2   Now read the article opposite and see if you were right.

3   Read the article again and write appropriate questions for the following answers.

1   It will automatically turn off the TV after a certain period of time.
2   Read or play outside.
3   Randal Levenson.
4   In order to reduce the amount his children watched TV.
5   The screen goes blank.
6   £49.
7   He thinks it has increased his vocabulary.
8   His neighbours.
9   Three thousand five hundred.
10   About two weeks.

4   Discuss the following questions.

1   What do you think about the general quality of TV in your country?
2   What do you think of the idea of a 'television ration box'?

Television Ration Box

1   PARENTS are soon to be offered the ultimate weapon to win the war over how much TV their children watch.

Instead of constantly fighting to ration viewing habits, they will have the job done for them by a coded electronic device.

It will switch off the set once an allotted period runs out, leaving the
10 child to turn to other activities such as reading or even playing in the fresh air.

The gadget, 'TV Allowance', was invented by Miami photographer Randal Levenson, a former engineer, who despaired of ever reducing his three children's screen time.

'There was a lot of anger in the house about the TV and Nintendo
20 usage,' said Mr Levenson, 47.

His response was to build the calculator-sized box which plugs into the TV.

The Levensons now use a code to set the four hours that Moss, 13, Cormac, 11, and Geddes, 6, can watch each week. Each has his own code, and when his time is up, the screen goes blank. He can find out how
30 much time is left by touching a button. The gadget, which will sell in Britain for £49 this summer, also controls video games and the video. It can block out specific periods such as homework time and cannot be disconnected by frustrated youngsters.

'They've got their lives back,' said Mr Levenson's wife, Rusty. 'Not that
40 they were total couch potatoes*, but they certainly spent too much time in front of the TV.

'The problem before was that we were giving up. We could only say "No" so many times. But the unemotional gadget can go on saying "No" for as long as necessary.'

'I thought, "Oh, this is really going to be horrible,' said Moss, recalling
50 the first time it was attached to the family set. 'Then you get to live with it and get used to it. I think my vocabulary's ten times bigger now because I'm reading more.'

But, being children and therefore devious, they have found ways of getting round the system, if not beating it.

The set is switched off for
60 advertisements and they barter with each other for TV time. They also decide which programmes more than one child wants to watch. Any time left over at the end of the week can be carried over into the next.

'It teaches kids time management and other business skills,' said Mr Levenson, who decided to market the gadget after neighbours asked him to
70 make units for them. So far, 3,500 have been sold without advertising and he believes that is only the start.

'If I make money, that will be fine. But it was worth it to cut back on the amount of TV my kids were watching. It takes about two weeks but then children accept the situation. They come to find that there are other things in life besides
80 sitting and watching TV.'

* a couch potato = someone who spends a lot of time sitting on the sofa in front of the TV

from The Daily Mail newspaper

Exam focus

Paper 2 Writing: Part 2 (discursive composition)

1   You are going to hear some people giving their opinions about the 'television ration box'. Listen and decide what different arguments you hear:

a) in favour of the idea.   b) against the idea.

2   In Paper 2 you may be asked to write an article of 120–180 words, in which you give your opinion on a certain subject. Here is an example of the type of question you may have.

An English-language magazine is investigating the views of people in different countries on the question:

Should parents limit the amount of television their children watch?

Write a short article for the magazine on this topic, based on your own views and experience.

1 Read the following answer to the sample question. In what areas is it good? In what areas is it weak? Think about:

- length
- grammar
- spelling
- handwriting
- vocabulary
- organisation of ideas and paragraphing
- use of linking expressions
- logical order of argument
- appropriacy of language for context

Should parents limit the amount of television their children watch?

First of all I think it is important to say that the qality of television has improved a great deal in recent years. There is now a wide range of programms suitabel for all ages and intrests. In my opinion, there are many things that children can learn from television. They can, for example, learn about other countrys, other ways of living and so on. As well as this, television can give parents a chance to be free of their children for a short time, which can be very important! On the other hand, sometimes children will just sit and watch rubish for hours at a time and oviously this is not a good thing and needs to be controled. Therefore, I think parents should discuss and aggree just how much TV the children watch. I do think, however, that it is important that children are invoilved in the desision and not just told, otherwise they will want to watch TV even more because it is something they are not alowed to do. To sum up then, parents need to think about how there children use TV and be prepaired to limit the time when it is on if they feel their children are becoming addicted to it in an unhelthy kind of way.

2 Work with a partner. Go through the sample answer above and:

a) correct all the spelling mistakes you can find (there are sixteen).
b) divide it into appropriate paragraphs.

3

1 Which of the underlined linking expressions in the above text are used to:

- give more information (e.g. and)?
- introduce a contrasting idea (e.g. but)?
- explain the consequence of something (e.g. so)?

2 Choose the correct alternative in the following sentences. Then add each new linking expression to the appropriate group above.

a) I like him although/in spite of he is rather selfish.
b) As well as this/In addition to having a lot of money, he is very good-looking.
c) It was raining so/therefore we decided to stay at home.
d) Building a road here will destroy an area of great natural beauty. Furthermore/And, all the local people are against it.
e) Not only/Moreover was the party awful, but we also had a flat tyre on the way home.
f) They lost the match despite/however playing very well.

3 Fill in the gaps in the following sentences with an appropriate linking word/expression from the completed groups in 1.

a) Television kills conversation in families. ...., it has led to an increase in violent crime.
b) We are going to be away for a few days, ... I have asked my mother to come in and water the plants.
c) Tom is a really nice guy .... of seeming quite unfriendly when you first meet him.
d) I really like the job I'm doing at the moment. ...., the salary is awful.
e) The hotel was miles from the sea and .... this, our room was small and badly decorated.
f) .... being very interested in the situation in the Middle East, I still don't understand it very well.
g) I finished reading that book, ... I didn't find it very interesting.
h) We decided not to go to the cinema .... the fact that we all wanted to see the film.
i) The cost of the proposed project is more than we expected and .... we do not feel we can go ahead.

127

21.5.03

4 Now write your answer to the question in Exercise 2. You should follow this procedure:

● Read the task instructions carefully. Think about what type of text you are writing and what sort of people you are writing for.

● Make a list of points to include in your answer. Turn the question into a statement: *Parents should limit the amount of TV their children watch.* How do you feel about this? Why might this be a good/bad idea? List your ideas under a positive (+) heading, like this:

> **+**
>
> ● *lots of unsuitable programmes*
> ● *too much TV reduces time when children should be studying*

● Now imagine someone arguing with your ideas and add their views under a negative (–) heading like this:

> **–**
>
> ● *children can learn a lot from TV*
> ● *children should learn to be selective by themselves*

● Write a draft. Organise your article into the following paragraphs:

1 Introduction: state the general situation/problem referred to in the question.
2 Give your opinion and specific examples to support your case where possible.
3 Refer to counter arguments. — *opposite argument*
4 Conclusion: summarise your view and possibly give advice or make recommendations to those concerned.

● Read your draft through. Does it answer the question? Is it effective in the various areas listed in Exercise 2 part 1?

● Write a final version.

Speaking

1 Describe in as much detail as possible what you see happening in the pictures. Say which picture best reflects how your family spends its free time.

A

book change

B

C

2 Work with a partner and imagine you have been put in charge of a new TV channel. Decide the following:

1 What kinds of programmes you want to have on your channel e.g. sports, documentaries, quiz shows, films, news, soap operas.
2 How you are going to make it different from existing TV channels.
3 What you are going to call the channel.
4 What a typical evening's viewing will consist of.

1 Choose the correct alternative below to fill the gaps in the following text.

	A	B	C	D
1	can	need	must	got
2	very	really	terrible	absolutely
3	by	through	up	down
4	despite	however	although	though
5	supposed	need	had	got
6	should	necessary	important	supposed
7	wonderful	completely	very	absolutely
8	well	addition	also	moreover
9	over	in	across	through
10	needed	should	must	could
11	from	with	to	off

... and, anyway, I (1).......... just tell you about a (2).......... awful thing that happened to me on Monday. I had just got (3).......... to cleaning the kitchen floor, when I heard this knock on the front door. I went and answered it and there was this man who said he had come to investigate a gas leak. I told him that I didn't have a gas leak, but (4).......... this he insisted on coming in and said he (5).......... to have a look. So, I let him come in. I knew I was (6).......... to check his identification card and he was (7).......... funny when I asked for it. He said he had left it in his van and as (8).......... as this he wasn't wearing the usual overalls. So, I popped upstairs and phoned the gas board to see if they had sent someone round. It took me a long time to get (9).......... to them, but eventually I did and they told me that they hadn't sent anyone and that nothing (10).......... to be done in my area. I went downstairs and the man was putting various things of mine into a large bag. When he saw me, he just dropped the bag and ran out. It gave me quite a shock as you can imagine and to think he nearly got away (11).......... it!

2 Answer the following questions using a word you have learnt in Unit 12.

1 If you gave money to a police officer so he wouldn't give you a fine for speeding, what would you be doing?
2 What is the noun from the verb *to explain*?
3 What is the noun from the adjective *wise*?
4 What phrasal verb means 'to recover from something'?
5 What is the word for the title printed in big letters above a story in a newspaper?
6 What verb means 'to talk or write about other people's private lives'?
7 What do you put on the top of a building so you can receive TV broadcasts?
8 What gadget can you use to change TV channels without actually having to leave your seat?

3 Complete the following sentences in a logical way.

1 Something I really must do this weekend is ...
2 In my secondary school we aren't/weren't allowed to ...
3 If you want to speak English well, you need to ...
4 When I was younger, one of the things I used to get up to was ...
5 The last time I had a really great time out was when ...
6 As well as being really good fun, my best friend is ...
7 I decided not to go to the party in spite of ...
8 It was an incredibly hot day so we ...

UNIT
13 It's a mad world

Reading

1 Look at the photos below and opposite and discuss the following questions.

1 Who do you think the people are?
2 What are they doing and why?

2 Read the following text and decide if the things described could happen in your country.

Mad as a hatter OR geniuses at work?

(1 ___ C ___)

British eccentrics are famous the world over. We breed eccentrics and we're fascinated[1] by them. Eccentrics are found in all walks of life, whether they are lords or lavatory cleaners, teachers or train drivers. Some wear odd clothes, some collect to the point of obsession, while others inhabit strange environments or hold unorthodox beliefs[2]. Provided they are in no way a threat to society, we usually just avoid them but let them carry on in their own sweet way.

(2 ___ D ___) F

David Weeks, an American psychologist has conducted the first in-depth psychological study of eccentrics and has concluded that Britain's are still the best in the world. Weeks did detailed personality tests and taped interviews with 130 eccentrics. 'A true eccentric is never acting,' writes Dr David Weeks. 'They are strong[3] individuals with strange inclinations of their own which they are not afraid to express. They refuse[4] to compromise.' He believes one in 10,000 people in the UK is a genuine eccentric, and that for every female candidate there are nine male eccentrics.

(3 ___ A ___)

One of his most interesting findings was the good health[5] that eccentrics enjoy. 'Almost all of them visit the doctor only once every eight or nine years; the rest of us go twice a year.' Eccentrics tend to live longer than the rest of us. The theory[6] is that if you have a particular obsession, whether it is eating cardboard or living in a cave, life becomes full of meaning and significance and the resulting happiness strengthens the body's immune system. 'Eccentrics are living proof[7] that one does not necessarily have to go through life

with a fixed set of rules,' says Dr Weeks. 'They are their own best leaders and poor followers, and do not feel a need to possess the ordinary things of everyday life. They are prepared to stand out from the crowd.'

(4 ___ E ___)

Some, like botanist Alan Fairweather, a potato fanatic, have turned their eccentricity into a career – he worked for the Ministry of Agriculture, Fisheries and Food as a potato inspector. He has lived for thirty years on a diet of potatoes boiled in their jackets, supplemented by Mars bars, baked beans and Vitamin C. He won't sleep in a bed and his idea of a break is a visit to the International Potato Centre in Peru. There are others who are spare time eccentrics, like Barry Kirk, a computer technician, who likes to paint himself orange and pretend to be a baked bean.

(5 ___ B ___)

Some of Weeks's collection – such as the man who climbs down tower blocks dressed as a pink elephant – would stick out anywhere, but most are unremarkable on the surface. Weeks believes that inside lie resources of creativity[8] and imagination that are not sufficiently used. 'They are neglected, or not taken seriously, because of the way they express themselves. Often they are convinced that they are ahead of their time and that others have stolen or exploited their good ideas.'

(6 ___ G ___)

What counts as eccentricity varies[9] with time and a person's sex as well as location. Adeline Brudenwell, countess of Cardigan, was regarded as extremely eccentric in the 1870s because she would bicycle around London in tight red military trousers and a leopard-skin cape. She would also go for walks in Hyde Park wearing a blond wig, followed by a footman carrying a cushion on which sat a pet dog. Nowadays people would just assume she was an actress or a singer with a new album to promote.

from *Focus* and *Living* magazines

Vocabulary: phrasal verbs (*out*)

1 Match each pair of sentences below to one of the following general meanings of *out* when used in phrasal verbs.

1 to be/go away from home *go out*
2 to pay attention (often because of danger) *look out*
3 to remove, get rid of *throw out*
4 to appear clearly (often suddenly) *come out, stand out from sth out*
5 an ending of something (often because there is nothing left) *sold out, run out*

a) They are prepared to *stand out* from the crowd.
   Don't *stick* your tongue *out* at me! 4

b) *Look out!* There's a policeman coming.
   If you don't *watch out*, you're going to get in serious trouble. 2

c) Shall we *eat out* tonight?
   Apparently, he *stayed out* all night. His mother was very worried. 1

d) I'm going to *throw out* all my old notebooks. 3
   You should *rub out* all the mistakes and start again.

e) I've got to stop playing. I'm *worn out*.
   I'm sorry, we've completely *sold out* of milk today. 5

2 Look at the phrasal verbs in the following sentences and add each one to the appropriate pair in Exercise 1 according to the general meaning of *out*.

1 *Mind out!* That chair has only just been painted. 2
2 I can't find any jam. We haven't *run out*, have we? 5
3 Look at this! I've *come out* in spots all over my face 4 and neck.
4 You should *get out* and enjoy yourself more. 1
5 I think they should have *cut out* more of the bad 3 language in that film.

3 Imagine you have just had the most awful week. Make some notes on what has happened to you. Then tell a partner all about it in two minutes, trying to include as many phrasal verbs as possible. Then listen to your partner and see who used the most phrasal verbs from above and from previous units in the book. You can refer to the *Phrasal verbs reference* on pages 196–198.

EXAMPLE: *You'll never believe what an awful week I have had. I'm absolutely **worn out**! It all started on Monday when my Mum told me she had **thrown out** all my old records ...*

3 Decide which of the following headings should go before each of the paragraphs in the text. There is one extra heading which you do not need to use.

A How to stay in good shape. — *stay in shape*
B Appearances can be deceptive.
C Live and let live.
D Measuring madness.
E Hobby or full-time occupation?
F Some serious research.
G How times change.

4 Put the numbered words from the text in the following sentences in the correct form.

EXAMPLE: 1 That book about the Amazonian Indians is absolutely **fascinating** .

2 He said it was *unbelievable* that she had failed all her exams. She normally gets top marks.
3 If that wall isn't *strengthened* soon, the whole thing will collapse.
4 His *refusal* to listen to her idea was typical.
5 I think it is very *unhealthy* the way you eat so much chocolate and drink so much Coca-Cola.
6 It's a *theoretical* possibility, but it's not likely to happen in practice.
7 Can you *prove* you were at home between 6 p.m. and 9 p.m.?
8 His sculpture was a marvellous *creation* and everyone admired it.
9 These T-shirts are available in a wide *variety* of colours.

7 Look at this cartoon. What do you notice about the grammatical form of the last sentence?

last event – present result

8 Decide which two of the clauses in Column B are most likely to follow the clause in Column A.

A	B
1 If you don't know,	a) you should ask. b) you would have asked. c) ask.
2 When I see him,	a) I might tell him what you said. b) I am going to tell him what you said. c) I will be telling him what you said.
3 If they wanted the house,	a) they will phone. b) they would have phoned by now. c) they would phone.
4 Do your homework	a) unless you want to be in trouble with your teacher. b) provided that you want to be in trouble with your teacher. c) if you don't want to be in trouble with your teacher.
5 If he hadn't been so stupid,	a) he might not have gone to prison. b) he would not be in prison now. c) he can't be in prison.
6 If I hadn't eaten the fish,	a) I won't be ill. b) I wouldn't have been ill. c) I wouldn't be ill now.

Vocabulary: animals

1 The words in the box are all parts of different animals. Decide which of the animals listed below have which parts. Use a dictionary where necessary.

wings	fur	claws	a trunk	hooves	paws
a fin	a tail	a beak	feathers	a mane	
a hump	a horn				

1 bat	5 cow	9 cat	13 snake
2 rhinoceros	6 shark	10 eagle	
3 dog	7 lion	11 fly	
4 elephant	8 horse	12 camel	

2 Work with a partner. Student A should look at the picture on page 203 and describe it for Student B to draw. Student B should look at the picture on page 205 and describe it for Student A to draw. Then look at each other's pictures to find out how like the originals they are.

3 Match some of the animals from Exercise 1 to the following sounds.

a) to purr   c) to moo   e) to hiss
b) to bark   d) to roar   f) to neigh

4 Read the following sentences and try to work out the meaning of the expressions in *italics*. Use a dictionary where necessary.

1 They were trying to keep their wedding a secret, but his father *let the cat out of the bag.*
2 As I was on the way to the shops I thought I would *kill two birds with one stone* so I went in and saw Mary.
3 I've decided to get out of *the rat race* and give up working in advertising. I'm going to move away and grow vegetables in Wales.
4 I am sorry that you and Steve have split up but there are *plenty more fish in the sea.*
5 When I tell my parents that I have failed all my exams, they are going *to have kittens.*
6 I'm afraid you are just going to have *to take the bull by the horns* and tell him you want to leave.
7 If she tells him what she knows, it will really *put the cat among the pigeons.*
8 You know, I heard it *straight from the horse's mouth*, so it must be true.

Exam focus

Paper 3 Use of English: Part 2 (open cloze)

About the exam: In Paper 3, Part 2 you will read a text with fifteen missing words. The missing words will be mainly 'grammar' words e.g. *has/the/by/might*.

Procedure

1 Read the text all the way through.
2 Read the text again and look at the words in the sentences before and after each gap. Think about the grammar and meaning of the missing word and the words before and after it.
3 Fill in the missing words on the question paper.
4 Read the text through to check that it makes sense with the gaps filled.
5 Transfer your answers to the answer sheet.

1 Why are people frightened of bats? Think of three reasons and then read the following text to check if you are right.

2 For questions 1–15 read the text below and think of the word which best fits each space. Use only one word in each space. There is an example at the beginning (0). In the actual exam you will write your answers on the separate answer sheet.

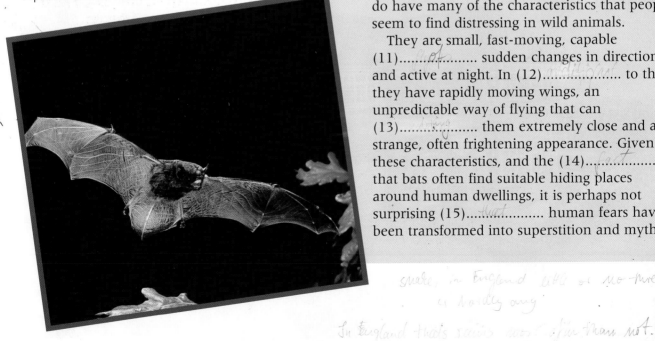

Fear of Bats

Bats are one of (0).......*the*.......... most numerous and successful groups of mammals that have ever lived on earth. Over 950 species (1)..................... known to exist – that's one quarter of all present-day mammals. Bats (2)..................... spread to almost every part of the world, from the Arctic to the stormy southern tip of South America.

However, bats all over the world are under pressure (3)..................... a fast-growing human population. Loss of suitable places to live, a fall (4)..................... food supply and environmental pollution are all (5)..................... life increasingly difficult for many bat species.

Strangely, there are some wild creatures which are, in fact, little or (6)..................... threat to humans, but consistently disturb people by their presence and cause irrational fear. (7)..................... them are such animals as cockroaches, spiders, mice and, more often (8)..................... not, bats. Exactly (9)..................... bats should frighten so many of us is hard to understand, (10)..................... they do have many of the characteristics that people seem to find distressing in wild animals.

They are small, fast-moving, capable (11)..................... sudden changes in direction and active at night. In (12)..................... to this, they have rapidly moving wings, an unpredictable way of flying that can (13)..................... them extremely close and a strange, often frightening appearance. Given these characteristics, and the (14)..................... that bats often find suitable hiding places around human dwellings, it is perhaps not surprising (15)..................... human fears have been transformed into superstition and myth.

Vocabulary: places

1 Look at the photos and discuss the following questions.

1 Which of the places would you like to live in? Why?
2 What do you imagine they are like inside?
3 What kind of people do you imagine live there?

2 Look at the following pairs/groups of words and decide what the difference in meaning is between each word.

1 a terraced house/a semi-detached house/ a detached house
2 a bungalow/a flat/a bedsit
3 a cottage/a hut
4 a caravan/a tent
5 a town/a city/a village/a suburb/the capital
6 a county/a country/a continent
7 a skyscraper/a penthouse

3

1 Match the words in the box to the letters in the picture.

lawn	porch	flowerbed	fence	shed	patio
pond	hedge	gate	pavement	cellar	attic
roof	chimney	drainpipe	TV aerial		

2 Describe the place where you live to a partner. What is it like on the outside and inside? Draw a diagram if necessary.

Watch Out! *country*

1 We went to a little hotel in the *country*.
2 It's a very nice *country* for a holiday.

What does *country* mean in each sentence?

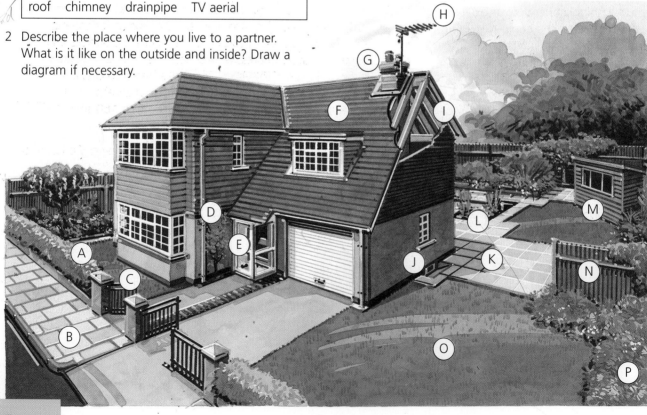

4

1 Say why people go to each of
the following places.

   a) a theatre   e) a museum
   b) a cathedral   f) a gallery
   c) a market   g) a factory
   d) a stadium

2 Tell a partner about when you
last went to these places. Why
did you go? Who did you go
with? What happened?

Use of English

Read the following description of Romania. There is one extra incorrect
word in each line. Try to find the word.

1 Romania's name itself suggests that what makes it different from
2 its neighbours. The connection is with the Imperial Rome and
3 coming from that is a language which sounds as like Italian. The
4 country where is about the size of Great Britain and has a population of
5 23 million, of whom ninety percent there are Romanians..

6 The scenery is varied: mountainous areas with a summer and winter
7 resorts, a very marvellous stretch of the Danube as it descends
8 towards the Iron Gates, not to be mention castles, palaces and
9 monasteries with so impressive frescoes. There are also historic
10 towns from the 13th of century, Black Sea beach resorts and
11 with the astonishing bird-life of the vast Danube delta. And if
12 this is not enough, there are no more fewer than 160 spas
13 offering cures for nearly of every illness known to man.

14 Romania is perhaps the most famous abroad for being the home of
15 Dracula the famous creation of the Irish writer, the Bram
16 Stoker. However, while the story is being fiction, the character
17 is based on a Romanian prince is called Vlad Dracula (son of
18 Dracul) or Tepes (the Impaler) because of such his cruelty
19 towards his enemies. On one occasion he is supposed to have been
20 sat down to a meal to enjoy himself the spectacle of some
21 prisoners having their arms and legs cut them off. He asked for
22 their blood to be collected and brought to him so as a dip for his bread.

23 So, when you visit Romania you may be like to visit Bran Castle
24 which was having built in 1377 and is the castle most closely
25 identified with Dracula. But, if you do, don't forget to how
26 much else there is for to see in Romania.

Describing places

In Paper 2 you may be asked to write a
description of a place such as the one on page 137
about Romania. Read the description again and
decide which of the plans below it follows.

A 1 Introduction: where the place is, how to get
there and why it became famous.
2 What you can do there.
3 Things to do and see nearby.
4 Conclusion: sum up opinion of place and make
a suggestion.

B 1 Introduction: when you visited the place and
why.
2 What happened while you were visiting the
place.
3 Another thing that happened during your visit.
4 Conclusion: how you felt about the trip when
you got home.

C 1 Introduction: factual information about the
place.
2 What there is to see and do there.
3 Why it is well-known.
4 Conclusion: some advice.

2 Read the following exam task and decide which
of the plans above would not be suitable. Why?

> You work for the local tourist information
> service. Your boss has asked you to write an
> article about a place of interest in your area for
> a tourist information magazine that is distributed
> free to young travellers. Write a description of a
> place you know well for the magazine.

3 You are going to write an answer to the
question above. You should follow this procedure:

- Look at the instructions carefully and underline the
key words.
- Choose a place to describe. Remember, it should
interest young travellers and you should know it
well.
- Choose one of the two possible plans in Exercise 1.
(You may change it if you wish.)
- Make a list of points to include. Answer questions
like these and think of others: *Where is it? How do
you get there from the airport/centre of town?
What is the first thing you notice about the place?
When was it discovered/built? When did it become
popular/famous? What do people usually do there?*
Decide in which paragraph you will include these
details.
- As soon as you have decided on the details and
where to put them, you can begin to write. Include
some conditional sentences with these patterns:
*If you take the road/train/bus from ..., you
reach/get to ...
If you have a little more time, you can also ...
If you visit ... during/in/at/on ..., you'll be able to ...*

1 Name each of the animals in the pictures and the parts of their bodies that are indicated.

a)
b)
c)
d)
e)
f)

2 Fill in the gaps in the following sentences with an appropriate verb in the correct form.

1 We're always .... out! Can't we have dinner at home tonight?
2 I'm afraid that we've .... out of that particular brand of soap, but we do have other types.
3 That class .... me out. They're such hard work!
4 .... out! You're going to drop those plates if you're not careful.
5 Don't .... out those toys. I might give them to my children one day.
6 You can tell she has had training. She .... out as being by far the best.
7 You should .... the bull by the horns and tell your boss that you've got too much work and you're not being paid enough.
8 I want to know who .... the cat out of the bag. Who said we are going to get married?
9 I thought I would .... two birds with one stone and visit my old school at the same time as we're in Edinburgh on holiday.

3 For questions 1–10, complete the sentence so that it has a similar meaning to the first sentence using the word given. **Do not change the word given**. Use between two and five words including the word given.

1 I didn't know he was going to the party so I stayed in.
   never
   I .... in if I had known he was going to the party.

2 My father advised me not to marry you but I wouldn't listen to him.
   taken
   I wouldn't have married you .... my father's advice.

3 Mike stole the money and went to prison as a result.
   not
   Mike .... to prison if he hadn't stolen the money.

4 With more effort you could have won the match.
   harder
   If .... you could have won the match.

5 Rain or very cold weather are the only things that will stop us having a barbecue.
   unless
   We'll have a barbecue .... or is very cold.

6 With fluent English you can apply for lots of jobs.
   fluently
   If .... you can apply for lots of jobs.

7 The boiling point of water is 100° C.
   if
   Water .... heat it to 100°C.

8 Winning the lottery would be an extraordinary experience.
   if
   I don't know what I would do .... the lottery.

9 She was very rude to me so I decided not to lend her my car.
   might
   I .... my car if she hadn't been so rude to me.

10 I didn't do my homework so it isn't getting wet in the rain.
   would
   My homework .... wet in the rain if I had done it.

14 Guilty or not guilty

Reading

1 Look at the people in the photos and discuss who they are and what they are doing.

A

B

2 Read the text and then describe what Batman does.

3 Answer the following questions in your own words.

1 Why had the Joker come to the museum?
2 What mood was the Joker in?
3 What did the water do to the Joker? Did it hurt him?
4 How did Batman get into and out of the museum?
5 What was the Joker impressed by?

C

1 Vicki could feel the trap close around her. The Joker and a dozen of his men had burst into the museum and set about methodically destroying the paintings. Vicki wondered if there was some way she could run for it, but, within seconds of their arrival, henchmen were covering both main doors and all of the emergency exits as well.

2 Then the Joker saw her. He waved pleasantly as he approached. His face was no longer ghostly white, but his unnatural smile was still there. His good cheer made Vicki feel even more trapped than she had before.

3 She had to keep him away from her. She needed a weapon. She grabbed a water pitcher from the cart and threw it at the Joker.

4 The pitcher missed, but it drenched the Joker with water.

'No!' He cried as his hands covered his face. 'No!'

He bent over double. The tan was coming off on his fingers, revealing the bone-white skin beneath.

'I'm melting!' He fell to his knees.

'I'm melting!' He writhed on the floor. 'Oh, God, I'm melting!'

'Help me!' the Joker croaked, staggering back.

Had she really hurt him? Despite herself, she took a step forward.

He leapt forward abruptly.

'Boo!' he screamed.

5 He was on top of her. She couldn't get away. All she could see was the purple flower, and that big, big grin.

Writing: making your writing more interesting

1 In the Batman text there are various words and expressions that add a dramatic, exciting atmosphere to the story. Find these words and expressions and match them to the following meanings.

1 to enter suddenly and dramatically (*para. 1*)
2 in order and with care (*para. 1*)
3 to take suddenly and roughly (*para. 3*)
4 to make completely wet (*para. 4*)
5 to show (*para. 4*)
6 to move in pain (*para. 4*)
7 to walk unsteadily (*para. 4*)
8 suddenly and unexpectedly (*para. 4*)
9 to cry out loudly in a high voice (*para. 4*)
10 a smile (*para. 5*)
11 to break in many pieces (*para. 6*)
12 to jump (*para. 9*)
13 very surprised (*para. 10*)

2

1 Match the following verbs with a general meaning to a group of verbs in the box.

1 tell   4 hold   7 throw
2 move   5 laugh   8 walk
3 think   6 say   9 eat

a) exclaim/mutter/insist
b) giggle/chuckle/snigger
c) writhe/wriggle/fidget
d) hurl/toss/lob
e) stagger/wander/tiptoe
f) munch/nibble/swallow
g) wonder/consider/reckon
h) order/inform/instruct
i) clutch/grasp/hug

2 Describe in what ways the verbs in each group differ in meaning from each other. Use a dictionary where necessary.

3 You can also make your writing more interesting by using interesting language to modify nouns and adjectives.

EXAMPLES: *His face was no longer **ghostly** white.*
*The tan was coming off on his fingers, revealing the **bone-white** skin.*

Look at the next part of the *Batman* story and discuss more interesting/dramatic ways of expressing the information it contains. Then rewrite it, incorporating your ideas.

Something shattered overhead. Everything was perfect until that noise, the Joker thought. He looked up. Something had come through the skylight, that same dark something that was dropping to the floor.

No, the Joker corrected himself. It wasn't just any old something. It was the Batman. He landed only half a dozen feet away. He pointed his fist at the Joker. There was something attached to the bat guy's wrist. Was Batman going to shoot the Joker? He was too young to die. The Joker considered running, but the bat guy would nail him before he took a step.

The Batman fired. The projectile split in two, each half embedding itself into the walls past the balcony on either side of the Joker. The Joker realized there were wires attached to each of the spikes, and another wire leading from the Batman to his skylight entranceway.

The Batman grabbed Vicki and swung out along the escape wires he had created for himself, plunging off the balcony and straight through an arched doorway marked 'Exit'.

It took the Joker a second to recover.

'Those toys!' he exclaimed at last. 'Where does he get those wonderful toys?' He looked around at his boys. They seemed every bit as flabbergasted as he was.

'Well, don't just stand there!' he yelled. 'Go and ask him!'

They went. The Joker sighed. Did he have to think of everything around here?

It took Vicki a little time to realize she had been rescued from the Joker. Batman held her and before long they were in Gotham Square. He told her to go down a small side street. He followed her and threw a small object behind them. Soon there was smoke in the entrance to the street.

'Get in the car,' he told her. At first she didn't know which one, but then she saw it. It was black and looked strange. 'Ignition,' said Batman and the car started.

4 Now write the next part of the story in an equally exciting style!

from *Batman* (the novel) by Craig Shaw Gardner

141

Vocabulary: crime

1

1 Work in four groups A, B, C and D. Each group should check that they know the meaning and pronunciation of the words in the appropriate box. Use a dictionary where necessary.

Group A

a thief.   a kidnapper   a mugger   a shoplifter
a pickpocket   a blackmailer   a hijacker
a forger   a smuggler   an arsonist   a rapist

Group B

a court   a judge   a jury   a witness
a defence lawyer   a prosecution lawyer
the accused   a verdict   a plea

Group C

a fine   Community Service   capital punishment
corporal punishment   a suspended sentence
a jail sentence

Group D

to arrest   to question   to accuse   to deny
to admit   to put on probation   to execute
to release on bail   to acquit

2 Now work in groups of four, one student from Group A, one from Group B, one from Group C and one from Group D. Explain the meaning and pronunciation of your words to the other students in the group.

2 Work with a partner and correct the mistakes in the following sentences, putting the stress on the corrected information.

EXAMPLE: A: A forger sets fire to buildings.
B: *No, an* <u>arsonist</u> *sets fire to buildings. A* <u>forger</u> *makes copies of things in order to deceive people.*

1 A mugger threatens to make secrets known to the public.
2 A shoplifter steals things from people's pockets, especially in a crowd.
3 A hijacker takes goods or people from one country to another illegally.
4 A jury questions the witnesses.
5 The judge pleads guilty or not guilty at the beginning of a trial.
6 You normally get a jail sentence if you are caught driving too fast on the motorway.
7 Some people think capital punishment is a more useful and positive way of punishing people than giving a jail sentence.
8 He denied stealing the car when he saw all the evidence against him.
9 He was put on probation until the case could be heard.
10 They executed him when they found the police had been lying.

┌───
Watch Out! *to steal/to rob*

1 You *steal/rob* things e.g. a watch.
2 You *steal/rob* people or places e.g. an old lady, a bank.

What is the correct alternative in each of these sentences?
└───

Use of English:
multiple choice cloze

In Part 1 of Paper 3 you will read a text with fifteen missing words. After the text you will be given a choice of four words for each of the gaps. The missing words will mainly be 'vocabulary' words and not 'grammar' words.

In the following example, all of the alternatives are words connected with crime, but in the exam the words will not be linked to a topic.

Read the text and choose the correct alternative to fill each gap. As you choose, look at each of the four words in the context of the complete sentence and think about:
- its exact meaning.
- its grammar, for example what prepositions or verb patterns it can be followed by.

THE CRIMINAL THEY CAN'T LOCK UP

Burglar, 14, walks free for 33rd time

BY CHRISTIAN GYSIN

Britain's most persistent young burglar walked free for the 33rd time yesterday.

Two hours later the politicians promised to take action against tearaways who the law says are too young to be (1)............ up.

Youngsters aged between twelve and fifteen who repeatedly (2)............ crimes will be held in ten new 'secure training centres' for up to two years.

The 14-year-old, in (3)............ yesterday, was responsible for a mini crimewave near his home totalling £58,000. As he was (4)............ his worried mother said, 'I really thought he would have been locked away.

'I'm worried that he'll be out (5)............ it again before the week's out.'

Her son had (6)............ clothes worth £28,000 and (7)............ into the same branch of one particular shop three times in one week. He played with the laces of his £100 trainers as the court heard he had also (8)............ his local chemist's at least six times.

Before one (9)............ a shop assistant was even handed his 'calling card' marked with his initials and advising: 'Ring the police'.

The boy, who cannot be identified for (10)............ reasons, (11)............ seven charges of burglary and asked for another 24 to be taken into (12)............ .

The court heard he was too young to be remanded in custody and that there was no place for him in secure accommodation.

The boy's mother added after the (13)............: 'I just find it astonishing that nowhere can be found for him. I've (14)............ him he's living on borrowed time.

'I've tried – but I can't (15)............ him.'

from *Today* newspaper

1 **A** put   **B** closed   **C** locked   **D** jailed
2 **A** commit   **B** do   **C** make   **D** practise
3 **A** trial   **B** court   **C** dock   **D** cell
4 **A** releasing   **B** freed   **C** innocent   **D** unlocked
5 **A** making   **B** taking   **C** burgling   **D** doing
6 **A** robbed   **B** hijacked   **C** stolen   **D** pickpocketed
7 **A** broken   **B** dropped   **C** popped   **D** smashed
8 **A** taken   **B** stolen   **C** burgled   **D** shoplifted
9 **A** raid   **B** action   **C** rave   **D** steal
10 **A** criminal   **B** illegal   **C** law   **D** legal
11 **A** denied   **B** admitted   **C** confessed   **D** accused
12 **A** consideration   **B** thought   **C** mind   **D** understanding
13 **A** court   **B** custody   **C** crime   **D** trial
14 **A** criticised   **B** explained   **C** warned   **D** pleaded
15 **A** check   **B** control   **C** limit   **D** prevent

143

Grammar: *make/let/allow*

1 Decide what difference in meaning, if any, there is between the three sentences in Column A.

A	B
1 They allowed him to go home.	a) He was allowed go home. b) He was allowed to go home.
2 They let him go home.	a) He was let go home. b) *No passive form*
3 They made him go home.	a) He was made to go home. b) He was made go home.

2 Choose the correct passive form in Column B of the sentence in Column A.

Grammar reference p.177 (19.2)

3 Fill in the gaps in the following sentences with the correct form of *make, let* or *allow*.

1 They were not .... to open their presents until Christmas morning.
2 Will you .... me go to the party if I promise to be home by 12.00 p.m.?
3 I am never .... to do anything I want. It's not fair.
4 They tried to .... him tell them where his friend was, but he wouldn't.
5 Don't .... him escape! If he gets out onto the road, he'll be run over.
6 He was .... to pay for the damage he had caused to the car.
7 If he hadn't .... me borrow his racket, I wouldn't have been able to play.
8 I am afraid you're never going to be .... to have a party in this house again.
9 If you won't .... him sit down and do his homework, I will!

4 What do you think the boy's parents in the article *The criminal they can't lock up* on page 143 should:

1 make him do?
2 let him do/allow him to do?

Speaking

1 You are going to have a meeting to decide what to do with the young man in the article *The criminal they can't lock up*. His name is Brian North.

Work in groups of five. Each student should take one of the following roles and spend a little time preparing what to say.

- Brian North
- Mrs North
- a representative of the police
- a social worker
- the manager of a local shop

2 Now work with the other students in your group and have the meeting. By the end of the meeting you should have a definite suggestion of what to do with Brian.

3 Finally turn to page 203 and read what actually happened to Brian. Was your decision similar or different?

4 Discuss what, if any, punishment you think would be appropriate for the following people.

1 Three children aged ten, eleven and twelve who deliberately damaged a railway line. As a result, a train came off the line and several people were injured.
2 A single unemployed parent with four children who stole £20 worth of food from a supermarket.
3 A successful businessman who was found to have deliberately not paid £20,000 a year in taxes for the last five years.
4 An animal rights activist who put a bomb in a university laboratory which experiments on animals. The laboratory was destroyed, but no animals or people were hurt.
5 A doctor who had been working for thirty hours without a break and gave the wrong drugs to a patient. As a result the patient died.

Grammar: passives

1   The passive is often used when the agent of the action is either not known or is unimportant.

EXAMPLE: *The boy cannot be identified for legal reasons.*

Look again at the article on Brian North on page 143 and find eight more examples of the passive.

2   Complete this table with the correct passive forms. Use the following words as the base of each sentence:

police/question/suspect

	Active	Passive
Present Simple	*The police question the suspect.*	*The suspect is questioned by the police*
Present Continuous	*The police are ...*	*The suspect is ...*
Past Simple		
Past Continuous		
Future Simple		
Future Perfect		
Present Perfect Simple		
Past Perfect Simple		
Modals (Present) e.g. *must*		
Modals (Past) e.g. *must have*		

3   Fill in the gaps in this letter with an appropriate active or passive form of the verbs in brackets.

Grammar reference p.171 (12)

Dear Julie,

Well, I arrived safely ... but my luggage didn't! After many enquiries I found that it (1)................. (send) to Finland instead of England! Apparently, it (2)................. (label) wrongly at check-in. Anyway, it finally (3)................. (arrive) three days ago and, other than that, I (4)................. (have) a great time ever since I arrived.

The people I am staying with are very nice and I (5)................. (already/show) all the local tourist sites. I (6)................. (treat) exactly like one of the family and I (7)................. (introduce) to all their friends. I share a room with Penny, the daughter in the family, who is my age. It's amazing ... every morning we (8)................. (wake up) by her mother with a cup of tea! Yesterday (Sunday), we (9)................. (even/give) breakfast in bed!

Today was my first day at my new language school. When I arrived, I (10)................. (take) to a special room where we (11)................. (welcome) by the Director. He (12)................. (explain) what was going to happen and who all the staff were. Then we (13)................. (go) to a large room where we (14)................. (give) a test to do. It was quite difficult, but it was soon over and then we (15)................. (have) an interview with a teacher who (16)................. (check) our spoken English. As we (17)................. (leave) we (18)................. (hand) a form to fill in with all our personal details and we (19)................. (tell) to arrive early tomorrow to give us time to find our new classes. In the afternoon we (20)................. (take) on a guided tour of the city by bus which was very interesting.

I'm really looking forward to tomorrow when we (21)................. (put) in our new classes.

I don't know yet what level I'll be in – apparently we (22)................. (tell) when we arrive tomorrow. At the same time we (23)................. (give) the various books that we need for the course. It's all quite exciting! I just hope I like my teacher!

Love,
Rosario xxx

Exam focus

Paper 4 Listening: Part 1 (multiple choice)

About the exam: In Paper 4, Part 1 you hear eight short extracts of people talking in different situations (e.g. friends chatting, a stranger asking directions, part of a radio programme). You have to answer one question about each extract by choosing between three alternative answers. The questions might be about who is speaking, what they are talking about or what attitudes, emotions or opinions are being expressed. The questions are in the question booklet and recorded on the tape. You hear each extract twice.

Procedure

1   Read the multiple choice questions before you listen and underline question words (*who, what, why, how*) and any other important words.
2   Listen carefully as each question and extract is played.
3   Answer the questions in the question booklet as you listen.
4   Check your answers and answer any questions you had difficulty with the second time you hear each extract.
5   Transfer your answers to the answer sheet at the end of the test.

You will hear people talking in eight different situations. For questions **1–8**, choose the best answer, **A, B** or **C**.

1   You hear a man talking in a pub.
    What is he expressing his opinion about?

    A shoplifting
    B mugging
    C bad driving / joy-riding

2   You hear a man talking to his wife.
    How does she respond to what he says?

    A She is understanding.
    B She is disappointed.
    C She is worried.

    they get let off scot free

3   You hear a doctor talking to a patient. What does she want him to do?

    A change his habits
    B go for some tests
    C tell her about some exercises

4   You overhear the following exchange on the bus. How does the man react?

    A He is surprised.
    B He doesn't believe the woman.
    C He is angry.

5   You hear someone phoning a restaurant. How does she react to what she is told?

    A She accepts it politely.
    B She tries to persuade the manager.
    C She threatens the manager.

6   You hear part of a radio programme on women in society.
    What does the speaker think about the position of women?

    A They now have equal opportunities with men.
    B They can't get any of the top jobs
    C They have more opportunities than before.

7   You hear a couple talking in a doctor's waiting room.
    What are they trying to decide on?

    A a birthday present
    B a present to celebrate academic success
    C a Christmas present

8   A woman speaks to you in the street.
    What does she want you to do?

    A comment on something
    B sign something
    C give money for something

Speaking

1 Work with a partner. Student A should look at the pictures below, and Student B should look at the pictures on page 203. The pictures are in jumbled order. Describe to your partner what is happening and together try to work out the complete story in the correct order. Use passive forms where appropriate.

2 Now read the story of what actually happened. Some of the lines are correct and some have one extra word which should not be there. Decide which lines have an extra word and correct them.

1 Jim Crawford had just been left his car in a car
2 park near his office when he was approached by a
3 mugger with a knife who demanded of his wallet. Jim
4 gave to him his wallet and the man ran off. Jim
5 decided to go to the nearest police station and
6 report the crime, but just as he was walking towards
7 it he was being stopped by a second man. This man
8 also wanted Jim's wallet, but Jim tried to explain
9 him that it had already been stolen. The second
10 mugger told him to hand them over his shoes and
11 socks. Jim did it as he was told and then, when the
12 man had gone, walked into the police station. The
13 police were absolutely surprised to see him without
14 any shoes and socks and questioned him about what
15 had happened. After having giving descriptions of
16 the two men, Jim was driven back to his car. But,
17 to his horror, when they got to the place at where
18 he had left it, he discovered that it had been stolen.

A

B

C

D

Listening: Guardian Angels

1 You are going to hear a conversation between a husband and wife. Listen and decide what connection there is between what they say and the picture below.

2 Listen again and decide if the following statements are True or False.

1 Guardian Angels began in America and have since come to Britain.
2 Only a few of them are paid or carry guns.
3 In Britain they will work patrolling the streets.
4 There is a 3-month period in which they are taught different skills.
5 They sometimes ask the police for help.
6 The official police view about the Guardian Angels is quite negative.
7 The view of the police on the streets is quite positive.
8 The man and woman having the conversation basically have the same view about the Guardian Angels.

3 Discuss the following statements.

● The Guardian Angels are a useful and necessary idea. Citizens should take more responsibility for preventing crime.
● There shouldn't be a need for groups like the Guardian Angels.
● The Guardian Angels are a dangerous idea. Keeping law and order must be left to the police.

Vocabulary: phrasal verbs (*make*)

● *As far as I can **make out**, the idea is that ...*

1 Replace the words in *italics* in the following sentences with a phrasal verb with *make* and an appropriate particle from the box. Use a dictionary where necessary.

up (x 3)   for   of   out (x 2)

EXAMPLE: Look ... why don't you go and say you're sorry and *become friends again* with Julie?
Look ... why don't you go and say you're sorry and ***make it up*** with Julie?

1 When it started to rain, we *went to* the nearest shelter.
2 It wasn't true, was it? You just *invented* it, didn't you?
3 He *pretended* that he had been with his best friend, but I knew it was a lie.
4 She tried to *get back* the lost time by getting a taxi.
5 He *couldn't read* what the sign said, because it was so foggy.
6 What do you *think of* that picture? I can't understand it at all!
7 Why don't we *prepare* the spare room for John in case he wants to stay overnight?

2 Work with a partner. You have fifteen minutes to write a short story involving a crime using as many phrasal verbs with *make* as you can. When you have finished, read your story to another group. Who managed to include the most phrasal verbs?

1

1 Write the meaning of the following words.

a) to drench   h) to smuggle
b) to stagger   i) a pickpocket
c) to grin   j) a jury
d) flabbergasted k) a witness
e) to yell   l) to deny
f) to fidget   m) to release
g) to nibble   n) illegal

2 Fill in the gaps in the following sentences with the correct form of one of the words above. You do not need to use all of the words.

a) He .... towards the telephone, but fell before he could pick it up.
b) The .... was out for several hours before they could all agree on a verdict.
c) He .... being anywhere near the bank on the day the money was stolen.
d) She never eats properly. She just .... at her food.
e) Please stop ....! Sit still.
f) It was pouring with rain and I got absolutely ....
g) I was absolutely .... when she told me I had won first prize.

2 The following sentences are all incorrect. Find the mistake and correct the sentences.

1 By the time I got there, John had been gone.
2 Why didn't you let him to borrow the car?
3 I haven't being allowed to stay out late for ages.
4 On one occasion the teacher was made me stand in the corner with my hands above my head.
5 I am be looked after very well by the doctors and nurses.
6 What do you think you will been doing this time next week?
7 He could have delayed by traffic on the way home.
8 You shouldn't be worry. I'm sure everything will be all right.
9 Mike really enjoys be asked to talk about his childhood.
10 You know he made up it all. He wasn't really on holiday at all.
11 We made for to the nearest telephone as quickly as we could.
12 It's very difficult to be make out what it says. The writing is so small.

3 Fill in the gaps in the following text with an appropriate word.

A COCK AND BULL STORY

There was never any doubt as to the guilt (1)..........of.......... the accused. In the French county of Valois, in the year 1314, he (2).....................had..... deliberately killed a man. Several people had witnessed the attack. The accused (3)............was....... sentenced to death and hanged soon afterwards. The accused was a bull.

Modern law does not recognise the idea that animals can (4)......commit....... a crime, but in medieval Europe it was quite common for animals to (5)..................... taken to court on all sorts (6)..................... charges – everything from witchcraft to murder. On one occasion the rats of Atun in central France (7)..................... called before the court on a charge of infesting local houses and barns. When they failed (8)..................... appear, their lawyer explained that their lives would have (9)..................... put in danger by the number of cats in the neighbourhood. He said that (10)..................... court would have to guarantee the safety of each of his clients on their way to and from the trial. The case (11)......was........... postponed indefinitely.

In the 15th century, a cock in the Swiss town of Basel was not so lucky. He was accused (12)..................... laying an egg, which the superstitious townsfolk saw as a sure sign that he was a sorcerer. As a result, the cock (13)......was........ tied to a stake and burned, along with the egg. And in Lavegny, France in 1457, a sow that had killed and partly eaten a child was hanged (14)..................... murder. Her six piglet accomplices (15)..................... not punished, however, on the grounds that they had been too young (16)......to........... know any better.

Reading

1 Look at the pictures of different people below and discuss the following questions.

1 What message do you think each person is trying to communicate?
2 Do people use these signs in your country? What other signs do people use?
3 Do you think it is possible for animals to 'talk'? If so, can you give any examples?

2 Read the following text which describes an experiment with animals and answer these questions.

1 What was the aim of the experiment?
2 Did the Gardners believe the experiment was successful?

CHATTING WITH CHIMPS

NATURALISTS have long known[1] that the apes, our nearest relatives in the animal kingdom, communicate[2] with one another through gestures, sounds and facial expressions. But it was long believed[3] that only human beings could use words and sentences. In the 1960s, however, determined researchers set themselves the task of teaching chimpanzees and other apes to talk[4] in English.

At first the scientists tried to make the animals speak. But no chimp ever managed to acquire a vocabulary of more than four words, and these were spoken with great difficulty as their vocal tracts are not well adapted for producing the sounds of human speech. The breakthrough came when Trixie and Allen Gardner, a husband-and-wife team of scientists at the University of Nevada, decided[5] to try American Sign Language (ASL), a system of gestures used by the deaf. After four years of dedicated effort they had taught their first chimpanzee, Washoe, to use 132 ASL signs correctly[6] to communicate her wants and needs.

Washoe clearly 'understood' words – when she was asked in sign language to fetch an apple, she would bring that fruit rather than, say, a banana. But her linguistic abilities[7] went much further. She would not only produce simple combinations like 'give apple' or 'please, hurry' to get what she wanted from her keepers, but also talked to herself in sign language when she thought no one was watching: she was often observed making the sign for 'quiet' for her own benefit alone as she crept stealthily across the yard towards an area that she had been forbidden to enter. Washoe even learned to swear, applying[8] the word for 'dirty' to anything or anyone she disliked.

The Gardners went on to assemble a small community of baby chimps that were constantly in the presence of adults who used sign language among themselves as well as with the animals. The researchers reported that the chimps grew accustomed to talking to one another in sign language. They even started inventing[9] their own words by combining signs they knew, for instance, 'water bird' for a swan.

Apart from sign language, apes have been taught by other scientists[10] to communicate using plastic tokens on a board, having learned that each token represented[11] an object, action, colour or concept. Some researchers have noticed that the apes prefer to use symbols in a particular order, and see this as evidence of a primitive grammar. For example, they will request something to drink by signing 'more drink' rather than 'drink more'. Yet other scientists still doubt whether the apes are using language in a truly human sense. They point out that the apes rarely put together more than two words in a sentence, and they spend most of their time exactly copying the series of signs made by their teachers. But the Gardners at least are in no doubt[12] that their chimps really can talk with their hands.

from Reader's Digest *Did you know?*

3 Decide which of the following things the chimps were able to do.

1 recognise the meaning of individual words ✓
2 ask for things
3 spell correctly
4 use bad language
5 talk to one another in sign language
6 name new objects by combining words
7 decide on correct word order
8 make grammatically correct sentences

4 Put the numbered words from the text in the following sentences in the correct form.

EXAMPLE: 1 His ..... *knowledge* ..... of Polish is extremely good.

2 I think there has been a breakdown in .... between the two departments.
3 Did you know that she has had these .... for many years?
4 He's so .... He just goes on and on. It's unbearable!
5 Why are you so .... ? Just make up your mind and tell me what you want to do!
6 I'm afraid number four is .... You'll have to do it again.
7 The facilities for .... people in this building are terrible.
8 Have you filled in your .... form for that job yet?
9 That's a really useful .... I wish I had thought of it.
10 There have been some remarkable .... discoveries this century.
11 I don't think his views are .... of the other people in the class.
12 It is .... whether Xavier is going to be fit to play in tomorrow's match.

5 Discuss whether you think there are fundamental differences between people and animals or whether people are just another type of animal. If you think there are fundamental differences, what are they?

Grammar: expressing hypothetical meanings

1 Complete the sentence in the speech bubble.

I wish I could talk to animals. If I could, I ...

2 Look at these sentences containing the verb *wish*. Then decide which of the rules below are true. If you think there is a mistake in the rules, correct it.

- I wish I had a bit more money.
- I wish I was/were more self-confident.
- I wish I could swim.
- I wish you wouldn't smoke when we are eating.
- I wish you didn't have to go to work today.
- I wish I hadn't argued with my parents last night.

1 When referring to the present or future, *wish* is followed by a present tense.
2 When referring to the past, *wish* is followed by the Past Perfect.
3 When we want to criticise someone else's irritating habit or we want something to change, we can follow *wish* with *would* + verb.

Grammar reference p.167 (8.1)

3 Choose the correct alternative in the following sentences.

1 I wish it *wasn't/wouldn't/isn't* so hot. I hate this kind of weather.
2 The holiday was a disaster. I wish we *didn't go/hadn't gone/weren't going*.
3 I really wish I *can/could/am able to* play the violin like her.
4 Don't you wish that we *didn't/don't/doesn't* have any homework to do.
5 I wish you *weren't/won't/wouldn't* talk with your mouth full. It's very rude.
6 He wishes his parents *are living/have lived/lived* nearer.
7 The party was very boring after you left. We all wish you *had stayed/stayed/would stay*.

4 Imagine your fairy godmother has given you four wishes which must be formed in this way:

1 *I wish* + Past Simple
2 *I wish* + Past Perfect
3 *I wish* + *could*
4 *I wish* + *would*

Write your wishes using the correct form.

5 Choose the alternative which correctly interprets the sentence in italics.

1 *It's time they left.* = They have already gone./They haven't gone yet.
2 *If only I hadn't gone to the party.* = I'm sorry I went to the party./I'm sorry I missed the party.
3 *I'd rather you came early.* = I am pleased you came early./I would like you to come early.
4 *Suppose somebody saw you take it. You'd be in real trouble.* = He is thinking about taking it./He has taken it.

6 Complete the following sentences in a logical way.

1 I wish I ... . I'm just so lonely at the moment.
2 If only I ..., I wouldn't have failed my exams.
3 I'd rather ... tonight because I've got so much work to do.
4 Suppose we ... . Do you think anyone would mind?
5 I wish he ... . It's so annoying.
6 It's time you ... . You've done nothing all day.
7 I think I'd rather ..., I haven't had much exercise recently.
8 Suppose you ... ? Surely that would put your dad in a good mood?
9 If only we ..., then we could come and visit you more often.
10 I'm afraid it's time ... . We both have to get up early tomorrow morning.

Watch Out! *'d rather/'d better*

1 I*'d rather* go to an Italian restaurant.
2 You*'d better* finish your homework.

a) Which of the phrases in *italics* means *should* and which means *prefer?*
b) Which *'d* is a short form of *had?* Which *'d* is a short form of *would?*

7

1 You are going to hear a song. Listen and decide what the singer wishes.

2 Match up the two halves of the following lines of the song. Then listen and check your answers.

1 You know I never meant	a) out of sight,
2 But I only passed by	b) right, yeah.
3 All this time I stayed	c) wondering why.
4 I started	d) in your life,
Chorus	e) as a friend, yeah.
5 You said you didn't need me	f) to cause you no pain,
6 Oh, I guess you were	g) I did it again, yeah.
7 Ooh, I never meant	h) to see you again,
8 But it looks like	
Chorus	

3 Look at the appropriate line in the song and imagine possible answers to these questions.

a) *line 1:* why do you think?
b) *line 4:* why what?
c) *line 7:* what pain do you think he caused?

Use of English: word formation

1 Look at each of the following verbs and decide when you might do this, in what situation and with whom.

1 to translate
2 to repeat
3 to whisper
4 to mutter
5 to chat
6 to gossip
7 to shout
8 to discuss
9 to row
10 to beg
11 to mention
12 to inform
13 to contradict
14 to speak up

Listening: extracts

1 Look at these written extracts from different types of text. Decide what kind of text each extract is taken from
EXAMPLE: A a TV guide

2 Now you are going to hear eight spoken extracts. Listen and decide which of the texts they are connected to and in what way.

2 For questions 1–10 read the text below. Use the word given in capitals at the end of each line to form a word that fits in the space in the same line. There is an example at the beginning (0).

A LOCAL ASSOCIATION

Our local (0) _neighbourhood_ association held their annual	**NEIGHBOUR**
(1) .... last week. Since I had recently been chosen as our	**MEET**
street's (2) .... I had to go along. The new president of	**REPRESENT**
the association made a long, (3) .... and very boring	**REPEAT**
(4) .... about plans to build a shopping centre in the area.	**SPEAK**
All the time he was speaking there was this (5) .... going	**MUTTER**
on at the back of the room. An (6) .... started between	**ARGUE**
two groups of people (7) .... after he finished speaking.	**IMMEDIATE**
One group were in complete (8) .... with the president	**AGREE**
while the others claimed his report was full of (9)	**ACCURATE**
By the end of the evening (10) .... seemed to have broken	**COMMUNICATE**
down completely.	

A
6.20 Blind Date
Cilla Black hosts the popular show which creates new couples and sends them away to surprising locations. This week we hear how Mike and Sandra got on during a cycling holiday in Holland.

B
Department meeting 13/7/96
1. Market share in Europe
2. Recent resignations
3. Projected sales figures for South America (cut off)

C
Wednesday
7.30pm. Squash with Carol

D
Insert the documents FACE DOWN. The unit can accept up to 10 sheets of paper at a time. Enter the phone number of the party to which you wish to send. Confirm in the display whether the phone number is correctly dialled. If you misdial, press the STOP/CLEAR button then enter the correct number. Press the START button. The unit will dial and transmit the documents.

E
I hate being separated from you like this, but just remember it's only another 4 weeks until we can see each other again. Please write soon. Your letters mean so much to me. Fondest love, Geoff.

F
ROWENA, CATCHING MORNING TRAIN TO PLYMOUTH. SHOULD BE WITH YOU FOR LUNCH, LOVE GUY.

G
O Romeo, Romeo, wherefore art thou Romeo? Deny thy father and refuse thy name, Or if thou wilt not, be but sworn my love ...

H
Directed by Ridley Scott, this is the story of Thelma (Geena Davis) and Louise (Susan Sarandon) who together decide to get away from their humdrum everyday lives (and men) and take a weekend break. However, a violent incident turns their trip into a nightmare and they end up trying to escape the law instead. The film is built around the relationship between the two women ...

Writing: a report (2)

1 In Paper 2, Part 2 you may be asked to write report. Look at the following task.

Your school plans to advertise its exam courses. The Director of Studies has asked you to prepare a report on what kind of advertising would be most likely to reach students like yourself and persuade them to come to the school. She has asked you to report on the potential benefits of television, radio or press advertising.

---

2 Before you start, look at the procedure for writing a report on page 72 and the model report in the Writing Reference on page 182.

When you have finished writing your report check to see that you have followed the instructions and written 120–180 words.

Grammar: *to have something done*

1 Look at the following two sentences and decide what differences there are in meaning and in form.

- I hope all the work you are having done on the house is going OK.   *has done*
- I hope all the work you are doing on the house is going OK.   *going to do*

Grammar reference p.175 (16)   *have my house painted*

2 Match a noun in Column A with a verb in Column B and write a sentence with *have* as in the example. Some of the nouns can go with more than one verb.
EXAMPLE: *You can **have your house painted**.*

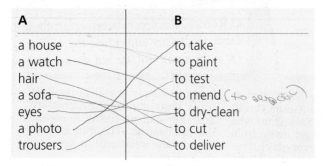

A	B
a house	to take
a watch	to paint
hair	to test
a sofa	to mend (*to repair*)
eyes	to dry-clean
a photo	to cut
trousers	to deliver

3 Look at this extract from Jack's diary. Imagine that today is Thursday. Write complete sentences about:

1 what he had done yesterday.
2 what he is having done today.
3 what he is going to have done tomorrow.

Wednesday

Pick up jacket from dry-cleaners.
Optician 12.15pm (eye-test).
New window in bathroom to be put in (between 3 and 4 pm).

Thursday

Delivery of new sofa (3-4 pm).
Ken Mills to paint bathroom.
Go to garage: mechanic will change oil and tyres.

Friday

11.00am TV repairman.
Need special photo taken of me to go with CV.
Don't forget hair-cut before tonight!!

---

4 Imagine you have unlimited money to spend. How would you change the place you live? What would you have done?

EXAMPLE: I would have a tennis court built in the garden.

┌─ **Watch Out!** ◄─────────────────

I must *have* my hair cut soon.

Which of these verbs can replace *have* in this sentence: *make/get/put/fetch/do?*

└─────────────────────────────

Exam focus

Paper 3 Use of English: Part 3 (key word transformation)

About the exam: Each of the ten items in Paper 3, Part 3 is worth two marks. All the other items in Paper 3 are worth only one mark.

Procedure

1 Try to work out what each item is testing (grammar, phrasal verbs, fixed phrases, for example *to look forward to + ing*).
2 Write the missing words in the spaces in the question booklet. Remember not to change the key word.
3 Read each new sentence to check that the meaning is similar to the given sentence and that all the words you have written are spelt correctly.
4 In the actual exam you will then transfer your answers to the answer boxes on a separate answer sheet. Here is an example of an answer box.

1	

5 Remember to transfer **only the missing words** to the answer box on the separate answer sheet.

For questions **1–10**, complete the second sentence so that it has a similar meaning to the first sentence, using the word given. **Do not change the word given.** You must use between two and five words, including the word given. Here is an example **(0)**.

Example:

0 I wasn't allowed to stay out after midnight when I was younger.
   let
   My parents .*would not let me stay*. out after midnight when I was younger.

1 I wish I could windsurf.
   love
   I would .... windsurf.
2 It was a real mistake telling Nigel how I felt about him.
   only
   If .... Nigel how I felt about him.
3 Your children are supposed to be in bed by nine o'clock.
   time
   It's .... in bed.

4 I wouldn't like you to mention this to anyone else.
   rather
   I'd .... mention this to anyone else.
5 I wish I had learnt a foreign language when I was younger.
   regret
   I .... a foreign language when I was younger.
6 What would happen if someone had seen you with her?
   suppose
   Just .... with her.
7 It really annoys me the way you keep tapping your fingers on the desk.
   wish
   I .... your fingers on the desk like that.
8 My grandmother gets the hairdresser to wash her hair for her.
   has
   My grandmother .... by the hairdresser.
9 Someone stole their car while they were at the beach.
   had
   They .... while they were at the beach.
10 Our house needs painting.
   must
   We .... painted.

Grammar reference

Index

1 Adjectives ending in -ed and -ing

1.1 Adjectives ending in -ed

These adjectives end in -ed or have the same form as the past participle of a verb (e.g. *thrilled, relieved, terrified*). We use them to describe people's feelings. The adjectives normally follow *be* or other verbs like *feel, seem, look*, etc.

*She was **excited** about going to the circus.*
*They both looked **astonished** when I told them I was getting married.*
*What's the matter with Iannis? He seems a bit **depressed**.*

1.2 Adjectives ending in -ing

We use these adjectives to describe experiences or events. They can be used before the noun or after *be* and other linking verbs.

*That was an absolutely **terrifying** film. I had my eyes closed for most of the time.*
*Jeff's party was really pretty **boring**.*
*What's that magazine? It looks really **interesting**.*

2 Adverbs of frequency

2.1 Adverbs of definite frequency

The following are common adverbs of definite frequency:

once ⎫
twice ⎪
five times ⎬ a day/week/month/year
several times ⎭

every day/week/month/year/morning/afternoon/evening
every three/couple of/few years
on Monday/Wednesday/weekdays, etc.

These adverbs usually come at the end of the sentence.

*My telephone rings **several times a day**.*
*She goes swimming **every morning**.*
*They visit their relatives in Greece **every few years**.*

2.2 Adverbs of indefinite frequency

These adverbs are used to talk about how often we do things. We can put them in order from 'most often' to 'least often' like this:

always   most often
almost always
generally/normally/regularly/usually
frequently/often
sometimes
occasionally
almost never/hardly ever/rarely/seldom
not ... ever/never   least often

In statements and questions these adverbs come towards (but *not* at) the beginning of the sentence depending on the main verb as follows:

- after *be* when it is the only verb in the sentence
  *I **am always** glad to see you.*
- after the first auxiliary verb when there is more than one verb
  *I **have often walked** down this street before.*
- before the main verb when there is only one verb
  *We **sometimes go** to a restaurant for lunch on Sundays.*
- before *used to*, *have to* and *ought to*
  *She **often used to** come and see me.*
  *We **never had to** wear uniforms when I was at school.*
  *You **sometimes ought to** phone your mother, you know.*
- in questions, after the subject
  ***Don't you usually go** home by bus?*

In negative sentences they come in the middle of the sentence as follows:

- *not* comes before *always* and usually before *generally, normally, often, regularly* and *usually*
  *She's **not always** so friendly. I wonder what she wants.*
  *I **don't usually** go out in the evenings during the week.*

- *not* comes after *sometimes* and *frequently*
  I *sometimes don't* enjoy parties.
  She *frequently doesn't* remember my name.

Always, *often* and *usually* can come at the end of the sentence.

I'll live here **always**.
Do you come here **often**?
I go out with friends on Saturdays **usually**.

Always and *never* come at the beginning with imperatives.

Always have a clean handkerchief with you.
Never say that to me again!

3 The article

3.1 The definite article: the

Use the definite article *the* to talk about the following:

- inventions
  When was **the telescope** invented?
- species of animal
  The domestic cat has lived alongside humans since the time of the Pharaohs.
- oceans and seas
  My sister says **the Pacific** is not as blue as **the Aegean**.
- mountain ranges
  Are **the Andes** as high as **the Dolomites**?
- island groups
  The Galapagos Islands are off the coast of Ecuador.
- areas
  There's flooding in **the northwest** and a terrible drought in **the south**.
- rivers
  You can take a cruise along **the Rhine**.
- deserts
  The sand on this beach was imported from **the Sahara**.
- hotels
  They spent the first night of their honeymoon at **the Ritz**.
- cinemas
  That film Robert Redford directed is on at **the Odeon.**
- theatres
  They're putting on a production of Miss Saigon at **the Palais.**
- newspapers
  You can get **The Times**, **The Guardian**, **The Independent** and several other British newspapers here.
- national groups
  The Welsh are famous for their singing.

Also use the definite article:

- with superlatives
  He's **the tallest, the most handsome** and **the nicest boy** in our class.
- when there is only one thing
  The sun was shining brightly, but it was still very cold.
  I sometimes think **the world** is not a very nice place.

- to talk about particular nouns when it is clear what we are referring to
  Where's **the dog**? I want to take him for a walk.
  Close **the window**, will you? It's freezing in here.
- to talk about previously mentioned things
  Take one egg, a small onion and a bunch of parsley.
  Break **the egg** into a bowl.

3.2 The indefinite article: a/an

Use the indefinite article *a/an*

- with (singular) jobs, etc.
  She's **an engineer**.
  Is your father **a football fan**, too?
- with singular countable nouns (mentioned for the first time or when it doesn't matter which one)
  I'd like **a small salad** and **a glass of mineral water**.
  What you need is **a decent holiday**.
- With these numbers: 100, 1,000, 1,000,000
  There were over **a hundred people** at the party.
  He wants **a thousand pounds** for that old car of his.
  He had made **a million dollars** by the time he was sixteen.
- in exclamations about singular countable nouns
  What **a fantastic view**!

3.3 The zero article

Use no article (the zero article) to talk about:

- continents
  They're travelling through **Asia**.
- countries
  Have you been to **Peru**?
- mountains
  They have reached the summit of **Mount Everest**.
- lakes
  Are **Lake Constance** and **Lake Como** both in Switzerland?
- villages
  San Andres is a village just along the coast from here.
- towns
  Horsham is a pleasant town near the Sussex coast.
- cities
  And now it's over to Jack Russell for the latest news from **Washington**.
- streets, roads, etc.
  Oxford Street and **Tottenham Court Road** are very busy shopping streets in London.
- magazines
  Do you read **Time** magazine?
- illnesses
  The twins have got **measles** and I've got **flu**.
  (**But:** I think I'll go and lie down – I've got **a headache**.)
- uncountable, plural and abstract nouns used in their general sense
  We buy **fruit and vegetables** at the market, but we get **bread** from a bakery near our house.
  I don't like **people** who try to impress you with how much **money** they've got.
  Love makes the world go round.

6 Countable and uncountable nouns

6.1 Uncountable nouns

These have no plural. The following are common nouns that are *usually* uncountable:

accommodation, advice, behaviour, bread, copper, (and all other metals), *English,* (and all other languages), *furniture, health, information, knowledge, luggage, news, progress, research, rice,* (and all other grains and cereals), *salt,* (and all other condiments e.g. *pepper*), *scenery, spaghetti, traffic, travel, trouble, water* (and all other liquids), *weather, work.*

6.2 Nouns which can be countable or uncountable

The following nouns can be both countable and uncountable:

1 Nouns we think of as single things or substances:
- egg
  *Would you like **a boiled egg** for breakfast?*
  *You've spilt **egg** on your tie.*
- chicken
  *I bought **a chicken** to have for Sunday lunch.*
  *There was a choice between **chicken** or fish on the plane.*
- iron
  *We'll have to buy **a new iron**. This one just doesn't get the creases out.*
  *People learned to make implements from **iron**.*
- glass
  *Pass me **a glass** and I'll pour you a drink.*
  *What did people use for windows before they invented **glass**?*
- hair
  *Waiter! There's **a hair** in my soup.*
  *She's got long blonde **hair**.*

2 Normally uncountable nouns which are used to refer to particular varieties.
*Would you like **wine** with your meal?*
*They produce **a very good white wine** on that island.*

3 Words for drinks e.g. *coffee, tea, beer.* The countable noun means *a glass of, a cup of, a bottle of,* etc.
***Coffee** is very expensive at the moment.*
*Why don't we stop for **a coffee**?*
*People in Belgium drink **beer** more than wine.*
*There's **a beer** in the fridge if you want one.*

4 *time, space, room*
*I'm sorry I haven't got **time** to talk to you now. Can you call me later?*
*We had **a really good time** at José's party.*
*All this old wardrobe does is take up **space**.*
*Fill in **the spaces** with a suitable word.*
*There's **room** for one more in this compartment.*
*Have you got **a single room** with a shower?*

6.3 Determiners used with countable and uncountable nouns

1 *few*
Use *few* with plural countable nouns. It means 'some but not many'. Before *few* you can use:
- the indefinite article *a*
  ***A few of my friends** and I are going out to dinner together this Saturday.*
  *There were only **a few people** on the bus.*
- the last, the first, the next, every
  *Over the next **few days** I want you to make sure you get plenty of rest.*
  *For the first **few months**, I felt a bit shy and insecure.*
  *We see them **every few weeks**.*

2 *fewer*
Fewer is the comparative of *few*. It can be followed by *than*.
*There were **fewer people** at the party **than** we had expected.*
*There will be **fewer jobs** in industry in the future.*

3 *a little; a bit of*
- Use *a little* and *a bit of* before uncountable nouns. It means 'at least some'.
  *I'll have **a little time** this afternoon if you would like to come and see me.*
  *Could I have **a bit of cheese**? It looks delicious.*
- *little* without the indefinite article means 'almost none'.
  ***Little money** was spent on the building and it began to fall down almost as soon as we moved in.*
  *She made **little effort** and didn't do well in the exam.*
  Note: use *a slice, a lump* and *a piece* with uncountable nouns for food.
  *How much sugar do you want? **One lump** or two?*
  *I'll just have **a small slice of cake**, thanks.*
  *Would you like **another piece of toast**?*

4 *many*
- Use *many* with plural countable nouns.
  ***How many twins** do you know?*
  *There are **many countries** in the world where you can enjoy excellent skiing.*

5 *much*
- Use *much* with uncountable nouns.
  *I don't have **much money**.*
  ***How much salt** does it say to put in the sauce?*

6 *lots/a lot of*
- Use *lots/a lot of* with plural countable and uncountable nouns.
  *I've had **lots/a lot of spaghetti**. I don't think I could eat another thing.*
  *They've got **lots/ a lot of friends and relatives** in Australia.*

7 Gerunds and infinitives

7.1 Verbs followed by the gerund form -ing

I **considered buying** a flat in Monte Carlo, but they were too expensive.

Here are some common verbs which are followed by the gerund:

admit, deny, appreciate, can't help, can't stand, consider, delay, deny, detest, dislike, enjoy, escape, excuse, face, feel like, finish, forgive, give up, imagine, involve, mention, mind, miss, postpone, practise, put off, resent, risk, suggest, understand

7.2 Verbs and phrases followed by the infinitive without 'to'

You **must answer** all the questions.

Here are some common verbs/phrases which are followed by the infinitive without to:

can, could, may, might, must, need, had better, would rather

7.3 Verbs followed by an object + the infinitive without 'to'

She **made me do** it.

Here are some common verbs which are followed by an object and the infinitive without to:
let, make, know, hear, feel, help.

Mum **won't let me go** to the beach today.
I've **never known him** be so rude.
I **heard her sing** in New York.
Can you **feel his heart beat**?
Would you **help me put** my bag in the overhead locker?

In passive sentences these verbs are followed by an infinitive with to.

He **was made to return** the money.
They **are known to be** very valuable.

7.4 Common verbs followed by an infinitive with 'to'

I can't **afford to buy** a new overcoat.

Here are some common verbs which are followed by an infinitive with to:

afford, agree, appear, arrange, ask, attempt, bear, begin, care, choose, consent, decide, determine, expect, fail, forget, happen, hate, help, hesitate, hope, intend, learn, like, love, manage, mean, offer, prefer, prepare, pretend, promise, propose, refuse, regret, remember, seem, start, swear, trouble, try, want, wish

7.5 Common verbs followed by object + infinitive with 'to'

He **encouraged me to try** again.

Here are some common verbs which are followed by an object and the infinitive with to:

advise, allow, ask, cause, command, encourage, expect, forbid, force, get, hate, help, instruct, intend, invite, leave, like, mean, need, oblige, order, permit, persuade, prefer, press, recommend, request, remind, teach, tell, tempt, trouble, want, warn, wish

7.6 Verbs followed by a gerund or an infinitive with a difference in meaning

1 **remember, forget, stop, try**

remember: the gerund is used when the action happens before the remembering; the infinitive refers to an action that happens after.
I **remember walking** along the beach holding hands.
Did you remember to tell Maria about the party?

forget: when used with the gerund this means 'forget what you have done'; when used with the infinitive with to this means 'forget what you have to do'.
I **had** completely **forgotten seeing** him in Paris that year.
I **forgot to post** the letter you gave me.

stop: when used with the gerund, this means 'stop something you do'; when used with the infinitive with to, this means 'stop in order to do something'.
I **stopped drinking** coffee because I couldn't sleep.
We **stopped to have** a coffee on our way into town.

try: when used with the gerund this means 'make an experiment' – doing the action may not be successful; when used with the infinitive this means 'make an effort' – the action may be difficult or impossible to do.
Try drinking a glass of water to stop your hiccoughs.
Try to study for two hours a day even if you are busy.

2 **can't bear/stand, hate, like, love, prefer**
When these verbs are used with the infinitive they refer to more specific situations. When they are used with the gerund they refer to more general situations. The difference in meaning is very slight.

I **prefer to go** to school by bus.
I **can't bear getting up** so early, but I have to.

8 Hypothetical meaning

8.1 wish

● We use wish + Past Simple to express a wish that has not come true in the present. We also use wish + Past Simple to talk about wishes that might come true in the future.
I **wish** Jackie still **lived** here.
Don't you wish you **played** tennis as well as she does?

- If the verb is *to be*, we can use the Past Simple (*I/she/it was; you/we/they were*) or *were* with all persons (*I/you/she/it/we/they were*).
  We all wish the exam **wasn't/weren't** *tomorrow.*
  I wish *she* **was/were studying** *here, too.*
- We use *wish + would* and *could* to refer to general wishes for the future.
  I wish I could come *to your party, but I'm afraid I'll be away that weekend.*
  I wish it would rain.
- *wish + would* is often used to talk about other people's irritating habits. This form is not often used with *I* or *we*. To talk about our own irritating habits we use *could*.
  I wish you would stop *tapping your foot like that. It's driving me crazy.*
  Don't you wish he wouldn't wear *that terrible old sweater?*
  I wish I could stop *eating so much chocolate.*
- We use *wish + Past Perfect* to refer to things we are sorry about in the past.
  I wish I had studied *harder.*
  She wishes she hadn't sold *her apartment.*

8.2 If only

- *if only* is used with the same verb forms as *wish*, and is used when your feelings are stronger. It is often used with an exclamation mark (!). It is used very commonly with *would/wouldn't* to criticise someone else's behaviour.
  If only I could *see her now!*
  If only grandfather were *here today.*
  If only I didn't have *to work so hard.*
  If only she hadn't stolen *the money.*

8.3 It's time

- *it's time* is used with the Past Simple to talk about the present or future. We mean that the action should have been done before. We can also say *It's* **about** *time* and *It's* **high** *time.*
  It's time you went *to bed, young man. It's already ten o'clock.*
  It's about time you started *doing some more work on phrasal verbs.*
  It's high time they were *here. Their plane landed hours ago.*

8.4 I'd rather (would rather)

- We use *I'd rather + Past Simple* when we want to say what we want someone or something else to do in the present or future.
  I'd rather you didn't stay out *too late tomorrow night.*
  Would you rather I came back *later? You look very busy.*
  I'd rather the meeting started *a little earlier.*
- We use *I'd rather + Past Perfect* when we want to say what we wanted to happen in the past.
  I'd rather you hadn't said *that.*
  I'd rather she had gone out *more warmly dressed.*

- *I'd rather + infinitive without to* is used to talk about our preferences or other people's preferences in the present or future.
  I'd rather go *to the beach than to the mountains.*
  They'd rather go *by bus.*

8.5 Suppose

suppose means 'What if ...?'. It is used with:

- the Present Simple to describe something that may possibly happen or may have happened.
  Suppose *someone* **knows** *she was with us.*
  Suppose *someone* **sees** *you going into the building tomorrow morning.*
- the Past Simple to talk about something that is just imagination or which is unlikely to happen in the future.
  Suppose she knew *you loved her. What would you do?*
  Suppose you won *the lottery. How would you spend the money?*
- the Past Perfect to talk about something that could have happened but didn't in the past.
  Suppose we hadn't studied *so hard. Do you still think we would have passed?*
  Suppose you had married *Ted. Would you have been happy together?*

9 Linking words and phrases

9.1 Addition

Use *as well as, in addition (to), moreover, furthermore, not only ..., but also ..., what is more* to add more information or reinforce (make stronger) what you have already said.

As well as *offering an excellent way of improving your English, the automatic translator is fun to use.*
In addition to *finding you a place to stay in London, our friendly staff will meet you at the airport.*

After *not only* use inversion (the word order you use in questions).

Not only was she *extremely rude to the customers, she also stole money from the till.*

9.2 Listing ideas, giving emphasis, describing a process

Use *firstly, first of all, in the first place, to begin with, secondly, thirdly, finally* to list ideas and emphasise them.

Firstly, *I would like to say that we have raised over £200 pounds.* **Secondly,** *I want you to know that we have raised that money by knocking on doors in the neighbourhood.* **Finally,** *I should tell you that all of that money will be spent on a day trip for disabled children in the area.*

9.3 Showing the relationship between causes and results

Use *as a result, because, because of (this), so* and *therefore* to show the relationship between causes and results.

She went out without an umbrella or a raincoat even though they had forecast rain. **As a result** she caught a terrible cold and had to spend a week in bed.

There are not many good basketball players in our country. **Because of this** teams try to recruit foreign players.

Because there are not many good basketball players in our country, teams try to recruit foreign players.

I told him I thought he had behaved very badly, **so** he's not speaking to me.

People whose diet is deficient in certain vitamins and minerals often become tired and depressed. **Therefore** it is important to make sure your patients eat a balanced diet.

9.4 however, although, in spite of, etc.

Use *however, although, even though, though, despite* and *in spite of* to show that what you are saying is surprising or unexpected in relation to something else you know to be true.

1 *however*

When you use *however*, you talk about the surprising thing in a sentence.

I was sure I was going to miss the plane. **However**, there was no traffic, so we got to the airport in plenty of time.

2 *although*, *even though* and *though*

When you use *although*, *even though* and *though* you can express the two ideas (the thing you know to be true and the surprising thing) in one sentence.

Although he trained every day, he couldn't improve his speed.
Even though it's summer, you still need a pullover.
Though there are a number of advantages, there are also serious disadvantages.

Though can be used at the end of a separate sentence that expresses the surprising thing.

We didn't have enough money to go out very much. We still had a nice time, **though**.

3 *in spite of* and *despite*

in spite of and *despite* are prepositions. They must, therefore, be followed by a noun (often *the fact*) or a gerund. *Despite* is slightly more formal.

In spite of the fact that it's known to be harmful, many people continue to smoke.
Despite the terrible weather, they reached the top of the mountain.
Despite arriving early we still could not get tickets.

9.5 but

But is used to link two contrasting ideas in one sentence. It is not normally used at the beginning of the sentence.

I eat chicken and fish **but** I don't eat eggs.
She is staying at home **but** we are going out.

9.6 On the one hand ... On the other hand ...

We use *On the one hand ... On the other hand ...* when we want to introduce an opposite point in a discussion. We don't always use *On the one hand ... .*

(On the one hand) if I do the exam in June, I'll be able to spend the summer with my family. **On the other hand** if I leave it until December, I'll have more time to prepare.

10 Modal verbs

FORM: modal verbs do not change in the third person. They are followed by the infinitive without *to*.

10.1 Ability

1 *can*

We use *can* to talk about present and future ability.

I **can pick you up** on Saturday morning.
Can't you ride a bicycle?

2 *could*

We use *could* to talk about general past ability.

I **could read** before I started school.
Could Einstein speak English when he went to live in the USA?

10.2 Asking for and giving permission

1 *can*

We use *can* to ask for and give permission.

Can I borrow your calculator for a few minutes?
You **can stay up** and watch the late night film, but then you have to go to bed.

2 *could*

We use *could* to ask for permission when you are not sure what the answer will be.
(**Note**: *could* is **not** used for giving permission)

A: **Could I ask** you a few questions?
B: Yes, of course **you can**.

3 *may*

We use *may* to ask for or give permission in formal situations.

May I leave early today? I've got a dentist's appointment.
You may leave the exam room after the examiner has collected your paper.

10.3 Possibility

1 **Theoretical possibility**

a) *can* We use *can* to:
  - say that things are possible without saying what chance there is that they will happen.
    Anyone **can learn** to use a word processor.
  - talk about typical behaviour of people or things.
    Dogs **can be** jealous of small babies.

- speculate or guess about past events
  (**Note**: this is only in questions and negative sentences.)
  FORM:
  can't + *have* + past participle
  can + subject + *have* + past participle
  Wh- word + *can* + subject + *have* + past participle
  She **can't have understood** *what you meant.*
  Can he have thought *we'd left already?*
  Where can they have gone?

  b) *could*
  We use *could* to talk about theoretical possibility in the past.
  Uncle Tony **could be** *very funny sometimes.*

2 **Factual possibility: *could*, *may* and *might***
  We use *could*, *may* and *might* to:
  - say there is a chance that something might happen in the future
    We **may go** *to Australia* **next Christmas**.
    It **could snow tonight**.
    She **might stay for a few days**.
  - say that something is possibly true at the moment of speaking
    She **might be angry** *about something you said.*
    He **may be away** *for the weekend.*
    We **could be wrong**.
  - talk about the possibility that past events happened
    FORM: *could/may/might* + *have* + past participle
    They **may have decided** *to stay the night there.*
    He **might have met** *her at Joe's party.*
    She **could have seen** *him leaving the building.*

10.4 Obligation: should and ought to

We use *should* and *ought to* to talk about obligations and duties in the future, present and past.

You **ought to/should** *treat your mother better.*
Oughtn't we to/Shouldn't we tell *someone about the accident?*
Shouldn't we have/Oughtn't we to have invited *Susan if we invited Charlie?*

Should + *have* + past participle is often used to criticise your own or other people's behaviour.

I **should have got** *some more soap when I was at the supermarket.*
You **shouldn't have said** *that.*

10.5 Strong obligation and necessity

1 **must**
  We use *must* to:
  - talk about present and future strong obligations and necessities that come from the speaker.
    You **must check in** *at least two hours before your flight departs.*
    I **must remember** *to tell Ted about the meeting.*

  - ask about what the listener wants you to do
    Must I eat *all the vegetables?*
  - tell people **not** to do things
    You **mustn't speak** *Greek in class.*

2 **have to/have got to**
  We use *have to/have got to* to:
  - talk about present and future strong obligations that do not come from the speaker. *Have got to* is used more in British English than it is in American English.
    We **have to wear** *uniforms at our school.*
    Do we have to write *in pen or in pencil?* (more common in American English)
    I **haven't got to go** *to school tomorrow.* (more common in British English).
  - talk about past and reported obligations of all kinds
    They **told us we had to check in** *two hours before departure.*
    We **had to wear** *uniforms when I was at school.*
    I knew I **had to do** *something. I meant to tell Ted about the meeting.*

10.6 Lack of obligation

1 **needn't, don't need to** and **don't have to**
  We use *needn't, don't need to, don't have to* to talk about a lack of obligation in the present or future.

  You **don't need to/needn't come** *to the airport. I'll get a taxi.*
  We **don't have to go** *to school tomorrow. It's a holiday.*

2 **needn't + have + past participle**
  We use *needn't + have + past participle* to say that somebody did something, but that it was unnecessary.

  You **needn't have written** *it out again.*

3 **didn't need to + infinitive**
  We use *didn't need to + infinitive* to say that something wasn't necessary without saying whether the person did it or not.

  You **didn't need to bring** *an umbrella.*

10.7 Deduction

1 **must**
  We use *must* to say that we are sure about something in the present or past.

  That **must be** *Elena when she was a baby*
  You **must have enjoyed** *your trip to Mexico.*

2 **can't**
  We use *can't* in negative sentences **not** *mustn't*.

  That **can't be** *Jack. He drives a Fiat.*
  Alex **can't have been** *away. The lights were on in his flat.*

11 Modifiers and intensifiers

a) We use the adverb *very* before gradable adjectives (that is adjectives that can be used in the comparative) and gradable adjectives followed by nouns. *Very* makes the meaning of the adjective more intense. *Very* can also be used before adverbs.

> The film was **very interesting**.
> She's a **very thoughtful girl**.
> That restaurant is **very expensive**.
> He drives **very slowly**.

b) Other intensifiers that can be used instead of *very* are: *so*, *rather* and *pretty* (weaker than *very*), *extremely*, *particularly*, *really*, and *terribly* (for extra emphasis).

> I felt **terribly embarrassed** when he gave me the flowers.
> She's a **rather shy** girl.
> I was **pretty pleased** when I heard I got a 'B' in the exam.

c) The following groups of non-gradable adjectives cannot normally be used with *very*.

- nationality adjectives e.g. *Peruvian, German, Japanese*
- colour adjectives e.g. *scarlet, navy, blue, purple*
- adjectives describing permanent attributes of activities e.g. **atomic** physics, **plastic** surgery
- extreme or absolute adjectives e.g. *terrible, disastrous, marvellous, wonderful*

Note: with the extreme or absolute adjectives, we can use *really* and *absolutely*.

> The party was **absolutely disastrous**. No one came!
> You look **really marvellous**. Have you been on holiday somewhere?

12 Passives

FORM: appropriate tense of *be* + past participle

Present Simple:	Audio and video tapes **are kept** in the resource centre.
Present Continuous:	Our car **is being repaired** at the moment.
Past Simple:	The parcel **was delivered** right on time.
Past Continuous:	I dreamt I **was being chased** by a tall blond man with a moustache.
Present Perfect:	**Have you been invited** to Simon's party?
Past Perfect:	We **had been told** to get there no later than ten o'clock.
Future *will*:	She**'ll be looked** after very well there.
Future Perfect:	The house **will have been** completely **repainted** by the time you get back.
going to:	The procession is **going to be led** by the Lord Mayor.
Modals:	The door **must have been left** open.
	Sale items **may not be returned**.
Passive Gerund:	Our cat doesn't like **being patted**.

Note:

1 Verbs that do not take an object (e.g. *ache, arrive, sit down*) do *not* have passive forms. It is not possible to say: *I was ached*.

2 Stative verbs like *have, fit, suit* are not used in the passive with the same meanings.
> Do you **have** a car? (have = own)
> They've only given us £5.00 change. We**'ve been had**. (have = deceived)
> Those jeans don't **fit** you any more. (fit = be the right size)
> The laboratory **is being fitted** with all the latest equipment. (fit = provided with)
> That dress **suits** you. (suit = look nice)
> Mary and Tom **are not really suited** to each other. (suit = are not compatible).

USE: the passive is used for the following reasons:

- to talk about actions, events and processes when the action, event or process is seen as more important than the agent. This is often the case in scientific writing.
> Santa Cruz **was founded** in 1495.
> The pigeons **were fed** a diet of seeds and lettuce.
- to put new information later in the sentence.
> The film **was directed** by Quentin Tarantino.
- to put longer expressions at the end of the sentence.
> **I was offended** by the way she pushed past me.

12.1 by + agent

When we are interested in the agent, we use the preposition *by*.

> The games **were designed by a new Japanese company**.
> They **were rescued by some climbers** who found them wandering along the track.

13 Questions

There are three main types of questions:

1 *Yes/No* questions (the expected answer is 'yes' or 'no')
> A: Are you from Greece?
> B: **Yes, I am**.

2 *Wh-* questions (*who? whose? where? why? what? which? when?* and also *how?*)
> **Whose** books are these?
> **Where** does he live?
> **Why** did they do that?

3 Alternative questions (which expect the answer to be one of two options)
> Do you want to **go out to eat** or **stay at home**?
> Which would you rather have, **coffee** or **tea**?

'**I might not be able** to stay for long,' she said.
She **said she might not be able** to stay for long.
'I think he **must be** ill', she said.
She **said she thought he must be ill**.

- the thing being reported contains the Past Perfect
'He **had been missing** for several months,' she said.
She **said he had been missing** for several months.

Other changes that occur in reported speech are:

Direct speech	Reported speech
tomorrow	the next day, the day after, the following day
yesterday	the day before, the previous day
last week	the week before
here	there
this/that	the
this morning	that morning
today	that day
next Friday	the following Friday
ago	before

15.3 Reported statements

FORM: verb (+ *that*) + clause
'I took the money,' she admitted
She **admitted (that) she had taken** the money.
'He studies during the week and plays volleyball at the weekend,' she said.
She **said (that) he studied** during the week and played volleyball at the weekends.

15.4 Reported questions

1 **Reported Yes/No questions**

FORM: when there is no question word in the direct speech question, we use *if/whether*. Word order is the same as in the statement. The verb tense and other changes are the same as for other types of reported speech.

'**Are you going** to Pete's party?' she asked.
She **asked if/whether we were going** to Pete's party.
'**Do you like** Greek food?' he asked.
He **asked us if/whether we liked** Greek food.

2 **Reported wh- questions**

FORM: when *wh-* question words are used, the *wh-* word is followed by statement word order, that is the subject followed by the verb. All the tense and other changes are the same as for other types of reported speech.

'**What's** your favourite colour?' **she asked** him.
She **asked** him **what** his favourite colour **was**.

'**Where do** Andy and Lucy live?' he **asked** her.
He **asked** her **where** Andy and Lucy **lived**.

15.5 Reported orders

FORM: verb + (*that*) + clause *or* verb + object + infinitive with *to*

'**Take up** sport,' the doctor **said**.
The doctor **recommended (that) I take up** sport.

'**Go** to the shops and get me some tea, will you?' she **said**.
She **told me to go** to the shops and get her some tea.

15.6 Reported suggestions

FORM: suggest + -ing
suggest + *that* + *should* + infinitive without *to*
suggest + Past Simple

'**Let's have a surprise party** for Eddie,' she **said**.

She **suggested having a surprise party** for Eddie.
She **suggested that we should have** a surprise party for Eddie.
She **suggested we had** a party for Eddie.

Note: we cannot say: She **suggested to have** a party for Eddie.

15.7 Reporting verbs

1 Verb + object + infinitive
She asked me to come.

Other verbs with the same pattern are:
advise, beg, encourage, invite, order, persuade, remind, warn

2 Verb (+ *that*) + clause
She says (that) she doesn't want to speak to you.

Other verbs with the same pattern are:
say, claim, admit, explain, promise

3 Verb + object (+ *that*) + clause
He told us (that) he worked for a big international company.

Other verbs with the same pattern are: *remind, warn*

4 Verb + gerund
He admitted lying to the teacher.

Other verbs with the same pattern are:
admit, deny, recommend, suggest

Note: verbs in groups 2, 3 and 4 can also be used with *that* + clause.
He admitted that he had lied.

5 Verb + preposition + gerund
She apologised for being so rude.
She discouraged me from taking up smoking.

Other verbs with the same pattern are:
accuse (of), apologise (for), blame (for), congratulate (on), discourage (from), insist (on)

6 Verb + infinitive
We agreed to meet again in September.

Other verbs with the same pattern are:
agree, decide, offer, promise, refuse, threaten

16 *to have something done*

FORM: *have* + object + past participle (the most common form)

get + object + past participle (also possible when people are speaking informally)

USE: we use *to have something done* to say that someone else did something for you because you wanted them to or to you even though you didn't want them to.

*Go and **get your hair cut**. It looks terrible.*
*We're **having the front of our building painted**.*
*How **will you have your suit cleaned**? The dry cleaner's is closed on Saturday afternoon.*
***Did those windows get broken** in the storm?*
*Charles I **had his head cut off**.*

17 Verb tenses

17.1 *Present Simple*

FORM: a) Positive statements
    *I/you/we/they **eat** chocolate.*
    *He/she/it **eats** chocolate.*

    b) Negative statements
    *I/you/we/they **don't eat** chocolate.*
    *He/she/it **doesn't eat** chocolate.*

    c) Questions
    ***Do** I/you/we/they **eat** chocolate?*
    ***Does** he/she/it **eat** chocolate?*

    d) Short answers
    ***Yes**, I/you/we/they **do**.*
    ***No**, I/you/we/they **don't**.*
    ***Yes**, he/she/it **does**.*
    ***No**, he/she/it **doesn't**.*

USE: we use the Present Simple:

a) with routine or regular repeated actions (often with adverbs of frequency like *always, often, sometimes, never, every Saturday morning, once a week*)
*We **go** to Greece for our holidays **every summer**.*
*She **doesn't drink** coffee **after midday**.*
*My father **goes** to the market **every Saturday morning**.*
*I **never get up** before nine o'clock on Sunday.*

b) in time clauses with a future meaning after *when, as soon as, if, until*
*I'll phone her **when/as soon as I get** home.*
*Say 'hello' to Tim **if you see** him.*
*I'm not going to speak to him **until he apologises**.*

c) when we are talking about permanent situations
*I **come** from Melbourne.*
***Does she still live** in a flat?*

d) when we are talking about the future as expressed in timetables, regulations and programmes.
*The train **leaves** at 5.33.*
***Do classes begin** at the same time as last year?*

e) with scientific facts
*Bees **make** honey.*
*The planets **revolve** around the sun.*

f) with 'state' verbs which are not normally used in continuous forms: *be, have, depend, know, think, understand, disagree, like, want, hear, love, see, smell, taste*
*I **don't have** much money.*
***Does she understand**?*
*I'm sorry, but **I disagree** completely.*
*That perfume **smells** too strong.*

g) in spoken instructions, sports commentaries, jokes and formal letters
*First you **put** the cassette in the machine.*
*Romero **runs** towards goal and he **kicks** the ball.*
*A man **goes** into a restaurant and orders some soup.*
*I **enclose** a copy of my curriculum vitae.*

17.2 *Present Continuous*

FORM: the present form of *be* + the *-ing* form of the verb.

Contracted forms: *I'm (I am), you're (you are), s/he's (s/he is), it's (it is), we're (we are), they're (they are)* + *-ing* form.

USE: we use the Present Continuous when we are talking about:

1 actions happening now
*I think she**'s having** lunch.*
2 changing/developing situations
*My toothache **is getting** worse.*
3 temporary situations
*I **am working** in my father's restaurant this month.*
4 plans and arrangements in the future
***Are you doing** anything special this weekend?*
5 annoying or surprising habits with *always*
*She**'s always losing** her belongings.*
*They**'re always holding** hands even after fifty years of marriage.*

17.3 *Present Perfect Simple*

FORM: *have/has* + past participle

USE: we use the Present Perfect Simple:

1 when we are describing situations that have continued from some time in the past until now
*Mike **has lived** in Japan for three years.*
*I**'ve been** in love with Bill since 1984.*
2 when we are describing recent events
*I**'ve eaten** two packets of crisps, a bar of chocolate a plate of spaghetti and four bananas so far today.*
3 when we are describing repeated actions that have continued from some time in the past until now
*We**'ve seen** three movies this week.*
*I**'ve been** to every one of their concerts since they started playing together.*
4 with 'state' verbs e.g. *be, believe, have, know, think, like*
*I**'ve disliked** bananas since I was a child.*

REPORT

(For work on reports see pp. 72–73 and p. 154.)

1 Question

The school where you study English has received a donation from an ex-student who has said the money should be spent on **either** computers **or** video equipment. You have been asked to write a **report** for the school council, describing the benefits to the school of both projects and saying which one you think should be chosen and why.

Write your **report**. (You should write between **120** and **180** words.)

2 Model answer

USEFUL PHRASES AND EXPRESSIONS

STATING THE PURPOSE
This report is intended to describe/evaluate/present …
DESCRIBING HOW YOU GOT YOUR INFORMATION
Local shopkeepers **answered a questionnaire** …
REPORTING YOUR RESULTS
Most people **said/expressed the opinion/told me that** …
PRESENTING A LIST
The following reasons were given for preferring the old library/buying a computer:
1 …
2 …
MAKING RECOMMENDATIONS
I would recommend, therefore, that we buy a widescreen TV for the student common room.

DO use headings.

DO use formal language.

Introduction:
The aim of this report is to describe the benefits of buying computers and video equipment and to suggest which resource our school should choose. I interviewed students from each class to get their opinions.

DO say how you collected the information.

Computers:
Many students (67%) thought that computers were very useful for language learning. They gave the following reasons for having this opinion:
1 English word processors are good for practising writing
2 Access to the internet and e-mail provides reading and writing practice
3 Computer games can be a fun way of learning.
Nevertheless, a small group (16%) said they did not know how to use a computer.

DO present information objectively. DON'T include irrelevant details.

DO use numbering to highlight main points.

Video equipment:
Although the school already has a video in classroom B2, many students (55%) said it would be a good idea to have a video in every classroom. All students enjoy it when their teachers use video in class.

DO include two or three points under each heading.

Conclusion:
Both kinds of equipment obviously have benefits. Although video equipment was a popular choice it is important to remember that we already have one video but no computers. Therefore, the computer option seems best.

DO express opinions impersonally. DON'T express opinions until the conclusion.

ARTICLE

(For work on writing articles see p. 63.)

1 Question

You see this advertisement in a local English language newspaper:

> Under 25 magazine is looking for articles in answer to the question 'Is life better for today's young people than it was for their parents?' There will be a prize of a trip for two to Disneyland, Paris for the best article we receive.

Write your **article**. (You should write between **120** and **180** words.)

2 Model answer

USEFUL PHRASES AND EXPRESSIONS

'TALKING' TO THE READER

I bet you don't want to spend the rest of your life living with your parents.

I'm sure you'll agree diet is even more important than exercise.

INFORMAL LANGUAGE

Let's look at the problem from two different perspectives.

So, the government should **clear up this mess** as soon as possible.

Another problem with banning cars from the city centre **is** deliveries to shops.

DO think of an interesting title. DON'T start and finish your article in the same way as a letter.

DO use informal language.

DON'T forget to express your opinion.

DO try and 'talk' to your readers.

DO finish your article in an interesting way.

The Good Old Days?

Our parents are always saying 'Things were so much better in the old days', but is this really true?

Let's start with entertainment. Our parents had pop music, TV and cinema. However, if you look at entertainment today, I'm sure you'll agree that we are much better off than our parents were. We have satellite TV, we can rent videos and all the best music is recorded onto CDs. Of course, there are computer games and the internet too.

Entertainment has improved, but has our quality of life? I don't think so. Thirty years ago pollution hadn't reached alarming levels and there wasn't nearly as much traffic on our roads. Although there was some unemployment, it wasn't as bad as it is now. What's more, life was less stressful.

So, despite having more fun than our parents did, we also live in a more polluted, more stressful world where many people are unemployed. Perhaps it wouldn't be so bad to go back to the good old days after all.

DESCRIPTIVE COMPOSITION (BACKGROUND READING TEXT)

(For work on descriptions of places see p. 138, and for descriptions of people see p. 81.)

1 Question

Which character in the book you read do you find least attractive? Write a **composition** briefly describing the character and explaining why you dislike him/her so much.

Write your **composition**. (You should write between **120** and **180** words.)

2 Model answer (on *Wuthering Heights* by Emily Brontë)

The character I find least attractive in Wuthering Heights is Hindley Earnshaw. Hindley is Catherine's older brother and from the very beginning of the story he shows himself to be an absolutely despicable person. In fact, Hindley Earnshaw is directly to blame for most of the other terrible things that happen in the novel.

One of Hindley's particularly unattractive characteristics is envy. When Mr Earnshaw brings Heathcliff back to Wuthering Heights Hindley is immediately jealous of Heathcliff and treats him very cruelly. Hindley also bitterly resents Cathy and Heathcliff's great friendship, and when Mr Earnshaw dies and Hindley inherits the house he treats Heathcliff as little better than a slave.

A second characteristic that makes me dislike Hindley so much is that he is a bully and a coward. He takes his anger out on those weaker than himself. He is seven years older than Heathcliff but regularly beats him and locks him up. Hindley is so weak that he ends up drinking and gambling away all the money he has inherited leaving his son, Hareton, to live the same terrible existence as Heathcliff.

> DO focus on what you have been asked to do. DON'T just tell the story of the book.

> DO describe a characteristic and then say why you like/dislike it so much.

> DO make links between paragraphs clear.

Paper 5: Speaking material (Units 1–5)

Work in pairs.

Part 1

Take it in turns to ask and answer the following set of
questions about yourself:

Where are you from?
Were you born there?
Have you ever lived anywhere else?
What are the people there like?

What about your family? Could you tell us something about them?
Do you live in a house or an apartment? What's it like?

Do you have a regular pattern to your day? What usually happens?
What do you normally do at the weekend?

Where do you spend your holidays?
Where would you most like to spend a holiday?

Part 2

Each student must talk about two photographs for about a minute.

Student 1: Compare and contrast these photographs, saying what you think it would be like to do work like this.

Student 2: When Student 1 has finished, say which of the jobs you think would be more difficult.

Student 2: Compare and contrast these photographs, saying why you think people enjoy doing activities like these.

Student 1: When Student 2 has finished, say which group of people you thought looked more experienced.

Part 3

Imagine that you have been asked to organise a programme of activities for a group of young people who will be visiting your country to learn your language. Below are some suggestions. Talk to each other about the various suggestions saying how they might appeal to different people and then choose one from each group that you think might help the students learn your language. You have about 3 minutes for this.

International students' visit

International Party Night

areas of natural beauty

places of historical interest

match

industries

local specialities

tradition

Part 4

Now discuss the questions below:

- How would you feel about going on a trip like this?
- If you are learning a foreign language do you think it is important to visit a country where that language is spoken?
- What do you think is the best way to learn a language?
- What other languages, apart from English, would you like to learn? Why?
- What are the most difficult things about learning a foreign language?
- Why do so many people want to learn English?

Paper 5: Interview 2 (Units 6 –10)

Work in pairs.

Part 1

Take it in turns to ask and answer the following set of questions about yourself:

Are you from this area?
What's it like to live here/ there?
Would you like to live anywhere else?
What are the people in this area like?

How many years have you been/were you at school?
What is/was your school like?
What do/did you like most about your school?
Which subjects did you least enjoy?
What are you going to do when you leave school?

What sort of music do you like to listen to?
Do you play a musical instrument?
What is your favourite instrument? Why?

Part 2

Each student must talk about two photographs for about a minute.

Student 1: Compare and contrast these photographs, saying what you think it would be like to work in restaurants like these.

Student 2: When Student 1 has finished, say which of the two restaurants you would prefer to eat in.

Student 2: Compare and contrast these photographs, saying how you think the children are feeling.

Student 1: When Student 2 has finished, say whether you would or would not like to work as a teacher.

Part 3

Below is a poster showing some ways that people like to spend their spare time. Talk to each other about these things saying which of them is most important to you and which you spend least time doing. You have about 3 minutes for this.

Part 4

Now discuss the questions below.
- What other kinds of spare time activities do young people in your country have?
- How do you think spare time activities will change in the future?
- How has the way people spend their spare time changed over the last fifty years?
- How much spare time do most students in your country have a week?
- What do you think would be the best way to encourage people to spend their spare time productively?
- What kinds of outdoor activities do you enjoy? Why?

Paper 5: Interview 3 (Units 11–15)

Work in pairs.

Part 1

Take it in turns to ask and answer the following set of questions about yourself:

Where are you from?
What's it like to live here/there?

What do you normally do at the weekend?
How do you normally travel to school/work?

What kind of food do you like most?
What kind of food do you dislike?
Are there any good restaurants in your area?
How often do you go to museums or art galleries? What do you like to see?
How good are the museums in your area?

Part 2

Each student must talk about two photographs for about a minute.

Student 1: Compare and contrast these photographs, saying why you think people enjoy these different media.

Student 2: When Student 1 has finished, say whether you prefer to watch the news on TV or read a newspaper.

Student 2: Compare and contrast these photographs, saying how you think people feel about art in settings like these.

Student 1: When Student 2 has finished, say which of the two paintings you prefer.

Part 3

Imagine that various proposals have been made to limit environmental damage to the earth. Below are some things that cause damage. Talk to each other about which of these things cause the most damage and decide how you would change the law in relation to one of these things. You have about 3 minutes for this.

Part 4

Now discuss the questions below.

- What other things cause damage to the environment?
- How would you make people more aware of environmental issues?
- What kinds of environmental damage affect you most?
- Do you think governments should make laws to prevent environmental damage?
- What laws are there in your country to prevent environmental damage?
- Do you think the situation will improve in the future?

Phrasal verbs reference

The grammar of phrasal verbs

There are four main types of phrasal verbs:

(1) **Verb + adverb (no object)** e.g. get on = have a good relationship with someone
Mike and Sally aren't getting on very well at the moment.

The verb and adverb cannot be separated by other words.

(2) **Verb + adverb + object/Verb + object + adverb** e.g. give away = distribute for free
He gave away all his money. OR *He gave all his money away.*

The verb and adverb can be separated, but if the object is a pronoun (e.g. it, me, them), the adverb must come after the object e.g. *He gave it away.* NOT *He gave away it.*

(3) **Verb + preposition + object** e.g. look after = take care of
He looked after his parents for many years.

The verb and preposition cannot be separated.

(4) **Verb + adverb + preposition + object** e.g. put up with = tolerate
I don't know how she puts up with his terrible behaviour.

The verb, adverb and preposition cannot be separated. the grammatical type of each phrasal verb below is indicated by the number in brackets.

break down (1) p.47: stop working, usually a machine or vehicle e.g. *If my car breaks down again, I am going to sell it.*

break (something) down (2) p.47: destroy something such as a door or wall e.g. *The firemen broke the door down and ran inside to look for the children.*

bring (someone) up (2) p.27: look after and educate a child e.g. *Do you think it is difficult to bring children up as a single parent?*

carry on (3) p.17: continue doing something e.g. *He carried on watching TV even though his mother had told him to go to bed.*

catch on (to something) (1) p.61: understand e.g. *The teacher explained it at least three times, but Helen still didn't catch on.*

close (something) down (2) p.47: end an activity e.g. *I read in the paper last night that they are closing my old school down.*

come down (1) p.47: fall to the ground e.g. *Did you see that the apple tree next door came down in the night?*

come out in (something) (4) p.131: often when your body develops spots or rashes e.g. *He came out in red marks all over his face and neck.*

cut (something) down (2) p.47: bring to the ground e.g. *If we don't cut that three down soon, it will fall down.*

cut down on (something) (4) p.47: reduce the amount e.g. *You must cut down on all the chocolates and cakes you eat. It's not good for you.*

cut (something) out (2) p.131: remove e.g. *If you cut some of these late nights out, you won't feel so tired in the mornings.*

die down (1) p.47: come to an end e.g. *She waited until the laughter died down before she continued her speech.*

eat out (1) p.131: eat in a restaurant instead of at home e.g. *I'd like to eat out tonight. How about going to that little Italian restaurant on the high street?*

get (something) across (2) p.61: communicate an idea e.g. *He had an interesting plan for reducing the level of pollution in the city, but it took him a long time to get his ideas across.*

get away with (something) (4) p.121: avoid being caught and punished e.g. *He is always late for work. How does he get away with it?*

get by (1) p.121: survive e.g. *It was hard to get by on one salary when Tom lost his job, but things are Ok now.*

get (something) down (2) p.47: make a written record e.g. *Simon, could you make sure you get his telephone number down?*

get down to (something) (4) p.121: start doing seriously e.g. *I really must get down to writing my Christmas cards otherwise it will soon be too late.*

get on (with someone) (1) p.27 = have a good relationship e.g. *My brother and I are different kinds of people. I've never really **got on** with him.*

get out (1) p.131: have time outside the home e.g. *You should **get out** more. It's not good always being inside with the children like this.*

get over (something) (3) p.121: recover from e.g. *Her grandmother died a couple of months ago and it's taking her a long time to **get over** it.*

get round (someone) (3) p.121: persuade someone to let you do something e.g. *My father doesn't want to lend me his car, but I know how to **get round** him.*

get through (to someone) (1) p.121: make contact, often by telephone e.g. *I've been trying to **get through** to you all day, but your phone has been constantly engaged.*

get up to (something) (4) p.27: do something, often naughty or bad e.g. *OK, kids, what did you **get up to** while we were away?*

give (something) away (2) p.81: 1 donate for free e.g. *I think we should **give away** all these old toys to the local children's hospital.*
2 show, reveal e.g. *His bored expression **gave away** how he really felt.*

give (something) back (2) p.81: return e.g. *Lend me £10, will you? I promise I'll **give** it **back** tomorrow.*

give in (to someone) (1) p.81: surrender, agree to what someone else wants e.g. *You shouldn't **give in** to him if you think he is wrong.*

give off (something) (3) p.81: produce e.g. *Plastic **gives off** a horrible smell when it is burnt.*
(Note that in this case the verb and the adverb cannot be separated.)

give (something) our (2) p.81: distribute e.g. *The teacher **gave** files and books **out** to all the students.*

give (something) up (2) p.81: stop e.g. *All my friends have **given** smoking **up** this year. It's incredible.*

go down (1) p.47: fall e.g. *The price of houses has **gone down** by five per cent in the last year.*

go on)1) p.17: continue doing something e.g. *She **went on** talking while he made lunch.*

grow up (1) p.27: become an adult e.g. *I **grew up** in the north of england, but I moved down to London for my first job.*

Hold on (1) p.17: wait e.g. *Could you **hold on** for a moment while I get a pen and paper?*

keep on (1) p.17: continue doing something e.g. *It **kept on** raining for the rest of the day.*

keep up (with someone) (1) p.61: maintain the same level e.g. *It's very difficult to **keep up** with her because she walks so fast.*

let (someone) off (2) p.61: give someone a light punishment or no punishment at all for something they have done wrong e.g. *As it was his first offence the judge **let** him **off** with a small fine.*

look after (someone/something) (1) p.27: take care of e.g. *Would you mind **looking after** our cats while we are away on holiday?*

Look out (1) p.131: pay attention, be careful e.g. ***Look out!** there's a car coming.*

look (something) up (2) p.61: find information, often in a reference book e.g. *He **looked up** all of the new words in his bilingual dictionary.*

look up to (someone) (4) p.27: admire, respect e.g. *I have always **looked up to** my mother. She's do patient and kind.*

make for (someone/something) (3) p.148: go towards e.g. *They **made for** the nearest café when it started to rain.*

make of (something) (3) p.148: think of e.g. *What do you **make of** that new book by Jason Bryant? I couldn't understand a word of it!*

make out (1) p.148: pretend e.g. *She **made out** that she had been at home all evening when in fact she had gone out to see Martin.*

make (something) out (2) p.148: see clearly e.g. *I can see someone coming towards us, but I can't **make out** who it is.*

make (something) up (2) p.148: invent e.g. *I don't believe what she told us about meeting Elton John. I think she is **making** it **up**.*

make (a room, bed, etc.) up (2) p.148: prepare e.g. *We need to **make** the spare room **up** if Jim is going to stay here tonight.*

make (time) up (2) p.148: get back e.g. *We left late, but if I drive fast, I think we can **make up** the lost time.*

make up (with someone) (1) p.148: become friends again e.g. *You shouldn't get angry with your sister. Please go and find her and **make up**.*

mind out (1) p.61: pay attention e.g. ***Mind out!** You nearly walked in that puddle.*

pick on (someone) (3) p.61: treat someone badly or unfairly e.g. *The other boys are really horrible to Michael. They're always **picking on** him.*

pick (something) up (2) p.61: learn e.g. *He's very quick. You just tell him how to do something once and he's **picked** it **up**.*

put (money) by (2) p.90: save e.g. *I try and **put** a little **by** each month. We'd like to go on a holiday to the Greek islands next year.*

put (an animal) down (2) p.90: destroy e.g. *It was very sad. Our horse broke its leg and was in terrible pain. We had to have it **put down**.*

put (someone) down (2) p.90: criticise someone or try and make them look stupid or insignificant e.g. *I think he **puts** me **down** in meetings because he never has any ideas of his own.*

put (something) off (2) p.90: postpone, make later e.g. *Can we **put** the football match **off** for a week because some of our team are ill with flu?*

put (something) out (2) p.90: extinguish e.g. *Could you **put** your cigarette **out**, please/ This is a no-smoking area.*

put (someone) through (2) p.90: connect (especially by telephone) e.g. *Could you **put** me **through** to Mr Jenkins' secretary, please? I need to change the time of my appointment.*

put (someone) up (2) p.90: give accommodation e.g. Of course we can **put** you **up** for a few days while you're looking for a flat. There's no problem – we've got a spare room.

put (the price) up (2) p.90: increase e.g. If we **put up** our prices again, we're going to lose some of our best customers.

put up with (someone/something) (4) p.90: tolerate e.g. I can't **put up with** the noise from next door's party anymore. I am going to ask them to turn the music down.

rub (something) out (2) p.131: remove something (usually with a rubber or a cloth) e.g. I think you should **rub** the first part of your essay **out** and try again.

run out (of something) (1) p.131: finish, have no more left e.g. Could you buy some more milk when you go to the shops. We have nearly **run out**.

sell out (of something) (1) p.131: finish because everything has been bought e.g. I'm sorry, we've **sold out** of bread. Why don't you try the supermarket?

slow down (1) p.47: reduce speed e.g. Please **slow down**. You're driving so fast, it's making me frightened.

speak up (1) p.61: say things more loudly e.g. You need to **speak up** a little, I'm afraid I can't hear very well.

Stand out (1) p.131: appear clearly e.g. He usually **stands out** in a crowd. He's well over two metres tall!

stay our (1) p.131: remain away from home e.g. Your mother doesn't like you **staying out** all night. Please be home by midnight.

stick out (1) p.131: appear clearly e.g. I'm going to really **stick out** at school. I'm the only person who hasn't got a pair of the right kind of trainers.

take after (someone) (3) p.27: be similar to in character e.g. He **takes after** his father, he's very friendly and outgoing.

take (something) down (2) p.47: write, make a note of e.g. Sharon, could you **take down** the following letter for Brian Stevens at CBC?

take (someone) in (2) p.40: make someone believe something which isn't true e.g. When he told her he had come to check the gas meter, she was completely **taken in**.

take off (1) p.40: suddenly increase, do well e.g. Interest in the environment **has taken off** in the last couple of years and I don't really understand why.

take (someone) off (2) p.40: imitate someone to make other people laugh e.g. You should hear Simon **taking off** the Prime Minister – he's very funny.

take (time) off (2) p.40: have a holiday/change e.g. You should **take** a few days **off** work, you're not looking at all well.

take (someone) on (2) p.40: employ e.g. I'm thinking of **taking** another secretary **on**. Do you know anybody suitable?

take (something) over (2) p.40: take control e.g. He's very dominating. When he joins a discussion, he usually **takes over** and no one else has a chance to say anything.

take (something) up (2) p.40: start a new hobby e.g. I've **taken up** yoga recently. It's changed my life.

take up (space/time) (2) p.40: occupy e.g. This sofa **takes up** far too much room in here. We should move it downstairs.

tell (someone) off (2) p.27: speak to someone angrily because they have done something wrong e.g. My Maths teacher **told** me **off** for not paying attention in class.

throw (something) out (2) p.131: get rid of e.g. Don't **throw** those boxes **out**. they might come in useful one day.

watch out (1) p.131: pay attention e.g. **Watch out!** There's a car coming.

wear (someone) out (2) p.131: to make very tired, no energy left e.g. I've spent the day shopping, cleaning and cooking and now I'm **worn out**.

work (something) out (2) p.61: calculate e.g. You've been trying to do that puzzle for ages. Haven't you **worked** it **out** yet?

Communication activities

Unit 1, Speaking Exercise 2, p.6

Scoring

Add up your total and see if the person described below sounds like you:

1	a) **1**	b) **0**	c) **2**
2	a) **1**	b) **2**	c) **0**
3	a) **1**	b) **2**	c) **0**
4	a) **2**	b) **0**	c) **1**
5	a) **2**	b) **0**	c) **1**
6	a) **2**	b) **1**	c) **0**
7	a) **0**	b) **2**	c) **1**

1–3 Very low on thrill-seeking. You like your comfort above all else. You'll do everything possible to avoid dangerous or unpredictable situations. Why not try taking an occasional risk now and then? You might surprise yourself!

4–6 You are cautious and sensible at all times. You occasionally think about breaking out of your normal routine, but you don't generally go through with it. Why not do something different and more exciting with a friend?

7–10 You seem to have found a very good balance between healthy excitement and unnecessary risk. You give yourself challenges which keep you alert and make you an interesting person to know.

11–14 The ultimate thrill-seeker. You're a bit of a wild one! Watch out though that you don't start taking stupid or dangerous risks just for the buzz. Remember it can be addictive!

Unit 3, Pronunciation Exercise 2, p.30

1 Shut the door, will you love?
2 Your uncle's got a bad cough.
3 Apparently they're having some trouble at the bank.
4 Give this cap to your mother.
5 There's blood on my ankle.
6 Your cousin came home. He won the match.
7 I drank too much on Monday.

Unit 3, Vocabulary Exercise 5, p.34

Student A

Unit 4, Grammar Exercise 6, p.43

Joke B

have	seem	be	go	sit	reserve
enjoy	remark	like	read	reply	

A wealthy man (1) .... in the theatre with his pet elephant. He (2) .... the best seats so they could (3) .... a good view. Everyone (4) .... very surprised at how interested the elephant (5) .... to be in the play and at the end of the play the manager of the theatre (6) .... up to the wealthy man and (7) .... on this.

   'Your elephant certainly seemed (8) .... himself. I must say I was surprised he (9) .... the play so much.'

   'So was I,' (10) .... the wealthy man. 'When he (11) .... the book the play was based on, he didn't like it at all.'

Unit 6, Reading Exercise 6, p.58

IQ puzzles

1 Four girls, Helen, Sharon, Claire and Donna, have an average age of twenty. Sharon is eight years older than Helen and fifteen years older than Claire. The sum total of Helen's and Sharon's ages is forty-six, whilst the sum total of Sharon's and Claire's ages is thirty-six. How old is Donna?

2 Ten of these shapes can be fitted together to form a circle. Which are the three pieces that are **not** needed?

Ten of these shapes can be fitted together to form a circle.

3 If you were given a 7-litre container and an 11-litre container and were asked to measure out exactly 8 litres of water using just these two containers, how would you do it?

4 Divide this square up into five segments so that each contains two dots, two squares and one circle. Four of the five segments must be of identical size and shape.

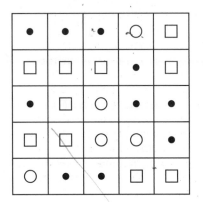

Turn to page 204 for the answers. How well did you do?

Unit 7, Grammar Exercise 4, p.71

Student A

In the small circle in the top left-hand corner, write the name of a hobby/free-time activity you have done for a long time and really enjoy.

In the rectangle in the top right-hand corner, write the name of the place where you live now.

In the square in the bottom left-hand corner, write down the number of times you have been abroad.

In the circle in the middle at the bottom, write down the most exciting thing you have ever done.

On the horizontal line in the middle, write the name of the most disgusting thing you have ever eaten.

Unit 8, Vocabulary Exercise 4, p.79 (student B)

Unit 8, Reading Exercise 3, p.80

Group B

> **Part B**

1 According to photographer Terry O'Neill: 'The public just don't realise how hard these supermodels work. They'll jump on a plane, go to Milan, go to bed, get up really early, do four fittings, do six shows a day for a week, no spare time whatsoever, jump on a plane, go back to New York, get up really
10 early, do a modelling assignment. **It**'s non-stop. I'm amazed the top girls have any private life at all. They work harder than Olympic athletes. Naomi is the best at it – she's there on the phone with her diary on her lap while she's having her make-up done, making appointments, running her life and her business affairs at the same time
20 as getting ready to be photographed. She's always doing twenty things at once. You've got to admire her.'
Whatever doubts there may be

about her book, the album is definitely her own work. Has a music career been a long-held ambition?

'It was something like that. I studied singing at school. Dance used to be my main subject and performing arts is what I've studied since I was five. So **it** was something I wanted to get back to. I love music ... listening to it, dancing to it. I know there are people out there saying, "She's just a model, can she sing, what's she doing?" But I wouldn't have got my contract and got other people to work with me if I hadn't got some voice. I've given it one hundred per cent and you can't feel bad about yourself for that.'

And how does a supermodel enjoy herself in time off from her busy schedule?

'Cooking, having friends over, going to clubs sometimes, if I know the DJs and if there's going to be good music.'

And how about men?

'Oh,' Naomi puts her head to one side and smiles sweetly. 'My ideal man is creative, intense, intelligent, humorous, very loving and affectionate.' She has had a number of celebrity boyfriends (including Mike Tyson, Sylvester Stallone, Robert De Niro, Sean Penn and U2's Adam Clayton), but now she talks about wanting a steady boyfriend and wanting babies,' ... but not for a while yet. I'll never give up travelling altogether – I like **it** too much – but at the moment I've got too much I want to achieve to be starting a family. Don't feel sorry for me, though. I live out of a suitcase, but I love my life – I really love it!'

201

Unit 9, Vocabulary Exercise 5, p.91

Student A mime the following actions for Student B:

1 Fry an egg.
2 Squeeze some lemon on an oyster, then eat it.
3 Ladle some soup into a bowl.
4 Boil some water and then make some tea.
5 Eat some peas with chop sticks.

Unit 10, Vocabulary Exercise 5, p.103

Student A ask Student B the following questions:

1 What's your home telephone number?
2 How much do you weigh?
3 How tall are you?
4 When were you born?
5 What percentage of the people in this room have black hair?
6 What is ¾ minus ¼?
7 What is the speed limit on motorways in your country?
8 What temperature does water boil at?

Unit 11, Reading Exercise 3, p.111

Group B

Weird Weather Facts

■ The study and forecasting of weather is called meteorology because it was once precisely that – the study of meteors. The idea that meteors were formed in the sky from various combinations of earth, water, air and fire, and that they contributed to weather conditions, goes back to the great philosopher and scientist, (2) ...., in the 4th century BC. It was believed in Europe until late in the 17th century.

■ In AD 582, it rained 'blood' on Paris. The terrified local people saw this as a sign from Heaven and responded by repenting for their sins. The true cause of the strange event was the (4) ...., the wind that sometimes blows from the Sahara across the Mediterranean into Europe. It carries a fine, red dust from the desert interior, and this had dyed the rain that fell on Paris.

■ On May 29, 1986, (6) .... in west China were sucked up by a tornado. It put them down again on some sand dunes 20 km away – completely unharmed.

■ The highest wind speeds ever officially recorded have occurred at (8) ...., where gusts have reached 370 km/hour.

■ The Algonquin Indians of North America believed that the earth lay on the back of a (10) ...., and when it shuffled its feet the Earth would quake. One ancient Japanese legend held that the movement of a vast underground spider caused earthquakes; a later account said it was a monster catfish. The ancient Greeks blamed huge (12) .... wrestling underground.

■ An average of 708 tornadoes strike the United States each year. In April (14) ...., 148 tornadoes hit thirteen states in just twenty-four hours, leaving 315 people dead.

■ If you are stuck out in a storm, never shelter under a (16) .... Try to get indoors, or into a car. Get away from metal objects and get rid of any metal you are carrying. If you're with other people, (18) .... Unfortunately, sometimes even being indoors is no protection. In July 1982 a woman was struck by a bolt that came through the window and hit the (20) .... she was holding. The force of the bolt threw her across the kitchen.

Unit 13, Vocabulary Exercise 2, p.134

Student A

Unit 14, Speaking Exercise 3, p.144

The boy was 'reluctantly' bailed to appear before the juvenile court again next month.

Magistrates ordered him to observe a 5 p.m. to 7 a.m. curfew because most of the offences have been committed at night.

They also ruled that he should live with his grandparents and report daily to his local police station.

Unit 14, Speaking, p.147

Unit 12, Exercise 2, p.124

Pictures for Part 3

Unit 3, Vocabulary Exercise 5, p.34

Student B

Unit 6, Reading Exercise 6, p.58

Answers to the IQ puzzles on page 200.

1 Donna is twenty-two years old.

2 Shapes 3, 6 and 9 are not needed.

3 Fill the 11-litre container and from this fill the 7-litre container, which leaves 4 litres in the 11-litre container. Empty out the 7 litres and pour in the 4 remaining litres from the 11-litre container. Then fill the 11-litre container again and from this fill the 7-litre container. This will leave you with 8 litres in the 11-litre container.

4

Unit 7, Grammar Exercise 4, p.71

Student B

In the small circle in the top left-hand corner, write the name of the friend you have had for the longest time.

In the rectangle in the top right-hand corner, write the name of the most awful place you have ever been to.

In the square in the bottom left-hand corner, write down the number of pets you/your family has had.

In the circle in the middle at the bottom, write down the name of the most interesting person you have ever met.

On the horizontal line in the middle, write down the most embarrassing thing you have ever done.

Unit 9, Vocabulary Exercise 5, p.91

Student B mime the following actions for Student A:

1 Eat a bowl of spaghetti.
2 Chop an onion.
3 Eat some prawns, taking all the shells off first.
4 Grate some cheese.
5 Whisk some egg whites together until they become light and fluffy.

Unit 10, Vocabulary Exercise 5, p.103

Student B ask Student A the following questions:

1 How old are you? (in years and a fraction)
2 What do you think is the average height of men in your country?
3 What's the home telephone number of a good friend of yours?
4 What is ½ times ½?
5 When is your mother's birthday?
6 What is the normal temperature of people?
7 How much did the last piece of clothing you bought cost?
8 What is ⅛ in decimals?

Unit 12, Speaking Exercise 3, p.124

Student A

Questions for Part 1
- Where are you from?
- How long have you lived here/there?
- What's it like living here/there?
- Why are you studying English? What might you do with your English in the future?
- What do you like doing in your free time?

Questions for Part 4
- How important is it that schools prepare pupils for life as well as teach academic subjects? Should school education be more practical?
- Should pupils go straight from school to university or should they have time off in between?
- What do you think is a good size for a class at school?
- Why do some teachers have problems keeping control of their classes at school?
- At what age do you think pupils should be free to leave school?

Unit 13, Vocabulary Exercise 2, p.134

Student B

Exam focus Paper 5, Part 2 (individual long turn) Exercise 3, p.53

Unit 10, Exam focus Paper 5, Part 3 Exercise 3, p.104

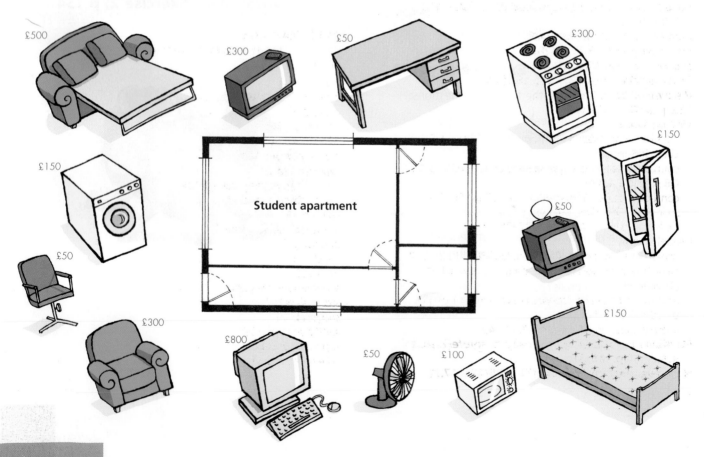